PRAISE FOR *PR TECHNOLOG*

MW00610501

Information and communication technologies, particularly those utilizing algorithms, machine learning, and other increasingly advanced applications of artificial intelligence, and the data and insights available through such technologies, are reshaping media and business and government communication. Therefore, public relations professionals, as well as journalists and marketers, need to be able to use these tools and the data and insights derived from them in ethical as well as effective ways. This book examines these developments, making it essential reading for PR professionals.
Jim Macnamara, PhD, Distinguished Professor of Public Communication, University of Technology Sydney

Mark Weiner is amongst those very few rational advocates of the need for a sounder professional credibility based on fact and data for the 3–5 million "artists" operating in the world today. His call to "Begin simple. Simply begin" strikes a bell when we look at ourselves in the mirror early in the morning in search for a convincing reason to persist. I strongly recommend both young, middle-aged and ancient professionals to "begin to begin".
Toni Muzi Falconi, Founding Chair, Global Alliance for Public Relations and Communication Management, and educator and polemist

Technology changed how people communicate and consume information, and also enabled speedy data collection and processing. Yet, it still comes back to communication professionals to uncover actionable insights from the data, execute communication plans, and manage public relations. Great possibilities of research-driven PR practice can be found in this book.
Patty Lin, Communications Director, Oracle

Weiner has written a classic! He has blended marketing and communication theory with the best practices of the profession. This should be on every communicators bookshelf.
David Michaelson, PhD, leading expert in communication research, measurement, and evaluation

Industry veteran and thought leader Mark Weiner has written a must-read guide for communications professionals looking to optimize the PR process and quantify the power of corporate communications. Read this book and benefit from his experience and expertise.

Chris Monteiro, communications consultant and former Chief Communications Officer, Mastercard and KPMG

Mark Weiner knows how to organize his experience into a logical framework and rephrase it in plain terms so practitioners can not only understand but also reference it in their daily work. *PR Technology, Data and Insights* will navigate you through the challenges of the big data revolution.

Koichi Yamamura, PhD, Principal, TS Communication

Like its author, this book brilliantly frames the current market and challenges for communicators in harnessing technology, data, and insights. The inclusion of specific resources makes this a road map for teams to build better-structured data to deliver communication value to the C-suite.

Johna Burke, CEO Global MD, AMEC (Association for the Measurement and Evaluation of Communications)

If you're serious about advancing—or protecting—your career in the strategic communications industry, this is the book you need to read this year. Mark Weiner provides fresh insights and a wealth of practical advice, with real-world examples. This book is the key to unlocking data analytics for applied business strategies.

Rowan Benecke, President, Cognito

PR Technology, Data and Insights

Igniting a Positive Return on Your Communications Investment

Mark Weiner

KoganPage

Publisher's note

Every possible effort has been made to ensure that the information contained in this book is accurate at the time of going to press, and the publishers and authors cannot accept responsibility for any errors or omissions, however caused. No responsibility for loss or damage occasioned to any person acting, or refraining from action, as a result of the material in this publication can be accepted by the editor, the publisher or the author.

First published in Great Britain and the United States in 2021 by Kogan Page Limited

Apart from any fair dealing for the purposes of research or private study, or criticism or review, as permitted under the Copyright, Designs and Patents Act 1988, this publication may only be reproduced, stored or transmitted, in any form or by any means, with the prior permission in writing of the publishers, or in the case of reprographic reproduction in accordance with the terms and licences issued by the CLA. Enquiries concerning reproduction outside these terms should be sent to the publishers at the undermentioned addresses:

2nd Floor, 45 Gee Street
London
EC1V 3RS
United Kingdom
www.koganpage.com

122 W 27th St, 10th Floor
New York, NY 10001
USA

4737/23 Ansari Road
Daryaganj
New Delhi 110002
India

Kogan Page books are printed on paper from sustainable forests.

© Mark Weiner, 2021

The right of Mark Weiner to be identified as the author of this work has been asserted by him in accordance with the Copyright, Designs and Patents Act 1988.

ISBNs

Hardback   978 1 3986 0042 3
Paperback   978 1 3986 0040 9
Ebook   978 1 3986 0041 6

British Library Cataloguing-in-Publication Data

A CIP record for this book is available from the British Library.

Library of Congress Control Number

2021930557

Typeset by Integra Software Services Pondicherry
Print production managed by Jellyfish
Printed and bound by CPI Group (UK) Ltd, Croydon CR0 4YY

*To Braden, Graham, Cameron and my family, whose
support and love nourish me always.*

CONTENTS

Foreword by Tina McCorkindale x
Preface xii
Acknowledgments xv

Introduction 1

PART ONE
Technology, Data, and Insights 21

01 Technology 23

Big Data 24
Artificial Intelligence 26
Audience Targeting Technology 31
Tools to Find Earned Media Opportunities 33
Earned/Owned Media Production and Distribution Tools 35
Technology for Engagement 37
Technology for Media Monitoring and Social Listening 40
Tools for PR Measurement, Analysis, and Evaluation 42
Will PR Technology Replace PR Professionals? 45
Endnotes 46

02 Data 47

Introducing Data to Public Relations 48
Objectives, Inputs, Outputs, Outcomes, and Business Results 49
Understanding PR Data 64
Data's Role in Corporate Communication 66
Conclusion 68
Endnotes 69

03 Insights 71

The Current State of Technology-Driven Data-Informed Public
    Relations Insights 72
The Public Relations Insights Discovery Process 79
Bringing It All Together 86
Endnotes 94

PART TWO
The Public Relations Continuum 95

04 The Landscape Analysis 97

The Benefits of a Landscape Analysis 98
The Landscape Analysis Process 99
The Public Relations Landscape Analysis Tool Kit 102
The Executive Audit 102
The Journalist/Influencer Audit 108
Surveys 113
Media Demographic Audit 114
Retroactive Media Analysis 116
The Landscape Analysis Process: Insights 119
Conclusion 119

05 Setting Objectives 121

The Importance of Setting Objectives 122
The Technology-Enabled, Data-Informed Process for Setting
    Objectives 124
Objectives Should Be Measurable 125
Objectives Should Be Meaningful 128
Objectives Should Be Reasonable 129
When to Review Your Objectives 131
The Do-It-Yourself Guide to Setting Objectives that are Measurable,
    Meaningful, and Reasonable 133
If Management Wants PR Objectives and PR Wants to Prove Value,
    Why Doesn't Everyone Set Objectives? 141
Thoughts and Implications 142
Conclusion 144
Endnotes 147

06 Strategy and Tactics 149

Separating Strategy from Tactics 150
The Benefits of Strategy 152
How to Develop a Strategy 152
Media Segmentation: Target Audience Reach is Better Than Gross
    Reach 154
Media Targeting 156
Message Development 163
Why Strategies Fail 165
Tactics 166
Tactical Public Relations 167
Why Tactics Fail 172
Conclusion 172
Endnotes 173

07 Evaluation 175

The Benefits of Evaluation 176
The Right Way to Evaluate Your Public Relations Performance 176
Evaluating Inputs, Outputs, Outcomes, and Business Results 177
Evaluating the Public Relations Continuum 181
Evaluating Objectives 185
Evaluating Strategy and Tactics 188
Evaluating Evaluation 199
Why Doesn't Every PR Person Evaluate Their Performance? 205
Endnotes 207

Epilogue 209
Index 211

FOREWORD

The ability to think intelligently, strategically, and to adapt quickly becomes more critical in public relations every day with the accelerated pace of change, technological innovation, and competition. Recently, I saw a great meme that featured two cartoon characters struggling to pull a cart fitted with square blocks instead of round wheels up a hill. A person carrying a set of round wheels is following them, trying to convince them to use his wheels rather than their square blocks, but they both decline, saying "no thanks" and that they are "too busy." Sometimes, I think this example represents how the public relations and communication industry treats data and the insights it derives from it.

In this book, Mark Weiner, a highly respected and trusted leader in our field, offers much-needed guidance on how people can generate a positive return on their communication investment through technology, data, and insights. He makes the case by emphasizing that it's better to "begin simply" than not to begin at all. The public relations industry needs to speak the language of the executives of whom we ask support, budget, and resources. But still, measurement and evaluation remain challenging tasks for many in our profession.

A few years ago, I attended an industry conference for top executives in the public relations industry. One of the presenters, a well-regarded chief communications officer, discussed a "successful" event her team hosted for her company. When an attendee asked how they measured its success, the CCO replied, "We didn't measure it. We're just not there yet." This CCO is not a rarity.

Mark makes a case with practical solutions for data-driven decision-making that can be done on any budget. At the Institute for Public Relations, our tagline is "the science beneath the art of public relations™" and that is exactly the case Mark makes here to marry the science and the art. Data can help. What you can do with the data and how you can leverage insights to drive impact on the business is the holy grail. Many want to do it but few actually find it. Mark's book can change that so all companies can find that holy grail. PR can absolutely be quantified.

With the rapid pace of change, our profession must evolve so we don't get left behind. Blockbuster could have been Redbox, and Yahoo! could have been Google. While this may be overly simplistic, we all can be better at harnessing the information accessible to us. As Mark Weiner states, "The absence of applied technology, data, and insights is a matter of 'unwillingness' rather than 'inability.'"

And I'm not just talking about media data—that's only one kernel on an ear of corn. We have a plethora of tools and techniques accessible to us that can help drive decision-making. Mark outlines how we can best collect data and choose the right analytical tools and techniques that harbor valid and meaningful insights, rather than contributing only to "success theater."

Big data and little data analyses, surveys, and stakeholder tracking are just some of the approaches to be implemented and implemented well. We still have an opportunity to be innovative in measurement, though. As Mark spotlights in his book, "Conventional thinking is the enemy of innovation and breakthrough results."

Mark emphasizes that businesses demand that whatever can be automated will. This allows more time for us to be more proactive, thoughtful, and strategic. Throughout the book, Mark uses his expertise and optimism to offer practical ways for us to be smarter. The lessons he draws show us there's no reason why we shouldn't. And Mark is the best of the best to lead us on this journey. As a top leader in the PR industry with extensive experience, Mark offers his book as an indispensable guide to understand what we need to do to succeed to be smart, brave, strategic, and better leaders to help our companies be stronger and more successful.

Tina McCorkindale, PhD, APR
President and CEO, Institute for PR

PREFACE

Corporate communications and public relations face a defining moment. Technology, data, and insights now shape the day-to-day practice of many thousands of professional communicators. Now, more than ever before, the way we practice public relations reflects both the science and the art. The most important reason for this? Public relations needed to evolve in response to the imperative everyone in business now faces: the need to deliver a quantifiable return on investment.

The good news: public relations delivers the most efficient returns on investment within the marketing and communications mix. We may not drive the highest sales volume, but we drive sales at an extraordinarily low level of investment. As such, the sales we deliver cost remarkably little when compared with advertising, price promotions, and other forms of marketing communication. Smart companies invest in PR for this reason. Smart CEOs recognize that the organizations they lead must listen to and interact with a much broader group of stakeholders than just shareholders. And the best chief communications officers recognize the growing importance of their ability to properly position the enterprise on rapidly emerging issues of extreme sensitivity. The status of public relations within this environment is primed for historic growth. Technology provides us with the data and insights we need to deliver positive business results and to represent the organization on matters that resonate beyond the investment community: environmental sustainability, diversity and inclusion, workplace environment. All within a heightened awareness of societal well-being, racism, sexism, and other extremely sensitive moral and ethical issues on which companies must take a position.

In Part One, we describe and explore the key elements shaping public relations today: technology, data, and insights. The three elements combine to deliver the return on investment that businesses demand. Note here that PR's future will be a function of our ability to marry the best of technology with uniquely human attributes. Technology enables us to execute efficiently and consistently, but humans provide the interpretive analysis, actionable insights, and strategic guidance on which organizations depend. Technology may enable "real time," but only human analysis and insights empower "right time" decision-making.

In Part Two, we show how communicators apply technology and talent in each phase of the public relations continuum. The continuum describes every communications effort: beginning with landscape analysis and proceeding through objectives-setting, strategy development, tactical execution, and ending with evaluation for continuous improvement. As such, the public relations process is cyclical rather than linear and improves with every rotation.

After starting my career in the newspaper business with *The New York Times* and Tribune Media, I've worked in research-based public relations for 35 years. I've worked in executive positions for organizations that provide research, analysis, evaluation, and insights. Throughout this part of my career, I've had the opportunity to counsel many of the world's greatest organizations. Along the way, I've learned valuable lessons beyond what you'll read in this book. Perhaps the most important lesson: learning is among the most difficult tasks we undertake. I've learned some lessons the hard way... perhaps that's why they're the most enduring. Here, I'm happy to share what I've learned in my career in communications research and analysis:

- If you're just getting started in data-informed communication and feel a bit overwhelmed by it, I suggest that you begin simply but simply begin. It's as true in business as it is in life.

- Being approximately right is better than being completely clueless.

- If you find yourself in debates over whether "data" is a singular noun or plural, or if you argue over the advantages of a five-point scale versus a seven-point scale, you need to refocus on what really matters: accurate, data-driven insights that inform better decisions. Concentrate on that and you'll succeed.

- Life isn't win or lose. I've led a more contented life by remembering that failure informs future success. As a business leader, I allowed for failure: rather than win/lose, business (and life) are win/learn propositions. It's up to us to make the most of every opportunity.

- Research and data bridge the gap between PR and business. Data is the language of business. Learn to speak the same language as the people who evaluate PR performance and who decide on PR budget allocation.

- It's true that PR enjoys the benefits of some amazing technology. Don't forget that, nowadays, *everyone* has a PR tool. *Everyone* has PR data. Focus your attention on the best way to *think* about the data, and how to *manage* the tool. Despite advancements, human ingenuity, reasoning, and critical thinking cannot be replaced... not yet, anyway.

When I began writing the book, I envisioned an intended audience comprised of professional communicators in corporations, agencies, government, and non-profits around the world. Public relations people will recognize some of what's featured here, but the approaches we recommend may be new to all but a small minority. Of course, the CEOs or CMOs who fund PR and evaluate PR performance will also benefit. Each chapter ends with a list of questions every PR investment decision-maker should ask of their PR team. As a communications professional, you should be prepared to answer them, as well.

A friend once told me, "Dinosaurs would still be alive today if they could only predict the weather." With this book in hand, you possess the tools and guidance you'll need to tell which way the wind blows. The keys to success include technology, data, and insights, certainly. We also need an open mind to recognize and embrace the irreversible changes in our public relations landscape.

ACKNOWLEDGMENTS

Writing this book wasn't easy. But how lucky I am to be supported by so many people (many of whom turn up later when I needed to invent a brand or product name to make a point).

I thank Braden Bledsoe, my bride, whose love and patience supported me through the late nights and long weekends required to complete the manuscript. My sons, Graham and Cameron, who have grown to be outstanding men. My parents and my sister Lesley gave me the framework I needed to navigate my life. I welcomed support from Susan and Bill Bledsoe as well as from Cresta and Tom Bledsoe and their twins Isles and Clary. They, along with lifelong friends Harlan Marks and Bob Pierce, provided me with a steady diet of "how's the book coming?" Without my family and friends, the book wouldn't have happened.

I've worked for fantastic companies in my career: I thank my colleagues present and past from whom I've learned more than I could have dreamed. I must thank our clients with whom we've accomplished so much and whose stories I share. In particular, I must recognize colleague and friend Chelsea Mirkin, whose intelligence and determination elevate everyone around her. Also, I've been lucky to experience blessed mentorship from Kevin Clancy, PhD, Larry Moskowitz, Dan Barber, and Jack Felton. I'm not sure they knew how they affected me but here's a chance to express my gratitude out loud.

Finally, I must recognize the spark behind it all: Kathe Sweeny, with whom I collaborated on my first book, *Unleashing the Power of PR*, who remembered me and reached out to gauge my interest in writing the encore. She kept the faith through ideation, conception, and an extraordinary slog through writer's block. She prevailed and, now, so have I.

Here, in this book, you hold the contributions of many people with whom and through whom I gained the experience and earned the opportunity to share my story.

Introduction

Harnessing Technology, Data,
and Insights for Public Relations

Technology, data, and the desire for validated insights are changing our roles as public relations professionals as well as the organizations for which we work. Beyond storytelling, media relations and creativity, your senior leaders expect you to understand business fundamentals as well as the technology and data sciences that propel business results. In order to raise the profile of the public relations function within the organization to elevate the success of the enterprise and advance the profession, corporate communicators must harness the advantages that business knowledge, technology, and data sciences provide. While this task may seem enormous, the solution starts with each of us making a humble commitment: *begin simply but simply begin.*

This book outlines the emerging methods and developments that allow you to optimize the PR process and quantify the power of corporate communications. We begin with a review of public relations technology, data and insights, and a discussion of the forces driving these trends. With a better understanding of these assets, we can look at how they can be applied throughout the communications continuum, including landscape analysis, objectives-setting, strategy development, tactical design and execution, evaluation and continuous improvement. The goal is to improve efficiency, performance, and return on PR investment with each rotation through the cycle so that we can better connect public relations outputs with business performance and the overall success of the enterprise.

Why the PR Profession Needs to Change

The business world typically sees PR as a "people business" combining the skills of stakeholder relationship management, ingenuity, and interpersonal communication. By this definition, PR is "soft," meaning it cannot be measured. In a world driven by data-informed decision-making, the absence of PR data means PR's value remains entirely subjective, an undesirable position which puts our professional standing at risk. And yet despite the many opportunities for public relations practitioners to evolve through the focused use of technology, data, and insights, many in the field make a deliberate choice to do nothing, opting instead to reinforce the notion that "public relations is an art" rather than recognizing the underlying science beneath the art. Timeworn canards that "technology is too sophisticated" and "PR data analysis is too complicated" are mere rationalizations since so many simple options are available at low cost, even free. Communications technology (or CommTech) allows PR professionals to execute more efficiently and speak the same language as corporate decision-makers. Communicating in the language of business positions us as invaluable counsellors to power. By not taking advantage of these assets, many practitioners purposely choose to limit their upside potential. Simply stated, the absence in any public relations program of applied technology, data, and insights is a matter of "unwillingness" rather than "inability."

While the concepts supporting technology, data, and insights may feel new to many professional communicators, the concepts are traceable to PR's earliest days of the twentieth century (discounting the very earliest examples of prehistoric public relations when cave paintings were the first forms of story visualization).

Public Relations Always Embraced Technology

If we define "technology" as "equipment and machinery," technology has always been central to public relations, though in forms we may not recognize now. For example, where we now have email, PRs once used the United States Postal Service; while we now compose content using our keyboards, typewriters have keys, too; whereas we now use streaming video, practitioners once relied upon VHS tapes and, before that, "industrial films." We now manage our journalist database on our PC or through a platform whereas public relations professionals once relied on their Bacon's books, Rolodexes and Addressograph plates. While we now capture news in real time using low-cost portals and Google Alerts, we once depended upon our clipping service to deliver a twice-weekly envelope of manually sourced, hard-copy clips snipped from newspapers and magazines. Before the internet, we had only the public library, encyclopedias, print media, radio, and television. And, perhaps among the greatest transformations, social media, which as a form of "unmediated media" simply has no antecedent other than the barber shop, the neighborhood diner, and the town square.

In the late 1950s into the early 1960s, PR underwent a technology boom. After the Second World War, the emerging practice of public relations grew to a point that it required special PR service companies to meet the needs of a quickly evolving profession to handle database management, printing and mailing, wire distribution, film production, press clippings, and more.

Today, we benefit from built-for-purpose technology to help professionalize public relations and to enable public relations departments and PR agencies to do more with less and for less. Emerging technologies apply artificial intelligence and virtual reality... and who knows about the advances of which we haven't yet dreamed that will continue to propel public relations forward.

Public Relations Always Embraced Data

Often called "the father of public relations," Edward Bernays referred to the practice as a "social science" because it was reliant on scientific methods to build theories that persuade, motivate, and explain the behavior of individuals, groups, and organizations. Bernays employed surveys to make a better case for his clients' positions and products. He also applied data as a means of generating publicity. Because of his efforts and the evolution of applied data in the profession, public relations research and evaluation now enjoy wider acceptance than in the past. And while communications data science may seem as if it's new, it may be that it's just *new to you* since it's been around for more than 100 years.

To illustrate the point, we once tabulated the volume of print clips and circulations but we now calculate print and digital circulation as well as TV audience, social followers, and unique visitors per month. In the past, we used mechanical adding machines and calculators. Twenty-five years ago, my older colleagues described how they used to apply specially designed adhesive tape to create bar charts on graph paper. Now we use low-cost PR technology to capture and visualize content exposure, and to produce reports with just a few mouse clicks. Through the 1980s, we were limited to simple clip-counting; now we analyze the quantity *and* the quality of the earned media content we generate, including the tone and presence of intended and unintended messaging, spokespeople, competition, opposition, reputation attributes, and much more at a highly granular, actionable level of detail. Before technology enabled instantaneous online surveys, researchers conducted in-person interviews and mailed questionnaires to capture public opinion for further analysis and evaluation. The time intensity and related costs meant that only the largest companies could afford anything more than semi-annual surveys, if they could afford it all. Focus groups were once the only way to capture people's organic commentary in their own words. Now, social listening and analysis enable researchers to capture unfiltered comments from thousands of people in a single day in ways that are statistically valid and projectable to a larger population (which focus groups are not).

Through the late 1990s, the only way to isolate PR's contribution to business outcomes happened in those rare cases where PR operated in isolation and by using A/B testing (which in and of itself was rarely done). In and around the year 2000, market mix modelling emerged as an early "big data" approach to clarify the connection between a marketing output and brand performance and business results. AT&T's Bruce Jeffries-Fox created the first marketing mix model to include PR data and first quantified PR impact. But even after that success, PR data was rarely integrated into marketing mix model data streams, and when it was, it was often lumped into the equation as "other" (in other words, "unspecified" and "unexplainable") without ever being attributed directly to the public relations function. The models reflected a *derived* impact based on algorithms rather than *actual* impact. They were expensive and slow, with most brands conducting the analysis only once a year on a single brand, even among the largest, most diverse consumer packaged goods companies. Now, attribution analysis connects digital earned media coverage with a quantifiable subsequent behavior. Advances in automated market mix modelling now offer sophisticated approaches to uncover the relative return from PR as well as any other marketing endeavor. Attribution technology and automated models enable fast and inexpensive big data analysis across the marketing and communications mix.

Public Relations Always Embraced Insights

The prestigious Arthur W. Page Society, one of PR's most exclusive professional associations, defines the role of communications in the fifth of its seven Page Principles: "As a management and policymaking function, public relations should encourage the enterprise's decision making, policies and actions to consider its stakeholders' diverse range of views, values, experience, expectations and aspirations."[1] Within this context, the public relations professional is a counselor to and a member of the leadership team striving to contribute directly to the performance of the enterprise. Quantifiable, reliable, and actionable insights are the foundation of good counsel.

Communicators strive to operate at the high levels achieved by Arthur Page, Vice President of AT&T and an extraordinarily rare example of a PR person serving on the board of directors of one of America's largest companies. High-achieving corporate communicators frequently bring insights, but those who support their insights with a rigorous foundation of data earn their coveted "seat at the table" because they speak the language of the board room: *data* (not "buzz" or "hits"). Many public relations practitioners subsist in vague and indeterminate service to what Chief Communications Officer and Page member Andrew Bowins calls "deli counter PR," fulfilling management requests for "'a pint of press releases' and 'a quart of press clippings.'"

Whereas executives expect public relations professionals to deliver creativity, too many communicators rely on variations of "what we did for that other client" or "this worked last time." Conventional thinking is the enemy of innovation and breakthrough results. The data-informed, insights-enabled communicator drives positive change and contributes measurable business performance through the intelligent and timely application of technology, data, and insights.

When public relations functions in a data vacuum, insights are unreliable. Where data resides, intelligence leads to insights that connect PR output to outcomes, more effective decision-making, and improved business performance. While public relations decision-making continues to rely on experience, observations, and hunches, insights based on rigorous data science coupled with expertise and experience lead to dependable and scalable strategy and execution.

The Forces Driving Change in PR

While many of the basic tenets of the profession—creative muscle, an ability to build and sustain relationships, an aptitude for interpersonal communication, and a gift for the written word—continue to be important, these skills require greater speed, agility, and decision-making power than ever before.

This is where technology, data, and insights become invaluable to us. Communications technology enables us to manage and execute quickly; communications data empowers us to navigate with less waste and greater confidence; and communications insights enable us to contextualize the present and plan the future.

What caused the need for greater speed, agility, and decision-making power in our profession? Technology, data, and insights in public relations are but a manifestation of changes in society and in business in general.

Accelerated Pace and Disruption of Business

The world we know changes constantly but the pace of change in the past five years accelerated at a spectacular rate. Most of us find ways to adopt and adapt to rapid change in ways that outpace the organizations for which we work. The rate of change and the threat of disruption cause distress to many business leaders who understand the importance of innovation, the need to mitigate advantages held by competitors, and the difficulty of transforming nimbly. Consider how quickly the iPhone disrupted the mobile phone sector (and others including social media, photography, social media, and more) or the impact Amazon had on traditional retail chains. Even the mightiest competitors of Apple and Amazon were slow to transform operations, initiate digital strategies, and attract the required talent to manifest the necessary change.

Adding to our collective anxiety is the perceived need for immediacy. Most organizations use a variety of real-time technologies to support instantaneous decision-making. Despite our ability to adapt so far, somehow the speed at which we operate will become even faster: the advent of 5G and WiFi 6 will hasten processing and wireless connection speeds by a magnitude of 3x. For fully automated operations like programmed stock trading, for example, that rely on algorithms to buy and sell large numbers of shares, a millisecond can make a material difference between profit and loss. However, the importance and immediacy of such technology diminish in cases where thoughtful decisions are required. In these cases, the technology serves as a platform to enable expertise and experience. These situations rely less on real time and more on "right time," which is to say, the speed of the decision being made.

For corporate communicators who must adapt to the accelerated pace of business, many technology platforms offer low-cost, real-time or near-real-time access for news and social media dissemination, social listening and media monitoring, analytics, and reporting. Problems arise when people assume that the real-time tool can do everything you need with uniformly high quality and efficiency. It can't. Since our focus is on technology, data, and insights, let us concentrate briefly on technology. The technology promises real time but communicators often overlook the time it takes to manage the platform. Selecting media lists for distribution; identifying target journalists; updating journalist/influencer contact information related to conversations and pitches; setting up search strings and dictionaries; filtering your media monitoring results for irrelevant content; checking the analytics data for inaccuracies... all of this takes time and effort. So while the technology may be real-time at the moment of execution, we must invest many hours to ensure quality and speed when we eventually employ it.

For data-informed insights generation, we must recognize the need to "challenge the data," to analyze the figures we produce and the analytics we apply to probe more deeply into the origin of the data, how it's been processed, and whether it's sufficiently reliable for communications decision-making. In short, the data may be accessible at speed, but we must think about the data and process the results through a critical thinking progression to understand its meaning. For us to optimize the data fully, we must consider it as less of a report card and more like a tutor. A report card tells you how you did last semester, but a tutor gauges past performance and tells you how to improve in the future: What do we know now? What do we need to know to perform even better? What new possibilities emerge through thoughtful analysis? Where should we focus our time and effort?

As corporate communicators, we play an important role as counselors, involving ourselves early in the strategic planning process. We must also seek opportunities within the practice and throughout the organization to uncover opportunities to partner with marketing, finance, and other areas of the organization to promote reasonable risk-taking and to enable positive transformation and growth. Such collaboration requires thoughtful proactivity since intra-company collaboration raises the stakes for public relations. As such, remember that while certain situations may require real time, integrational thinking requires a common platform for planning, execution, and evaluation. Data connects everything within the organization. The chances for successful integration improve when purposeful data-informed collaboration drives the conversation.

Artificial Intelligence and Machine Learning

From autonomous vehicles to SIRI to online shopping recommendations, artificial intelligence promises to do for us what we once could only do for ourselves, only more efficiently. While most of us interact with artificial intelligence in some way every day, we can agree that it continues to develop. But who hasn't been amazed by technology that mimics human intelligence? The technology replicates actions once considered unique to animate beings. Every day and in almost every industry, we deploy technology to take action, to make judgments based on its ability to mirror human attributes like cognition, perception, and ingenuity. Machine learning, a more common form of artificial intelligence, is a method of developing computer systems that absorb information and evolve based on the computer's experience. Some common machine learning applications include medical diagnoses, self-driving cars, investment fund management, legal discovery, and work evaluation. The publisher of this book applied AI to help with editing and proofing. As such, expectations for the technology are high and optimism among business leaders remains great. At the same time, concerns over disruptions in the labor markets, unsupervised weapons deployment, and increased vulnerability to cyber terrorism, among other risks, cause hesitation among others. The full potential of artificial intelligence confronts industries and companies to consider, assess, and plan for certain obstacles, the most notable of which are a true understanding of what the technology can do and what it cannot, the skills required to manage the technology, and funding requirements for all this.

Like business everywhere, public relations must evolve. The ripest opportunities for artificial intelligence and machine learning in business relate to tasks described as repetitive or dangerous, which hardly describes public relations as we know it. However, as public relations practitioners, we need to recognize that the companies we represent and the media with which we collaborate face enormous challenges as the new technologies emerge. Communicators must prepare to respond to fast-breaking/high-risk situations, for instance automated market trading losses or an accident related to an autonomous vehicle. Many newspapers already use artificial intelligence to "write" routine announcements such as earnings and sports scores, to uncover fake news, and to fact-check reporting.

Business priorities demand that whatever can be automated will be automated. While we explore artificial intelligence in Chapter One, many of public relations' unique and valuable contributions are distinctly human. Artificial intelligence promises to monitor news and social media, inform media targeting, and enable better message detection and planning, but someone needs to manage the technology. And while artificial intelligence and machine learning may generate data used for better communications decision-making, the process requires human expertise to think about the data and to generate the actionable insights that empower breakthrough communication.

Globalization

Through globalization, individual economies around the world seek to streamline the marketplace, elevate competitiveness, limit international skirmishes, and spread prosperity more equitably. What's more, global organizations pursue lower taxes and lower cost of labor, some of which they find outside the borders of their headquarters nation. Despite recent trends toward a heightened sense of nationalism, tariffs, protectionism, and, for some organizations, an "anti-globalization backlash," institutions of all kinds continue to depend on one another regardless of location. The success of economic openness and international governance will be measured by the extent to which nations compete, collaborate, and achieve their respective goals.

Those of us in public relations must think globally and act locally. As economies around the world become more and more closely linked, developments in communications technology enable us to monitor international trends, analyze data on a worldwide scale, and uncover insights which enable us to execute local communication programs *from* any place *to* any place at the pace of business. Internationalization places an increased burden on the public relations professional as social/cultural sensitivities and language must be simultaneously coherent and nuanced (not to mention political, economic, and business frameworks that make everything even more difficult). In recognition of these challenges, large multinational organizations and PR agencies employ resident communications teams to execute programs that drive local outcomes that quantifiably contribute to their headquarters' objectives (wherever headquarters reside). Diverse stakeholder groups—employees, investors, consumers, regulators, and the communities in which organizations operate—deserve localized information and intelligence to better navigate their relationship with your company.

Ubiquity and Mobility of Technology

Sometime around 2016, the number of smartphones in use worldwide surpassed that of laptops and desktops, according to GlobalStats.[2] In their earliest iterations and reflecting the origins of desktops and laptops, manufacturers considered smartphones primarily for business applications because of their high cost. However, with the convenience of an all-in-one device for voice communication, video and photography, messaging, personal information management, social, and wireless, the smartphone became essential to most of the world's population. For communicators, the "always on" culture produced through mobile technology translates into a 24/7/365 culture for public relations along with the stress that accompanies it. Inaccessibility comes only because of a deliberate choice to disconnect, so much so that some companies felt forced to create "phone off" policies to enforce a better work–life balance. But disconnecting means you might be absent from even the small chance that your organization or your client may encounter an imbroglio requiring instant access and immediate response to an emerging crisis (commentary about which can be made even more compelling and viral when accompanied by video and photos taken by citizen journalists using—yes—smartphones). Mobility equals accessibility for all concerned: you, your management, your stakeholders, your competition, and your opposition. Your ability to manage the technology, your skill in thinking about data, and your capacity to contextualize at the speed of business is a measure of your professionalism and a modern-day requirement.

Shifting News Consumption Habits

With new and archived information at our fingertips via the internet and social media, an organization's stakeholders are more informed than ever with instant exposure to a vast array of sources, opinions, facts, and figures. For communicators, public relations materials endure for years if not decades. Stakeholders can access a press release and the media coverage that resulted from it whether it appeared this morning or a decade ago. For public relations—unlike advertising and other forms of marketing for which there may be no digital footprint—this enables an extraordinarily slow decay rate for earned media coverage that can be either good or bad depending on the news and information for which one searches. Positive reviews inform decisions for years while an unmitigated crisis results in the opposite, including diminished market share, lost market capitalization, and, in some cases, extinction. With more and more decisions—even small decisions—based upon online search, including elections, regulatory actions, purchases, employment, healthcare, investments, and practically every aspect of daily life including what's for dinner, the internet now represents the fabric of everyday living. As such, professional communicators must act both with immediacy and for the long term as every PR action remains searchable, retrievable, and educational to inform attitudes, preferences, and behavior for many years to come.

In 2018, the Pew Research Center declared that social media outpaced print news as the most frequent source of news for Americans (TV news was most popular).[3] Moreover, reflecting another important shift, in 2019 Pew reported that "mobile outpaced desktop when it comes to… occasional use of digital devices for news. Eight-in-ten US adults get news on mobile devices either sometimes or often."[4] Public relations is more than just media: it's employee communication, investor relations, reputation management, and more. Nonetheless and for the most part, "media" continues as a central theme across most public relations departments and agencies. As such, we must be even more nimble to initiate and respond to the media with the highest penetration among our target stakeholder groups. The media mix may be in flux—as it always has been—but the need to identify and communicate efficiently remains a constant, with the added challenge to reach each of our stakeholder concentrations using the channels they prefer. Survey panels and new technology, called "attribution analysis," provide demographic and firmographic data to identify the best media matches to enable greater efficiency and information consumption among the right people. When contextualized, communicators develop insights into which journalists and influencers resonate most strongly among target audiences; which journalists and influencers are most receptive to your organization's news; and which can be reached most efficiently using the channels preferred by the tier-one journalists and influencers your research identifies.

The Media Business

The rapid introduction and domination of social media place it on top of information dissemination including news, elections, regulatory and legislative action, and marketing. Far beyond its origins, social media now leads our modern discourse. Especially as it relates to news, business, government, and politics, social media's potential for good and evil increases because it's "unmediated media." Influencers—some of whom display a naked interest in presenting a particular side of an argument—leverage an advantage in going directly to the public and bypassing any journalistic principles supporting balanced reporting "without fear or favor."[5] Building on the last point, the public tends to trust "people like me" rather than experts, government, and the church. Where better to find people just like us than among our circle of social media friends and family?

Despite many challenges, professional journalism is alive if not exactly thriving. The advertising model, which fueled the media business for three centuries, has crumbled. In 2019, according to the Hussman School of Journalism and Media at the University of North Carolina, "more than one-in-five papers has closed over the past decade and a half, leaving thousands of our communities at risk of becoming news deserts. Half of the 3,143 counties in the country now have only one newspaper, usually a small weekly, attempting to cover its various communities. Almost 200 counties in the country have no newspaper at all."[6]

Nick Newman of the Reuters Institute for the Study of Journalism, reporting in "Journalism, media, and technology trends and predictions 2020," asserts: "The last ten years were defined by the twin technological disruptions of mobile and social media, which fragmented attention, undermined advertising-based business models, and weakened the role of journalistic gatekeepers. At the same time, social and political disruptions have affected trust in journalism and led to attacks on independent news media in many countries. The next decade will be defined by increasing regulation of the internet and attempts to re-establish trust in journalism and a closer connection with audiences. It will also be rocked by the next wave of technological disruption from AI-driven automation, big data, and new visual and voice-based interfaces. All this against a backdrop of economic and political uncertainty which will throw up further challenges to the sustainability of many news organisations."[7]

For the professional communicator, the new media landscape represents both opportunity and risk. Research tells us which media, journalists, and social influencers are most and least receptive to a particular theme. At the same time, data informs which media perform most credibly and efficiently in reaching a specific target audience. Research also reports the degree to which we deliver organizational messages directly, persuasively, and credibly. Through the dominance of social media, we risk losing the benefits of higher standards that come with professional journalism, which greatly reduce the potential for "fake news" and weaponized social media. Public relations and journalism are intertwined and each of us shares an interest in the viability of the media business. With shrinking margins, consolidations, and bankruptcies, print media in particular are under siege. As the journalist's partner, we should all do our best to support them.

Trust and the Truth

The 2020 Edelman Trust Barometer[8] reports that despite a strong global economy and near full employment preceding the Covid-19 pandemic (which may perpetuate even *lower* degrees of trust), neither government, business, NGOs, nor the media are trusted. The decline in trust for the four societal institutions the study measures, Edelman says, "can be found in people's fears about the future and their role in it, which are a wake-up call for our institutions to embrace a new way of effectively building trust by balancing competence with ethical behavior." Trust dissolves with the malleability of "truth" (as opposed to "fact"). As we see too often in our political discourse, accusations of "fake news" and the increasing popularity of fact checkers, "Pinocchio counting," and "truth-o-meters," which exist to highlight trans- gressions. "Truth" is based on reasoning, and if you're persuasive enough, you can convert me from my truth to yours. On the other hand, a "fact" is a "proven truth." As such, every fact is true but not all truths are facts.

For the corporate communicator, we must be mindful of the consequences of lost trust as we have in some ways contributed to it. Product claims for "new and improved," "made in America," and "all natural" often come from public relations and advertising departments only to be proven false or misleading under scrutiny. In terms of our day-to-day, professional commu- nicators must tell the truth with honest and good intention to portray an organization's character and values. What's more, we must embody the truth and our values by proving them through our behaviors. People judge an enterprise more by its actions and less by what it says.

Purpose and the Rise of Corporate Social Responsibility

Perhaps as a result of lost trust across our great institutions (government, politics, religion, and the media, for example) or maybe because businesses have earned our trust by supporting corporate social responsibility (CSR) and environmental, social and corporate governance (ESG) initiatives, more and more of the world's populations now look to companies to contribute posi- tively to our planet, our nations, and our individual well-being. As a reflection of this change, Business Roundtable, an association of chief executive officers of America's leading companies, shifted its emphasis in August, 2019 from "shareholder primacy" to "an economy that serves all Americans" including "customers, employees, suppliers, communities, and shareholders."[9] Earlier incarnations emerged in the late nineteenth century as Andrew Carnegie, among other titans of industry, committed to building libraries, parks, and performing arts centers as a way of sharing wealth among those in need. Corporate social responsibility emerged in the 1970s as a similarly focused social contract for "doing good," including but not limited to funding, and companies began to incorporate social practices into their business models ("sustainability," for example). Now, corporate social responsibility is an essential business strategy for companies large and small around the world.

More recently, environment, social, and governance (ESG) has emerged as an extension of CSR and as a means to quantify the degree to which a company operates ethically, sustainably, and with respect to social causes for investment purposes. Theorists, financial analysts, and investors believe that companies that reflect these priorities perform better than those that do not. As such, asset managers and other financial institutions increasingly rely on ESG ratings to measure, evaluate, and compare companies' ESG performance. Socially responsible investors synthesize the three domains—social, environmental, and corporate governance—to create an ESG score. Once a niche investment area, responsible investing now stands as a major measure of corporate performance and guides the preferences of those who wish to invest within ethically defined parameters. In recent years, it has become a much larger proportion of the investment market. As such, ESG's standing within the C-suite became increasingly important, too.

Also related to corporate social responsibility, "purpose" seeks to connect business performance with society. In November 2019, for example, the United Kingdom's Institute of Directors (IoD) introduced a Manifesto on Corporate Governance[10] that set out three objectives for new standards:

- Increase the accountability of the UK corporate governance system to stakeholders and wider society.
- Improve the competence and professionalism of UK board members—whose role is central to business decision-making.
- Enhance the ability of board members to pursue long-term, sustainable business behavior—including addressing the challenge of climate change.

The movement toward creating corporate purpose motivates employees, supports communities, and engages customers to recognize that a corporation and its brands aspire to go beyond profits to contribute a sustainable global guiding force. Purpose forms a foundation as well as a reflection to articulate why an organization exists, what problems it solves, and who it wants to be for all stakeholders: to attract and retain the best talent and to earn customer loyalty, to cite two examples. When companies align their business with societal purpose, they build deeper connections that often lead to higher market share, lower cost of business, and higher sales. Increasingly, businesses are harnessing the power of purpose to achieve profitability as well as contributing to the betterment of society. As an example, PepsiCo introduced "Performance with Purpose" in 2006 to support its products, the planet, and the people who occupy it. The company reduced its use of plastics in packaging, introduced reduced-salt and whole-grain options for its snacks, and made its delivery fleet more fuel-efficient. At the same time as upholding its purpose, the company delivered strong financial results.

For professional communicators, we must tell our CSR, ESG and purpose stories authentically, engagingly, and credibly to maximize impact. For example, Procter & Gamble's push to be "a force for good and a force for growth" depends, in part, on its PR team's ability to share compelling stories to support the company and its brand commitment to diversity, equality, and the environment. However, more important than "telling the story of purpose," public relations professionals must encourage the enterprise to "act with purpose." When companies and brands communicate with purpose in ways that are trustworthy, genuine, and persuasive, and then legitimize what they say through action, they earn trust and loyalty by elevating humanity to the heart of the initiative. Organizations must embed corporate social responsibility, ESG and purpose into every action while remaining flexible and agile to meet changing social dynamics. Covid-19 and Black Lives Matter responses revealed the readiness of organizations and the communicators who serve them. In March–April of 2020, companies and brands were limited by the permissions granted from the media and the public. By the last week of March, 2020 when the US rate of infection continued to climb while the pandemic rates in other parts of the world began to flatten, an analysis of news coverage in the USA revealed that Covid-19 news in combination with President Trump dominated roughly 90 percent of the domestic capacity for news in digital/print media. Forward-thinking communicators applied data and analysis to realize the limitations they faced: an insightful review of the data revealed that the media's appetite for corporate and brand news was limited to themes related to helping others—especially healthcare workers, furloughed employees, and the sick—lest they seem insensitive and uninformed. Routine proactive public relations activity like new product announcements died on the vine (if they were even tried at all). Companies and brands found ways to demonstrate caring and commitment that aligned with and supported efforts to help one another. By understanding, updating, and preparing, communicators knew their positioning, targeting, and timing while others were caught flatfooted. And the best communicators made sure that their company positioning was known throughout the organization so that one spokesperson reinforced every other.

The Public Relations Profession Adapts to a Changing World

The evolution of the profession continues, sparked by the many changes in society and business in general but also by some changes specific to public relations.

Professionalism of Public Relations

Earlier in the history of public relations, most practitioners expatriated from marketing or journalism and simply migrated to PR without formal training. Many universities began offering public relations courses in the 1980s (although New York University was among the first colleges to offer a class in public relations in 1923). Now, the Public Relations Student Society of America (PRSSA), which identifies itself as "the foremost organization for students interested in public relations and communications," upholds rigorous standards for public relations education and ethics. The organization began in 1968 with nine qualified colleges hosting PRSSA chapters; it now numbers 415 qualified institutions in the USA alone. Public relations master's and doctorate programs offer postgraduate continuing education for the ascending practitioner and teacher. The graduates of these programs represent more and more of the total population of communications professionals as their predecessors retire. This group of communicators reinforce their creative and writing ability with public relations theory as well as a more formal understanding of business, finance, statistics, technology, and more. Many are now emerging into leadership positions and they expect their subordinates to be as qualified and well versed as they are.

Reinforcing the move toward higher standards, professional associations around the world established and regularly reinforce principles with which members must comply. The Arthur W. Page Society as well as the Institute for Public Relations, the PRSA, IPRA, PRCA, CIPR, ABERJE (Brazil), and the International Association for Measurement and Evaluation of Communication (AMEC), among many others, hold members accountable for upholding standards for professionalism. Nowadays, many chief communications officers hold a Master's in Business Administration so they know how to harness data-informed business processes for continuous improvement. What's more, they expect public relations to abide by these processes to make a quantifiable contribution to positive business outcomes.

Reputational Risk

Just as companies that behave well earn rewards, the degree of punishment for bad corporate behavior has never been more severe. Consider these examples:

- **Samsung:** Lost $10 billion in market value according to *The Wall Street Journal* (WSJ) due to its exploding phone problem and the airline warnings that followed.

- **United Airlines:** Lost $1.4 billion in stock value after dragging a customer off a plane and the subsequent CEO's leaked letter to employees defending the action.

- **Boeing:** Lost $11 billion of market value within two days as it struggled to communicate its intentions for the troubled 737 Max. The former CEO's lack of transparency and failure to listen compounded matters.

Warren Buffett famously said, "It takes 20 years to build a reputation and five minutes to ruin it. If you think about that, you'll do things differently." The pain felt by each of these companies continues to haunt them years after the events occurred. For the most part, they recovered by saying and doing the right things, a process empowered by good corporate communications.

While the public relations department is not responsible for developing new safe technology or for designing aircraft controls, leaders often call upon the public relations person to clean up the mess. It's important for leaders to know that, just like any other asset, reputation can be managed through foresight, authenticity, and responsible action. Using technology to capture real-time alerts while there's time to mitigate, using data to quantify the potential impact of bad behavior and applying insights to guide authentic, ethical conduct are the responsibilities of the evolved public relations executive.

Emergence of Search

Search engines enable stakeholders to retrieve news, information, and other forms of content for years… even decades. In this way, news—both good and bad—lasts forever for whomever wants to see it. As such, public relations people must plan for future retrieval of press releases, news items, and social media posts. The repository of earned media coverage, reviews, and organic news acts as one of PR's unique assets when the content is positive. As opposed to other forms of marketing communication which appear and then disappear without a trace, public relations activity endures, affecting awareness, understanding, preference, and behavior long after the campaign ends. Ordinarily, public relations budgets relative to advertising and other forms of marketing are extraordinarily small—sometimes less than one-half of 1 percent (which means it often rounds down to zero). Whereas the effectiveness of a mass market television commercial, for example, may last for a week or two, and the effects of a price promotion may last only as long as the two-for-one offer is valid, the impact of public relations on sales can last for months or years. When combined with low PR budgets ("$0"), PR's long-tail effects translate to extraordinary efficiency relative to other agents within the marketing and communications mix.

Within this context, search engine optimization (SEO) has emerged as a requirement for professional communicators to enable social sharing at the same time as it "future proofs" output over time. Done properly, SEO involves audience research to uncover target audience triggers for content consumption such as messages and media that are both compelling and credible. Beyond content, the data-informed communicator also needs to know about the paths stakeholders take to raise awareness, gain understanding, and spark a buying decision.

Conclusion

While many of the basic tenets of public relations—such as creativity, an ability to build and sustain relationships, an aptitude for interpersonal communication, and a gift for the written word—will continue to be important, these skills require greater speed, agility, and decision-making power than ever before. This is where technology, data, and insights become invaluable to us. Communications technology enables us to manage and execute at speed. Communications data empowers us to navigate with less waste, better performance, and greater confidence. Communications insights enable us to contextualize the present, plan for the future, and optimize business outcomes for the benefit of the enterprise.

Technology, data, and insights become fundamental elements in the public relations/corporate communications mix as technology drives execution, data propels analysis and understanding, and insights enable corporate vision and the consultation required to achieve it.

In the following chapters we'll look more deeply at public relations technology and its many applications; we'll explore sources, methods, and uses for PR data; and we'll consider approaches for uncovering actionable insights. Finally, we'll review the public relations continuum and how it can be better informed through technology, data, and insights to achieve breakthrough results.

QUESTIONS PR INVESTMENT DECISION-MAKERS MUST ASK

- To what degree do we combine technology, data, and insights to understand our business environment?

- Does our public relations balance the best of tools and talent?

- How well do we integrate our public relations data into our business decision-making?

- To what extent do our enterprise leaders look to public relations for business counsel?

- Do we consider the impact of our statements and actions on all stakeholders, in every place we operate?

Endnotes

1 Arthur W. Page Society, The Page Principles, https://page.org/site/the-page-principles (archived at https://perma.cc/N7ZZ-WEVC)

2 GlobalStats (2020) Desktop vs mobile vs tablet market share worldwide – November 2020, https://gs.statcounter.com/platform-market-share/desktop-mobile-tablet/worldwide/2016 (archived at https://perma.cc/A98Y-467L)

3 Shearer, E (2018) Social media outpaces print newspapers in the U.S. as a news source, https://www.pewresearch.org/fact-tank/2018/12/10/social-media-outpaces-print-newspapers-in-the-u-s-as-a-news-source/ (archived at https://perma.cc/2ZRC-DW8V)

4 Walker, M (2019) Americans favor mobile devices over desktops and laptops for getting news, Pew Research Fact Tank: News in the Numbers, https://www.pewresearch.org/fact-tank/2019/11/19/americans-favor-mobile-devices-over-desktops-and-laptops-for-getting-news/ (archived at https://perma.cc/9Z3F-6BZH)

5 Ochs, A S (1896) Business announcement, https://www.documentcloud.org/documents/2271357-business-announcement.html (archived at https://perma.cc/3ZXJ-ZHNJ)

6 Abernathy, P M (2018) The expanding news desert, Center for Innovation and Sustainability in Local Media, University of North Carolina at Chapel Hill, pp 5–6

7 Newman, N (2020) Journalism, media, and technology trends and predictions 2020, Reuters Institute Digital News Project

8 Edelman (2020) Edelman Trust Barometer 2020, https://cdn2.hubspot.net/hubfs/440941/Trust%20Barometer%202020/2020%20Edelman%20Trust%20Barometer%20Global%20Report.pdf?utm_campaign=Global:%20Trust%20Barometer%202020&utm_source=Website (archived at https://perma.cc/8UMZ-4SL7), p. 5

9 Business Roundtable (2020) Statement on the purpose of a corporation, https://www.businessroundtable.org/business-roundtable-redefines-the-purpose-of-a-corporation-to-promote-an-economy-that-serves-all-americans (archived at https://perma.cc/FE9M-2VPX)

10 Institute of Directors (2019) IoD manifesto, corporate governance, https://www.iod.com/Portals/0/PDFs/Campaigns%20and%20Reports/Corporate%20Governance/IoD%20Manifesto%20-%20Corporate%20Governance.pdf?ver=2019-11-19-082215-783 (archived at https://perma.cc/B9KF-4VFC), p 3

PART ONE

Technology, Data, and Insights

01

Technology

I consider any technology that fosters better communication and engagement to be a form of *public relations* technology whether purposely built for public relations or not. From the printing press, telephone, and IBM Selectric typewriter to today's artificial intelligence, technology helps modern communicators operate at the pace that business demands. At present, communicators access purpose-built tools to help them at every stage of the public relations continuum. These tools enable PR people to micro-target stakeholders, develop strategies, create and distribute content, execute campaigns, and evaluate performance in real time, with quality and in ways that contribute to meaningful business outcomes. In this chapter, I provide an overview of these technologies and shed light on how to manage them, along with useful guidance for PR technology decision-makers. Communications technology enables public relations professionals to accomplish their objectives more efficiently and more consistently by removing rote work. Free from time-consuming routine tasks, communicators enable themselves to expend more time and energy on the uniquely "human" aspects of the profession, such as creating and managing compelling campaigns, counseling clients and senior executives, and interacting with various stakeholders including journalists, influencers, policymakers, employees, and customers. At the same time that technology sparks efficiency in the completion of routine tasks, it still requires expert oversight to think about the application, to manage the technology, and to execute at the right time.

While communications technology quickly evolved, the day-to-day responsibilities for effective public relations haven't changed: the need to manage stakeholder lists; the need to disseminate information; the need to monitor media; the need to understand our stakeholders... all these responsibilities live on. The technology of the past faded away but the essentials remain. Gone may be the days when PR technology meant your Rolodex for targeting; printing and mailing for release distribution; scissors for media monitoring; and tabulations of clip count, circulation, and advertising value equivalency for PR evaluation, but PR professionals continue to perform similar tasks today.

Most of the technologies we discuss in this chapter are purpose-built for the professional communicator, but two overarching trends affect much of business as we know it: Big Data and artificial intelligence. The terminology is quite common but the number of true PR applications are surprisingly rare. Through the lens of corporate communication, let's briefly explore each development.

Big Data

Big Data is the name applied to advanced technology that enables extremely large datasets to be analyzed and applied to generate more holistic organization-wide decision-making. Big Data systems are the culmination of many small data streams, of which PR data is one (although often overlooked). As organizations seek answers to business questions related to customer demand, competitive intelligence, and community trends, news and social media deliver unique data which, when combined with other information, helps to achieve business solutions.

When Southwest Airlines, one of the world's most admired airlines and Consumer Reports' top carrier for on-time performance, faced declining results in 2015, the company introduced a multi-disciplinary task force including representatives (and data) from finance, customer service, and operations to explore what was happening, why it was happening, and what needed to be done about it. The communications team contributed PR data from traditional and social media sources that referenced flight delays, on-time, and early arrival. The PR data stream was married to a variety of other data streams, including the Department of Transportation rankings, weather data, customer complaints, and "number of minutes delay per passenger" data to assess performance. With the addition of PR's input, the airline gained better context of its situation. Beyond the Big Data analysis the company's internal communications reinforced the importance of individual contributions to improve on-time departure. Because of the integrated Big Data analysis and the programs enacted as a result (including internal communications initiatives), on-time performance rose five basis points and the carrier rose two places in the Department of Transportation rankings. The following text and illustrations tell the Southwest story from the Institute for Public Relations white paper entitled "The Big Data revolution."[1]

- **Background:** Southwest Airlines integrated its communications data stream to solve a big business challenge. As one of the top domestic carriers of passengers and their bags in the United States, Southwest Airlines has a history of more than 40 years as an efficiency machine. For many years, it held the top spot in the U.S. Department of Transportation Monthly Air Travel Consumer Report as the best on-time domestic airline. Several years ago, those statistics began to slip, as the airline was working to bring together the schedules of Southwest and its newly acquired subsidiary, AirTran Airways. The airline also pivoted to a more long-haul scheduled airline with a greater number of connecting itineraries, all of which created a more complex operating environment. As a result, Southwest struggled with on-time performance (OTP). It is important to note there is a direct correlation between poor OTP and customer complaints, and a low net promoter score. Using a Big Data strategy, the business improved its OTP, a result of new programs and procedures in place to help improve turn times, originator flights, etc, along with diligence and dedication by Southwest employees.

- **Strategy:** An enterprise-wide effort began with many moving parts to attempt to improve the airline's operational performance. Initiatives like "Start Strong" were implemented to ensure the first flights left on time, thereby creating a better operational day. The communications team was asked to participate in the enterprise effort and contribute data to a comprehensive view of operation for a holistic view of on-time performance. Then, a cross-functional team analyzed the data to assess trends more accurately with the traveling audience (i.e. complaints, customer service calls, refunds etc).

- **Execution/Implementation:** Southwest's ops recovery team pulls information monthly from various teams and departments to get a holistic view of business performance and OTP, specifically in the areas of operations, customers, and finance. As part of the monthly ops recovery team report, under the customer umbrella, the communications team supplied data and insight on news coverage and real-time social conversation (sentiment, topics, and volume) that mentioned OTP directly, or, as customers often reference it, "flight delay," "on time," or "late flight."

- **Effectiveness of assignment:** The communications data included the number of news and social media mentions daily, daily sentiment, sample comments, and examples of news coverage. The communications analysis drew attention to major news announcements on a given day, like Department of Transportation rankings, or an event that may impact on-time performance (weather, or ancillary service issues, such as an air traffic control tower shutdowns). This data was married with the number of customer complaints recorded by the customer relations department, as well as the actual arrival delay in minutes per passenger. The resulting data analysis gave the team a surgical view of how external factors could be affecting OTP, and helped reiterate that poor OTP will drive an increase in customer calls and inquiries via the telephone and social channels. Just as important, poor OPT linked directly to downturns in the airline's Net Promoter Score. The business implemented several new programs and procedures to help combat some of the cause and effect results of sluggish on-time performance. Initial results, based on stats from the Department of Transportation, showed Southwest's on-time performance rate rose to 72.5 percent, or eighth place when compared to other airlines. This was a significant improvement over June 2014, when OTP was 67.6 percent and tenth place overall.

Artificial Intelligence

In 1950, at the dawn of computerization, the late Alan Turing, British mathematician and logician, first referenced "thinking machines." The term artificial intelligence came six years later when computer scientist John McCarthy coined the phrase and referenced efforts to develop computer programs that could think and solve problems as well as humans could. While the promise of artificial intelligence for public relations generates great optimism in areas related to audience targeting, media list development, content creation, media monitoring, analysis, and evaluation, verifiable case studies are rare. At the time of writing, thorough research related to the impact of AI on public relations produced few references, most of which referenced marketing promises and mentions of what's in store for the future. After asking a panel of PR research experts who comprise the membership of the Institute for Public Relations Measurement Commission, the response was clear: lots of excitement but very few verifiable case studies. But even if we found only a few cases, it's worth discussing the current and future states.

Analytics software entrepreneur and former CCO/CMO Mark Stouse is the CEO and founder of Proof Analytics. On October 28, 2020, we spoke about AI's utility for PR: "A key attribute of AI is that it 'thinks for itself' after having been trained. Through this lens, most of what we see in marketing and communications analytics today is not artificial intelligence at all, but various levels of automation and augmented intelligence." He continued, "There's very little that the communications profession can derive from AI at this time, other than basic targeting, given that the profession has done so little with the sort of linear and non-linear regression analytics commonly used to train artificial intelligence and machine learning." Until the profession commits fully to developing these solutions, it's clear that AI will continue to be more aspirational than practical for most PR and communications applications.

One peer-reviewed example of artificial intelligence applied to corporate communications came from another expert, PR research pioneer Katie Paine ("never wrong, just early"), who responded with a case study of how she worked with analytics company Fullintel and Texas A&M University professor W. Timothy Coombs to test the ability of an artificial intelligence system to identify crises and recommend responses. Their results show very high accuracy and effective response recommendation. Here's their story.[2]

In a 2019 presentation to the International Public Relations Research Conference (IPRRC), the guru of crisis response, Professor W. Timothy Coombs, and his co-author, Elina R. Tachkova, argued that the "preventable crisis" (i.e., one that an organization brings upon itself caused by human error or management misconduct) requires a very different response than disastrous events caused naturally. They suggested that while a lot of research exists to support recommended responses for other types of crisis, there was no research-supported effective response for self-inflicted crises.

At her annual Summit on the Future of Measurement, Paine challenged several media measurement vendors to prove Dr. Coombs wrong by using AI to identify the best response. Gaugarin Oliver, CEO of Fullintel, offered to take up that challenge and the two met with Professor Coombs to map out a research project to present at the upcoming IPRRC 2020. The research would test the hypothesis that AI could be used to help organizations determine the best response to a self-inflicted crisis. An effective response was defined as "the shortest time to neutrality"—the time it took for negative media coverage to be reduced to neutral. The process began by collecting many thousands of articles of traditional media coverage on three recent crises caused by human error and management misconduct (the Boeing 737 Max, the demise of WeWork, and an accidental toddler death). The researchers then applied definitions of different types of responses from Professor Coombs' Situational Crisis Communications Theory (SCCT). Fullintel taught its machine-learning technology how to identify a crisis, how to classify the type of crisis, and how to identify different responses which included options such as attack the accuser, denial, scapegoat, excuse, justify, apologize, compensate, and no comment.

The next step was to calculate the length of time it took to move *negative* news coverage to *neutral*. The algorithm then identified the most effective response that produced the shortest time to neutrality. The research revealed that the shortest time to neutrality was the result of an organization issuing an apology or providing information, and the longest time to neutrality was denial and scapegoating the victim. To test the validity of the findings, the researchers compared the accuracy of the AI-produced results against human analysis and reported a 97 percent agreement in determining what was or was not a crisis. The AI also performed well with 97.4 percent agreement when asked to identify the type of crisis and 94 percent agreement on the crisis response.

The crisis identification and response experiment indicates the potential for artificial intelligence for the profession by parsing thousands of possible choices to focus the communicator's attention on only the best choices for consideration. The experience also reinforces the point that as good as technology is and all the potential it represents, artificial intelligence requires human expertise to "train" the computer, to think about the results, and to make decisions.

Another application for artificial intelligence relates to content creation. In simpler applications, AI can support one-on-one conversations through social media, customer service, and email. But even in more complex situations, AI-driven content creation offers more. In one case, a service provider used a form of machine learning to generate localized press releases with great results. To introduce a new car, a major automobile manufacturer traditionally sent a generic release to every news outlet whose audience and readership might buy a car. In other words, every media outlet in the USA received the same release. To generate more coverage by appealing to local media interests (which implied the opportunity to sell advertising to car dealerships), the company generated localized releases that contained all the generic car attributes and specifications but tailored other aspects to each city and town in the USA. Instead of announcing "New car coming soon," the individualized release headlines read "New car coming on September 20th to Graham Motors on Stratfield Road," with the release quoting the dealership manager. Press release pick-up performance increased by 700 percent. While the releases required dealership data to produce them, the dealers were excited to appear in the headlines of their hometown papers. After the first experiment, the extraordinary results motivated every dealer to participate. As an alternative to funding relatively expensive co-op advertising, the car manufacturer underwrote the entire release distribution program for every dealer in America at a small fraction of the cost of advertising. Call this "co-op public relations." Once the localized database was constructed, upkeep was minimal and the process became even more efficient. With the benefit of technology doing what could not be accomplished manually, the PR staff focused on those job aspects that required the most communications savvy and creativity.

The news media's progress with artificial intelligence and content creation outpaces that of public relations. Major news organizations like *The Washington Post*, Bloomberg, the *Los Angeles Times* and Associated Press employ "automated journalism" to report earnings, recap sporting events, and publish weather reports. Public relations must approach content generation and dissemination with robot-generated reporting in mind. At present, the news robots work from third-party content (often provided by PR people) to identify key elements for publication. Similarly, public relations practitioners can apply purpose-built technology to derive bullets from data-driven content to inform speeches, events, and press materials. For example, most corporate earnings stories composed for publication using the technology begin with basic financial performance data; it's reasonable that technology will be more widely adopted for similar story types that don't require a great deal of creativity. In this way, PR professionals can focus on those activities that require a uniquely human contribution. Business leaders like the software because it allows their increasingly stressed staff to increase output by focusing on those stories—or aspects of stories— that require the human ingenuity and creativity that the technology lacks. The software requires only a few bullets to establish a theme and tone for the content, after which the AI uses its language skills to complete whole paragraphs that then just require human proofreading to validate before finalization.

It makes sense that if technology accelerates productivity for routine tasks, it ought to enable breakthrough "ideation" and "content creation" as well. That technology exists, too, but not necessarily in the form of purpose-built artificial intelligence. In fact, some of it is available to everyone at no cost via Google and other search engines. In essence, ideation technology, if you want to call it that, scans trending topics, key words, and search terms to isolate the most common or the fastest accelerating themes. Google Trends, for example, uncovers search patterns related to your areas of interest. The tool can also tell you the degree to which the subject is seasonal or evergreen, current and trending, or older and tapering down. With these simple queries to inform your efforts, you can focus your creative resources on the content that is most likely to succeed.

A more advanced example of an AI creativity enhancer involves facial coding and emotional AI that enable content creators to monitor facial reactions to digital content. Focused now on owned and paid media, the technology maps smiles, frowns, and raised eyebrows to gauge emotional reactions and to pre-test themes and images before identifying the optimal combination.

On top of this, automated media and research analytics technology enables communicators to evaluate trends in traditional and social media or in the minds of a stakeholder group to determine which topics are most compelling and most credible for an organization. This type of market research is a proven approach to positioning and brand messaging where the data enables the communicator to focus their talent on the factors that are most likely to deliver positive results.

In these examples, content creation and ideation technologies require human involvement, including even the content robots that seem to originate text. Each technology depends upon experts to write the material that the robot rewrites, to conduct and understand the Google Trends search data, and to interpret the AI readings to reflect emotions and intentions of the author.

Experts say that while AI-generated content doesn't equal all of the aspects of expertly crafted human content, it's good enough for many situations. Even though the technology is incapable of intuition, insights, and judgment, it can aggregate and organize vast amounts of content and data for human experts to accelerate their creative and analytical abilities, uncover insights, and judge various perspectives to improve communication and business outcomes. Most importantly, the communicator's irreplaceable contributions involve uniquely human abilities for creativity, judgment, and storytelling, each of which is required to make the most of every communications opportunity.

Artificial intelligence is widely recognized as a part of everyday life but it's still not fully understood, and applications for public relations are not as common as one might think. Nevertheless, the more we understand AI's potential and test its reliability, the more likely it is that AI will become a regular part of public relations and will be deployed more fully over time.

Audience Targeting Technology

In many ways, highly targeted personal "micro-communications" have replaced mass communication and broadcasting. Because of a highly fractionated society bombarded with many simultaneous sources of information, breaking through with generic content is nearly impossible. Modern communicators must speak to increasingly diverse audiences including customers, employees, shareholders, donors, regulators, and influencers, and opposition each with their own thematic preferences and penchants for favored sources of information. As such, communicators must reach these audiences through favored channels at the right time, with the most compelling content, using the most authoritative voice. In some cases, the authority may be a politician, a billionaire, or a member of the clergy. In other situations, the channels may be Facebook or the local TV news program. And so it goes: communicators must manage many more factors than in the days of mass communication when three broadcast networks reached the overwhelming majority of the US population.

Consider the findings of the Cision 2020 "Global state of the media" study that reported on a survey based on interviews with 3,253 journalists around the world. When asked for the "number one piece of advice" on behalf of PR professionals everywhere, 37 percent of the respondents said the number one thing PR pros could do to help was to "understand my target audience, and what they find relevant." One journalist went on to add, "Understand your target audience and ours to make sure your story pitch works with our publication's demographic, area of coverage, and subject matter. Random press releases and generic pitches not tailored to our publication are useless and annoying."[3]

Audience-targeting software, much of it adapted from marketing to meet public relations purposes, enables the communicator to pinpoint individuals and the media they consume. The software offers a variety of selection criteria, including area of geographic focus, demographics, firmographics (company size, industry, and annual revenues), and psychographics, which groups a variety of factors to create personas like "Graying Hikers and Travelers" and "Digital Nomads." In some cases—mostly in business-to-consumer categories—communicators can target the media with the highest penetration among specific publics based on what they own, the products they use, shopping preferences, and purchase intentions, among many other behaviors. Targeting databases also enable targeting by brand, including cars, banks, retailers, food and beverages, grooming, and more. The final piece to the equation is media targeting: the databases match all of the preceding attributes with the media with the highest penetration among these targets. In this way, Coca-Cola can target Pepsi drinkers and Pepsi can target Coke drinkers to persuade them to switch. At the same time, they continue to target their own customers with reinforcing messages to encourage brand loyalty.

Some of the audience-targeting software provides access to panel data, which offers survey results based on the answers to hundreds of questions from thousands of respondents who are paid to complete the questionnaire (which can take an entire day to complete). Another approach applies the same marketing technology used to micro-target digital advertising (cookies) based on search patterns. The application, which maintains anonymity and abides by privacy laws, captures the inquiring party's IP address and applies individual search queries for the individualized marketing of goods and services. Most people share this experience: you search for an item for purchase on Thursday evening and then alternative brands appear in your *New York Times* feed or in your email on Friday morning. The technology, known as attribution analysis, delivers product information drawing from your search and purchase behavior as collected from thousands of digital resources. In addition, geographic, demographic, and firmographic information is captured every time you register a warranty, apply for a credit card, or answer a pop-up survey online. In this way, you (maybe unknowingly) create your individual profile and feed the technology. That is what makes it extraordinarily accurate. As opposed to panel data that tells you how to reach certain groups, attribution technology micro-targets the individual IP address (people remain anonymous). What's more, it's based on individual behavior as opposed to the survey based on an individual's memory. For instance, the technology reveals the frequency with which you checked movie reviews and bought a ticket online rather than asking survey respondents to remember and guess at how many movies they saw in the past year and where they first heard about that movie. In this way, the technology eliminates the biggest vulnerability of the micro-targeting process: the flaws of being human.

Audience-targeting software identifies opportunities beyond conventional wisdom. In one example of the benefits, a luxury sports car manufacturer applied its PR to generate sales activity. The PR team devoted all of its resources to car buff magazines to reach their primary target buyers: men who loved going fast, feeling young, and enjoyed a day at the races. For decades, the PR team assumed that car buff magazines offered the highest penetration among this select audience. The auto company devoted all of its public relations outreach to editors at magazines like *MotorTrend*, *Car and Driver*, and *Road & Track*. "Media relations" amounted to inviting auto journalists to a day behind the wheel at the racecourse followed by drinks and dinner. Much to the PR team's surprise, the targeting software revealed the flaw in the strategy: the ideal subject was, in fact, female and of a certain age and income. In one of the most fundamental targeting decisions, they chose the wrong gender! What's more, the car magazines ranked in the bottom half of the top 100 media. The optimal media choice to reach luxury import buyers with a stated intent to purchase such a car in the next six months? *Martha Stewart Living*, the lifestyle magazine devoted to food, home decorating, gardening, beauty, and entertaining. Understandably, the shaken PR department needed to rethink how to best contribute to the company's success through product sales. The targeting technology revealed that while car buffs may love the automobile, they were much less likely to buy compared with their female counterparts. The programs were retooled to gain traction with women while dialing down the resources devoted to buff books (where the brand earned credibility among enthusiasts but not sales).

Tools to Find Earned Media Opportunities

You enhance the chances for placing earned media content when your content aligns with the editorial interests of the media you target. In this case, alignment means areas of editorial focus (music, technology, or cooking, for example), timing (Caribbean resort features during winter months), and timeliness (a hot trend or an evergreen story). To help, public relations services providers help proactive communicators by gathering information from the media themselves to create journalist databases, online editorial calendars, and editorial "match-making" forums. For "reactive communicators," HARO (an acronym for Help A Reporter Out) provides professional communicators with a source to retrieve and respond to reporter queries on a particular topic. Let's look at all of them.

Much more common than the audience micro-targeting referenced above, media-targeting software enables communicators to access journalist and influencer profiles to make target media lists. These databases maintain information about journalists, influencers, and bloggers across print and broadcast, trade, consumer, and business, as well as digital and social media for domestic and international outlets. The databases are searchable and updated constantly for contact information (name, title, phone, email, and social accounts), editorial interests (topics, "beats," geographic, etc), business data (circulation, lead time, political affiliation, etc), and contact preferences (phone or email, for example, or time of day and day of week). In some cases, one-on-one interviews reveal even more about biographical information and pitching tips ("lives in Hawaii but writes for *New York Magazine*" or "Tuesday deadlines so pitch only Wednesday through Monday"). Like other contact databases, these offer archiving and list-building capabilities as well as modules that help to communicate directly with journalists and to catalog interactions. What's more, some of the databases suggest journalists for consideration (like Amazon: "people who bought this item also bought these...").

Editorial calendars are available online and through PR platforms, and they offer creative sparks to tie your brand with what someone in the world is celebrating. Media outlets develop editorial calendars to help media planners strategize their advertising investments for the year ahead. The themes into which the advertisers buy are just as appropriate for public relations: Back to School, Mother's Day, Independence Day: each triggers an association for, respectively, pens and pencils, flowers and chocolates, and hot dogs and hamburgers, giving PR people with related products and services the opportunity to pitch their stories. While these widely celebrated holidays are natural and easy to recognize, editorial calendars go beyond the common knowledge. For example, February 9 is National Pizza Day; October 25 is Greasy Food Day; April 7 is National Beer Day; July 10 is National Pina Colada Day. During my five years at university, I observed these holidays three times each week but with different motives and decidedly different outcomes. For the professional communicators who represent restaurants and bars, not to mention companies that market beer, spirits, and mozzarella cheese, these special days offer opportunities to promote tie-ins of interest to consumers and editors alike.

Editorial calendars take many forms, including free online templates, Excel spreadsheets, and modules on do-it-yourself PR platforms. Editorial calendars offer specific days, weeks, and months of a wide variety of activities, including special events and holidays (even lesser-known celebrations like those mentioned above). They also provide lead times as you may need to pitch your "Summer Time is Potato Salad Time" feature to long-lead magazines in February while promoting the same story to a food blogger in July. While the calendars provide guidance, we must also consider current events, for instance an earthquake in California may supersede a fun nutrition feature about National Orange Juice Day (May 4).

Journalists continually seek subject matter experts, case studies, opinion leaders, and executives to add to their reporting. One free app is Help a Reporter Out, which enables journalists to connect with sources (whether they're PR people or not) in ways that help both the reporter and the respondent. Once you register and complete the form identifying your areas of interest, you'll begin receiving email alerts every day with queries matching your specifications. By providing journalists with the information they need when they need it, the likely success of your story is greatly enhanced as long as you abide by general courtesies (don't spam, don't respond to queries for which you're not qualified, etc). Major media use HARO and similar services to enhance their reporting and inform their readers, viewers, and listeners.

Earned/Owned Media Production and Distribution Tools

Despite the many manifestations of public relations—counseling, strategic positioning, crisis planning, and more—media relations continues to occupy a great deal of time and effort for most PR agencies and corporate communications departments. To most executives, public relations is synonymous with media. Some of the earliest examples of public relations technology were devoted to the production and distribution of press materials. Today, while the modes of technology have changed dramatically, some of the largest and best-known PR technology brands rely on press release production and distribution as major drivers of their businesses. For example, in the late 1950s, PR Newswire created a better way to distribute press releases to satisfy the Securities and Exchange Commission's requirements for simultaneous disclosure of earnings and other material announcements. Huge newsroom teletype machines replaced couriers to ensure simultaneous disclosure. Dot-matrix printers and then direct-to-computer delivery in turn replaced the teletype machines. PR Newswire, BusinessWire and their and peers can produce, distribute, and monitor content across print, social, digital, TV, and radio. The teletype machines are long gone but the needs that spawned the technology decades ago are just as valid today: speed, accessibility, and consistency.

Press releases and text-based public relations materials have evolved from the printing press to photocopier to fax to email to digital and social. Each stage of progress reflects a migration from outsourcing to do-it-yourself thanks to the benefits of technology. Through it all, the public relations newswires continue to provide the necessary services especially, as noted previously, when the release is one requiring instantaneous and simultaneous disclosure. Apart from paid release distribution services, communicators manage a lot of the process on their own by simply emailing their pitch, release, video, and photos directly to their contacts.

Similarly, video and audio production has evolved from film and tape to digital production and distribution. Up until the early 2000s, streaming video did not meet network and local news standards that required "broadcast-quality" video and content. Over the years, the internet's capacity for high-quality digital video changed all that. The point was driven home during the Covid-19 social distancing phase when major news anchors broadcast from their home studios, many using laptop cameras. The circumstances required it and viewers, being similarly homebound, accepted it. What is more, video conferencing became a standard procedure during the pandemic, as did editorial board meetings, CEO interviews, and expert appearances. Everyone grew accustomed to self-produced "home" video.

Podcasts combine the intimacy of radio with the self-selectivity of your digital library. Listeners download digitized audio files to mobile devices or a computer. They usually are available as a series featuring interviews, commentary, storytelling, and instructional content. Their impact is remarkable. Now, more than 104 million listeners consume podcasts and the frequency continues to rise.[4] The great majority of Americans are familiar with podcasting and the medium continues to gain acceptance.

There are three primary reasons why podcasts have become so popular. The first is that podcasting technology makes production fast and easy, and allows podcasters to deliver a wide variety of content. Available as a downloadable app, the tool works with any internet connection. For the beginner, one can produce audio segments, add an introduction, add theme music, and more. In addition, it enables the podcaster to "publish" their content online. The second reason podcasting is growing so dramatically is the ubiquity of listening technology: phones, smart speakers, desktops, and Bluetooth in our cars make podcasts available wherever we are whenever we are there. The third reason reflects the intimacy of the listening experience. Often heard using headsets, the listener devotes an extraordinary amount of attention with fewer distractions.

Ultimately, podcasting represents a low-cost, easily accessible, and highly engaging means of communication for the public relations professional. Based on these facts, and the tendency for technology to reduce costs over time and to make tasks even easier, it's reasonable to expect podcasting to grow even more in the coming years.

Conversely, virtual reality in public relations generated a lot of hype when it was introduced as a communications tool but failed to live up to its potential. Poor user experiences during the early stages limited the potential of virtual and augmented reality. However, certain communications situations lend themselves to virtual reality's unique capabilities. For example, imagine putting yourself in a virtual environment to "experience" a theme park or to "visit" a hotel conference center for an upcoming event (especially during the pandemic). At its best, virtual reality enables a lower-cost experience with a product or service. Some intrepid retailers like Ikea use virtual reality to help customers visualize the products they sell by creating simulated rooms.

While the potential for virtual and augmented reality is high for product demos, interesting trade show experiences, and more, very few people have the necessary equipment to use the technology at home or at work. The future may be bright, but it's not here yet.

Technology for Engagement

Email may seem like just one of life's everyday conveniences but professional communicators rely on email to make contact with journalists and stakeholders, so we should not take it for granted. When using email to deliver important information, it's essential to proofread the content, use compelling subject lines, avoid attachments when possible, and keep the message brief and to the point. General rules of email etiquette apply.

Video conferencing is another common communications technology that helps bring people together virtually for information sharing, mediation, and organizational problem solving. Video conferencing provides an efficient platform to achieve face-to-face interaction without travel, to communicate to large audiences conveniently, and to disseminate information to stakeholders. Even before the Covid-19 pandemic, video conferencing was an asset to communicators. During the pandemic, video conferencing became essential for business. However, one disadvantage exposed during the early days of the pandemic related to privacy. Now repaired, hackers found ways to eavesdrop on and interrupt video conferences. Even though conference call cadence can be tricky, with awkward interruptions, speakers on mute, kids playing, dogs barking, and people speaking at once, the convenience and efficiency of web conferencing make it an exploitable asset for the smart communicator. Interestingly, video conferencing during the pandemic made business surprisingly human. Where participants were once uptight about sharing the reality of their lives on-screen, it soon became normal as everyone experienced unexpected incidents at home and learned to take it all in stride.

Webinars are another tool useful for engaging audiences. Organizations use them for training, product demonstrations, and virtual roundtables during which participants exchange information and advice, often with the help of a moderator or subject matter expert. Webinars can be recorded for future use on your website or as an email attachment. During the pandemic, as physical conferences and classrooms became a health threat, organizations turned to webinars to carry on with networking and learning via digital seminars.

Websites/Newsrooms

While your website may not be under the control of the corporate communications group or its agencies, it is one of your most important assets. Through your press materials, social media posts, and more, SEO, when done properly, will lead stakeholders to your website where they can learn more about your organization, your leadership, your mission, employment opportunities, market information, and, in some cases, e-commerce. Yet, communications people do not always see an organization's website as a PR tool. To optimize your website for public relations, be sure to make it easy for stakeholders to find your site. SEO helps. As a professional communicator, it's important to stay tuned to the latest SEO developments to make sure the content you generate for internal and external audiences is loaded with SEO assets.

The most important properties on your website relate to making the site easily navigable, with compelling content in the form of press releases, your contact information, your logos, and photos of the leadership team, your headquarters, and products and services. This content can be diverse, in the form of text, visual, video, and audio. Your website assets must service your stakeholders directly and indirectly. Examples of direct assets include content for investors, journalists, customers, potential and current employees, partners, and the communities in which you operate. To satisfy journalists and investors in particular, many organizational websites create special "online newsrooms" to house these assets. An example of an indirect asset is those key words which enable search engine algorithms to lead interested parties to your website for additional information.

To demonstrate the need for PR and website managers to align, there's the case of a new product introduction which achieved impressive results in driving interested earned-media consumers to the company website. Using attribution technology which links earned media to subsequent behavior by tracking click-throughs, the PR team tracked the number of people who clicked on the story and then, afterward, visited the company site for more product information. Unfortunately, the website and the PR team did not coordinate, so when interested parties searched the site for the new product, it was nowhere to be found. In response, the attribution analysis revealed that after potential customers found no information, they left the site in frustration to find the information they originally sought at the company's chief competitor. The worst of all possible outcomes!

Social Media

Social media changed everything for our global society as well as for public relations: it changed the how, when, what, where, and with whom people communicate. For public relations, the emergence of social media offered a way to communicate directly with and listen discretely to publics and individuals (bypassing traditional "mediated" mass media). The effects have been profound: social media accelerated the pace of communication and, with it, the news cycle (most social media contains hyperlinks to traditional media); it encouraged more fully integrated marketing communication; and it created a platform for more mutually beneficial two-way communication. Given its importance, many social media engagement platforms help public relations professionals to communicate more efficiently through the medium. Certain elements have become essential for social media management technology, including content creation, scheduling, targeting, distribution, monitoring, and analytics. Trends suggest that social media engagement is becoming even more complicated. As a result, brands need to rethink their social media targeting to identify the channels in which their target audiences most commonly engage.

Dozens—perhaps hundreds—of social tools purposely designed for social engagement across text, video, visual, and audio channels emerge each year. More and more, communicators expect a social tool to do some, most, or all of the following:

- Technology to prioritize their social posts.
- Scheduling capability to publish at the right time.

- Serial posting tools to plan for a sequence of posts.
- Mobile connectivity to enable social interaction wherever and whenever they do business.
- Content-tracing tools to insert the company's URL into the content automatically.
- Authorization technology to ensure all posts from within the organization are approved.
- Response management reporting to track speed and frequency.
- Aggregated listening systems which compile a variety of feeds into an integrated inbox to simplify responses.
- Conversation archiving to capture, retain, and recall interactions.
- Social listening to ensure all references to the company or brand are captured.
- Timing tools to indicate the optimal time and day to post.
- Localization technology to account for languages and time zones.
- Alerting functionality to instantly notify them when the brand or company is referenced OR to set certain thresholds to alert them on emerging issues.
- Team analytics to optimize performance throughout the organization.
- Message tracking analysis to determine the effectiveness of individual posts and responses to identify what's working and what's not.
- Quantitative trends analysis to determine the volume and frequency of brand mentions versus those of competitors and opposition.
- Assignment modules to delegate tasks to designated individuals and subject matter experts.
- Account authorization capability to designate levels of authority over who can post what and when.

Technology for Media Monitoring and Social Listening

Media monitoring changed dramatically with the advent of two irreversible developments: digital news and social media. These services enable the user to catalog and apply Boolean search terms and dictionaries to help identify and retrieve content. The technology platforms capture news according to the specifications provided by the user: organization names, brands, spokes-people, and events are entered into the search engines. The platforms generate all the news featuring these references culled from thousands of sources, delivered through the platform, and organized by date, by media type, by geography, by campaign name, and more. Results appear instantly where embargoes allow. Specialty monitoring companies capture digital print, broadcast, and social media from around the world. Some platforms provide instantaneous translations and content categorization systems (by brand, by business unit, by territory, etc).

Print News

While certain industries and geographies still depend largely on hard-copy print media (for example, the beauty media sector and Japanese media), most traditional media are available online. Digital news enables the corporate communicator to retrieve content in real or near-real time, to access news archives belonging to the content owners, and, in many cases, to monitor news at no cost via Google. In the cases of the most influential media, including *The New York Times*, *Financial Times*, and *The Wall Street Journal*, paywalls prohibit unfettered access. Many sources are available through news retrieval services like LexisNexis and Factiva as well as through media monitoring platforms such as Cision, Meltwater, and Burrelles.

Broadcast Media

Broadcast media—television and radio—are also available via technology platforms as streaming video. In many cases, service providers rely on TV closed captioning required in the USA by the Americans with Disabilities Act. The captions deliver a way to capture content using text search. Recent developments using image recognition identify logos even when the brand name is absent from the captions. Historically, the technology for tracking analog radio has been difficult to capture and this continues today. Once digitized and archived online, as with NPR's Fresh Air, the content is more easily retrievable, but smaller market stations are often overlooked.

Social media

Hundreds of social listening companies dot the world with services to capture social media posts and conversations 24/7. The biggest challenge for most communicators is the volume and velocity of social channels that are so high—and growing—that the only solution is automated listening.

Executive Briefings

Executive briefings are a daily digest of the news required by organizational leaders to manage the information they need for the day ahead. They deliver a "news of the day" update into the email in-boxes of those designated to receive them. Optimally, the news items are limited to just the most salient news to make for easy, swift reading, and the deliverable is mobile friendly. The formats range from a simple automated roster of hyperlinks that can be managed in-house, to expertly curated content summarized by expert analysts to make it easier for the reader, to make the digest more accessible, and to make the content copyright compliant. When using do-it-yourself software or news-retrieval databases, it may seem easy to cut and paste content, but this practice violates copyright and places your employer or client at risk (and yet, many people risk legal action by continuing to do this).

Real-Time Alerts

Automated real-time alerts help professional communicators and news-rooms alike stay up-to-the-minute on breaking news. For public relations practitioners, real-time alerts identify emerging issues and potential crises while there's time to act. The best technology spans languages, countries, and media channels, and tracks for text, video, and digital images to bring a wide range of events—risks and opportunities—to the forefront. Some plat-forms add a human element to verify content and eliminate "fake news."

Tools for PR Measurement, Analysis, and Evaluation

While measurement, analysis, and evaluation may seem like interchangeable terms for the same thing, the data-informed communicator knows they represent very different stages within the mix:

- Measurement is akin to counting.
- Analysis involves the interpretation of data to uncover opportunities and insights.
- Evaluation requires a judgment—did the PR campaign work or not?

For media analysis, technology performs the first task very well—tabulations for media placements, social shares, circulation, and audience size are standard features even on free PR platforms. Assuming the campaign sets a measurable quantitative objective such as "number of hits," the technology will be able to deliver a calculation to determine whether the measure meets or exceeds the goal. Unfortunately, most platforms underperform on differentiating valid content from invalid. Despite "training" the technology using Boolean search terms and inclusion/exclusion dictionaries, the automation often includes irrelevant content such as ads, obituaries, and more. For example, automated monitoring for brands like Visa and Ford leads to the erroneous capture of content featuring verbs ("to *ford* a stream") and sentences which confuse proper and common nouns (Life-brand cereal and "get a life"). A level of human validation may be required to meet a higher standard since even simpler tabulations may be inaccurate and misleading.

Survey technology is used both to generate story ideas ("9 out of 10 dentists agree…") and to measure, analyze, and evaluate performance. For evaluation, surveys determine the effectiveness of a campaign by the degree to which a certain public's awareness, perceptions, understanding, and behavior may have changed. Like media analysis technology, automated surveys offer both advantages and disadvantages. A primary advantage is lower cost as the price per completed survey is limited to the cost of an email rather than alternative methods like telephone or in-person interview. Further, online surveys are less intrusive because they are available to anyone with email and a computer wherever and whenever the respondent chooses to participate. Finally, online surveys often come in a package which takes advantage of the all-in-one convenience of questionnaire design, questionnaire distribution, data collection, data analysis, and reporting.

Whether you work with survey data or media data, analysis is more challenging for technology alone. Focusing on media analysis, determinations of tone/sentiment, the presence of intended and unintended messaging, and other qualitative assessments tests the technology's abilities (despite promises of artificial intelligence and machine learning). Here, technology alone may be "good enough" because PR departments may lack the resources of a dedicated data scientist or research expert. Most platforms allow the user to override the determination of the automation—for example, changing a news item deemed by the technology to be "negative" to "positive" (it rarely happens in the opposite direction). In these cases, a member of the PR team is assigned the task of filtering the automated content feed for irrelevant content (ads, wedding announcements, obituaries of employees, etc) and then double-checking the tone attribution to improve the accuracy.

Evaluation necessitates the greatest level of human involvement as it requires judgment of the degree to which a campaign succeeded or whether it succeeded at all. Setting measurable objectives prior to the campaign ensures a relatively easy way to determine the degree to which quantitative measures met or exceeded the goal. Other success variables require a more nuanced approach that supplements the technology with sector expertise along with statistical acumen to deliver a judgment. The best forms of evaluation go beyond determining what happened, when, among whom, and by how much to uncovering actionable insights and strategic guidance to improve performance over time, versus objectives, and against competitors and best practice.

Attribution analysis for public relations repurposes aspects of marketing technology used for digital advertising planning, tracking, and evaluation and applies them to earned media. Just as advertising attribution technology monitors click-through from digital ad to website or e-commerce site, the earned media version tracks click-through from a digital news item through the journey from news site, review site, website, and e-commerce site. The technology has the potential to redefine public relations/media relations from above the sales funnel to a quantifiable contributor to the entire sales funnel, from awareness to engagement, understanding, preference, and purchase. In this way, billions of impressions may not measure PR success in the future, replaced instead by the number and profitability of sales. While too many public relations departments are evaluated on "big number" measures like impressions or hits, the efficiency of public relations in driving sales far exceeds that of any other agent within the marketing and communications mix. As this reality becomes better appreciated, public relations being characterized as "soft" will be redefined as an important and efficient driver of business performance.

In addition to strategic and tactical public relations technology, specialty platforms deliver back-office functionality related to project management, campaign resources and deadlines, client relations management, and monthly reporting. For agencies in particular, technology solutions provide help for billing, collections, and general bookkeeping (hours per project, profitability per project and per client).

The rise of communications technology requires us to rethink what we do as well as how and why we do it. As in almost every area of society and business, technology has and will continue to transform our profession. Across the board, technology enables professional communicators to reinforce our unique contribution to the enterprise while improving our efficiency and return on investment (ROI).

Will PR Technology Replace PR Professionals?

While artificial intelligence and new technologies promise to enhance our productivity, efficiency, and creativity, they have also made more and more jobs obsolete—and those jobs aren't coming back. In certain lines of manufacturing, robots are faster, more accurate, more consistent, and less expensive than humans. In addition, they never ask for sick days or vacations. For public relations, however, robots lack the essential qualities of the professional communicator, while other professions like accounting may disappear in the next twenty years.

A positive outlook for public relations' ability to withstand automation and artificial intelligence is not surprising. While computers can manage many repetitive data-centric tasks and communicate well with one another, they cannot relate to the human audiences with whom PR people engage. Technology cannot contextualize or empathize—it's easy for most humans but nearly impossible for automation. What's more, creativity, while enabled by technology, cannot replicate human ingenuity. Robots may write an adequate press release when the release is sufficiently standardized, but a computer cannot place the proper emphasis on the most salient points in the most accessible way in which readers, viewers, and listeners choose to engage. Ultimately, the frequent role of the public relations professional is to *persuade*. Persuasion requires the consent of both parties and robots can't pick up the social cues to adequately engage in a persuasive conversation.

The time may come when rote tasks take certain responsibilities away from interns and entry-level communicators, but no one gets into PR to be the person who builds media lists, monitors the platform to track earned and social media, or produces charts and graphs. The sooner these young professionals begin experiencing the real fundamentals of public relations—writing, composition, persuasion, pitching, relationship building, strategic thinking, purposeful creativity—the sooner they become fully realized professionals.

QUESTIONS PR INVESTMENT DECISION-MAKERS MUST ASK

- What are your objectives for the technology? What do you hope the technology will achieve for you?
- What systems do you already have in place? To what degree must these technologies interact and communicate with one another?
- Do you want to integrate your PR technology with other platforms used by marketing and sales? How will you integrate the systems?
- What are your information requirements? How frequently and how quickly does information flow in and out of the solution? For media monitoring, do the feeds refresh in real time 24/7/365?
- How flexible is the system? Can you customize the display and the outputs?
- How will you measure the ROI of the platform? To what degree will the technology enable you to improve the ROI of your communication?
- How will you migrate from your existing system to the new system?
- How intuitive is the technology for a novice?
- What resources are available to support the system (financial, human, and technological)?

Endnotes

1 Weiner, M and Kochhar, S (2016) Irreversible: the public relations big data revolution, Institute for Public Relations, https://instituteforpr.org/irreversible-public-relations-big-data-revolution/ (archived at https://perma.cc/RV5K-Z3TB), pp 25–26

2 The Measurement Advisor (2020) Yes you can use artificial intelligence to predict a crisis, Paine Publishing, http://painepublishing.com/measurementadvisor/yes-you-can-use-artificial-intelligence-to-predict-a-crisis/ (archived at https://perma.cc/B83R-SPBD)

3 Cision (2020) Cision's global state of the media 2020, https://www.cision.com/us/contact-us/thank-you/state-of-the-media/ (archived at https://perma.cc/8MUP-3NCD), p 18

4 Based on research conducted by Edison Research and Triton Digital in 2020

02

Data

Traditionalists view public relations as a people business, focused on creative activities, media relations, and speech writing. By that definition, public relations is little more than an indeterminate endeavor reliant on verbal acuity and ingenuity, the contributions of which are unquantifiable and not attributable to the benefit of the enterprise. Within this context, even executives who appreciate public relations consign it to the periphery without the advantage of data-driven proof of performance. Even with low-cost/no-cost tools designed to generate PR data, many communicators make a deliberate choice *not* to measure. These regressive PR practitioners insist, "PR is an art. And how do you measure art?" Well, ask Sotheby's, one of the world's largest auction houses: they measure the value of art every day, and without a data-informed marketplace some "valuable" art might not hold any monetary significance at all. As such, the notion that you can't measure public relations is a myth, especially based on the outmoded premise that PR is a form of art.

Earlier in my career as a research-based communications consultant, I assumed every PR agency and corporate communications department measured its public relations programs and applied data to inform decisions. After all, research and evaluation appeared in every textbook, and all of the major PR awards programs required research for setting objectives and evaluating performance. Considering the fundamental primacy of research in these instances, it struck me as very strange that almost every public relations person with whom I spoke avoided talking about data, research, and evaluation. Naively, I assumed they had developed a secret method that couldn't be revealed. "Of course they measure," I rationalized. "But for whatever reason, they simply choose not to talk about it with *me*." For years, I supposed that communications research was so precious to these individuals they chose not to disclose their approach and I simply moved on.

After ten years in the profession, I met the president of a mid-sized New York agency at an industry event at which he casually revealed the truth by declaring, "There's no way we'd measure: I'd gladly forego being a proven success in exchange for never being a proven failure." Despite representing some of the world's greatest brands—including several from a company recognized as one of the world's most successful data-driven marketers—the agency managed to retain the client without ever quantifying the value or return on investment of its work. Twenty years from the time that agency president's casual cocktail chatter revealed so much to me, many practitioners furtively take the same approach to data and research in their PR work, principally as a way to avoid quantitative evaluation. This breed of unenlightened PR person lingers, choosing a career filled with the uncertainty of never knowing what worked, what didn't, and what could be done to improve. In the meantime, the C-suite to whom they report evolved significantly. Data is the language of the boardroom and to conduct any aspect of business without quantification impedes the success of the organizations for which we work, the teams on which we serve, and our profession (not to mention our career potential). The choice against data-informed public relations equates with surrendering our ability to quantify PR's unique contribution to the enterprise, to erase opportunities to improve over time, and to earn the coveted seat at the table.

Most public relations professionals find themselves on the path to communications research enlightenment: some journeys are just beginning while others find themselves well on their way. At the journey's end, public relations research and evaluation accomplish what most of us seek: the ability to quantify PR's ability to drive business results, the insights we need to execute productive campaigns consistently and to full effect, and an increased role for public relations, accompanied by adequate funding and resources. For those readers who are not familiar with public relations measurement, analysis, and evaluation, let's start by beginning simply but simply beginning.

Introducing Data to Public Relations

Data are specific units of information that people use for decision-making. The conventional wisdom is that data is comprised only of numbers, but words, concepts, facts, and statements are also elements within the equation. Data in today's business environment is essential and billions of dollars in investment support the current and future demands for more and better data. Given this level of expenditure, it's no wonder that among the most common anxieties in a data-driven world is that we are drowning in data while bearing the responsibility to apply it intelligently, to drive better business decisions, and to generate a return on our data investment.

Despite the high levels of expenditure—or perhaps in some cases *because* of it—working in a data-driven business world comes with a variety of challenges which apply to PR just as they apply to every industry and professional sector. The biggest challenge today is not so much the need for data but getting the right data, ways by which to filter out the surplus, and new approaches to thinking about and applying the good stuff. Sophisticated communicators collect and analyze data from a variety of direct and indirect sources to leverage what they gather in the communications process. Data informs objectives-setting and strategy development by leveraging stakeholder patterns and their preferences for information, delivery, and consumption. Data also informs campaign development that combines the best elements of timing, messaging, and targeting to trigger the desired outcome.

In the following sections, we review the essential considerations for any communications professional interested in making the most of their public relations research and evaluation journey. We begins with applications.

Objectives, Inputs, Outputs, Outcomes, and Business Results

Public relations investment decision-makers want to know whether their outlay and your effort yield an effect, and if so, the degree to which it "moved the needle." They ask, "Do our public relations efforts change awareness, understanding, preference, and behavior?" If so, what are we changing, by how much, within what timeframe, and among which audiences? To answer these questions, communicators collect data to represent five types of activity and yields:

Objectives

The PR data process depends on setting objectives. Without measurable objectives, the public relations professional has only a vague idea of their destination and no idea of when they've arrived. In the absence of data-informed objectives, the PR department risks being out of place with the enterprise, PR team members risk being misaligned with one another, and the PR individual risks devoting resources to goals that don't matter to the team or the enterprise. What is more, measurable objectives make it easier for leadership to assess PR performance in the language they understand: data. When agreed to in advance, communicators predefine public relations success along with the measures by which success is determined. When professionals base their objectives on data, the goals they set are more easily negotiable and navigable to achieve results that meet the key criteria for "reasonable, meaningful, and measurable." Objectives-setting is examined more thoroughly in Chapter Five, but the following items contribute to every phase of the public relations continuum from landscape analysis, objectives-setting, strategy development, tactical creation and execution, evaluation and ongoing refinement, each of which we visit later in the book.

Inputs

Inputs include the data representing time, resources expended, levels of investment, and activities. When the time comes to evaluate "efficiency," you'll need to know the requirements of each campaign relative to the result. For example, if one campaign generates 100 positive earned media stories after investing $10,000 and 100 hours of time, you can compare that with other campaigns, some of which may have yielded fewer stories against less time and money, or may have generated double the stories against the same levels of time and budget invested. Ideally, over time, each campaign will generate better results with greater efficiency, which equates to doing more with less and for less. Without measuring the inputs, your ability to measure the efficiency of the related activities limits your ability to prove value and improve performance. In some cases, top executives may not know enough about PR other than to check off the boxes you negotiate with them: the number of activities undertaken and completed as well as the degree to which you completed them on schedule and with high quality. Some PR clients seek only "the big number" (outputs, outcomes, and business results), but input data points seek to reveal the *biggest outcome* number in relation to the *lowest input* cost. When you accomplish this and improve the ratio over time, you demonstrate PR value and improve PR ROI.

Input data reflects the time and money invested in the creation and execution of a program or campaign. When measured against the outcomes, simple division reveals a "cost per X" equation that allows you to assess cost per percentage point of increased awareness, cost per thousand positive messages, and cost per engaged customer. Recommended input considerations include:

- total hours for planning, strategizing, execution, and evaluation;
- cost per hour factored by the number of hours and the hourly compensation rates.

Measurable input activities include the following:

- **Background research on company/brand priorities, executive preferences, etc:** At the beginning of the year or before the campaign begins, teams invest time and effort in evaluating the public relations landscape to create a foundation upon which to improve the likelihood for success and minimize risk. This usually involves speaking with internal stakeholders from the C-suite, marketing, consumer insights, and other areas with an impact on PR. It may also involve external conversations with journalists, agencies, and the like.

- **Meetings to ideate, conceive, and plan the campaign to begin the strategy development process:** These include setting objectives, messaging, and audience targeting.

- **Informal pre-testing time and effort:** This may involve checking back with the original stakeholders from the first bullet to inform, discuss, and refine.

- **Preparation of the PR brief or playbook to formalize the public relations plan:** Designed to be part proposal and part execution document, the PR brief/playbook identifies target audiences, intended messaging, spokespeople, events, and budget. Use this document to finalize the campaign with executive sponsors, and to refine and deploy the public relations plan.

- **Emails, phone calls, texts, and letters:** These are some of the first steps in the execution phase. Time and effort go into these routine tasks and they need to be accounted as a measurable input (agencies typically track their hours for billing purposes; PR department staffers can do the same).

- **Budget and costs:** These include agency budget, out-of-pocket production and distribution costs, monitoring and evaluation expenses, etc. Ultimately, the budget and out-of-pocket costs determine a lot about the effort, whether it's an annual program or a simple one-day promotion. The budget-setting process is an essential input metric that contributes to the overall inputs measurement of time and resources, working with vendors, service providers, and the like.

It's a long list, but each bullet represents another way to win. Unless you are working against a billable hourly time sheet in which one accounts for every hour of every day, you and your team may find this difficult to initiate. If so, pick the biggest input drivers and confirm with your client—whether an internal or external client—to set the stage and gain buy-in from the person who will eventually evaluate your performance.

Outputs

Outputs include data reflecting what we produce as part of our everyday work, from a simple press release to a big-budget campaign (not to mention the entire annual program). Output measurement includes tracking the number of people attending a press event, calculating the number of placements from a press release, or tabulating the reaction to a social media post. Like all measurement, monitoring the quality and effectiveness of our outputs enables us to refine our approach and course correct while there's still time to effect change. Ideally, output data should align with inputs, outcomes, and business results data so we can learn and plan even more productive public relations programs in the future.

Output measures represent a unique and critical component to capturing and evaluating communications performance. All forms of marketing and communication feature outputs. Examples of marketing outputs include an advertisement, a billboard, or a newspaper insert. For public relations, outputs are media pitches, news releases, social media posts, and events as well as the media coverage and attendance they produce; output data points measure the degree to which communications efforts generate exposure to an audience.

Similarly, all marketing and communications seek to generate and measure an outcome or a business result. The primacy of outputs data in understanding the overall effects of marketing and communication within the organization centers on the fact that as opposed to "controlled" communications like advertising, direct, and price promotions, public relations is only semi-controllable at best. In "uncontrolled" situations when an organization becomes the focus of public scrutiny in the media, public relations is often the only communications presence, especially when confronting a crisis. While a conduit to outcomes and business results, outputs are limited to exposure rather than the effects of that exposure. Since outputs do not connect directly to behavioral change or revenue generation, for example, some communications professionals discount their importance.

Many factors contribute to outcomes, such as awareness, understanding, attitudes, and behavior. Isolating the effects of an individual marketing communications agent can be challenging because most campaigns include more than one element. When it comes to uncontrolled communication, apart from competitive marketing, most of this type of exposure relates in some to way to public relations. Everyone generates positive outputs and everyone lays claim to the positive effects, but most of the negative or critical exposure requires output measurement to capture and assess what's being communicated, by whom, and to what end. As such, outputs measurement is an essential dataset and should not be overlooked or undervalued.

Because advertising and other forms of paid communication maintain 100 percent control over their messaging and media placements, their outputs measurement relies on a simple formula of frequency and reach called a gross rating point. Since budgets are limited, marketers carefully calculate a balance of reach and frequency to ensure the optimal levels of exposure. The gross rating point determines a cost per thousand (whether by frequency or reach) by dividing the level of advertising buy by the number of thousands of media consumers. Public relations-earned media outputs, meanwhile, rely on the discretion of the journalist and editor. That means that PR output measures require a broader range of factors. The output data points shown below reflect what may be called a public relations gross rating point (PR-GRP). The PR-GRP elements fall into the three categories previously defined as quantitative, qualitative, and comparative.

Quantitative measures are simpler tabulations. Almost every public relations measurement program includes them.

- Frequency denotes the total number of stories and posts in which your company, brand, or placed message appears in print and broadcast, trade, business, and consumer media as well as social.

- Reach includes print media circulation, television, and radio audience. Unique visitors and page views reflect the number of people who were either exposed to your content or had the potential to be exposed to your messages (not everyone who subscribes to a newspaper reads every story, hence "probability to see" rather than "saw"). Also known as exposure, circulation, and audience. Impressions are a variation which communicators sometimes abuse by arbitrarily assigning a multiplier to reflect "PR's added credibility" or an assumed "pass-along rate." Multipliers range from 2.6 to 8 or more. Since no formal standard exists for any aspect of the general use of multipliers, they should be avoided and discouraged.

A better variation of reach is target audience reach, which introduces a hierarchical element reflecting the fact that the *big* reach number is not necessarily the *best* reach number. High-circulation magazines and popular television news shows may generate big numbers, but they may not be the right readers and the most valuable viewers. Target audience reach quantifies the degree to which your target audiences read, watched, or heard your key messages through your media placements. *The New York Times* is not the only newspaper to reach business leaders, policymakers, and influencers, but it's more likely to reach those audiences than a placement in a rural farming journal. Similarly, communicators should look to media other than *The Wall Street Journal* to reach farmers looking to buy a tractor in the next six months. A small daily newspaper in a rich suburb to an urban business hub may reach just as many executive decision-makers through their home news as would be reached through more conventional—and more competitive—choices like the *Times* or the *Journal*.

- Total mentions reflect another aspect of frequency by tracking the number of times your company or brand appears in an individual story as well as in the media overall. The underlying premise is that a positive story with a single reference to a specified brand is less desirable than a positive story with many references to that brand as each mention reinforces the overall positive messaging. Conversely, a negative story with many brand mentions is less desirable than a negative story with a single brand mention as the communicator hopes that fewer brand references attached to negative themes are less visible and the best result under the circumstances. In this way, generating 100 positive stories with 500 total brand references achieves more than 100 positive stories with 100 total brand references. References may be explicit or implicit and may include brand attributes or company spokespeople as supportive and qualified mentions beyond direct references to the brand itself.

- Advertising value equivalencies directly translate the advertising gross rating point to public relations without any of the subtleties that make public relations unique. This is calculated by multiplying a basic advertising unit cost by the time and space acquired through that investment. AVEs, as they are commonly known, generate criticism as an invalid metric misappropriated from paid advertising to earned media. Despite the controversy surrounding them, ad value equivalency continues to appear frequently as a low-cost representation of the "value" of earned media. Of course, public relations differs from advertising in the way readers, viewers, and listeners digest and process the content, and the implied credibility of a journalistic imprimatur. PR also differs in terms of its inability to control the message, as advertising does. What is more, any experienced advertising executive knows that ad buys are heavily negotiated while AVEs apply the highest book rate. AVEs at their worst apply a dollar value to coverage both good and bad (no sane person would pay for critical or negative advertising as a way to promote sales of that brand). Finally, earned media sometimes appears in places where ads do not, such as the front page of the newspaper. Many of the top public relations award competitions prohibit the inclusion of AVEs and disqualify any award submission that features them. In many cases, the executives who fund public relations programs demand ad value equivalencies as a way to apply a dollar sign to PR efforts. Perhaps developed at a time when advertising agencies managed most public relations campaigns, the measure was an acceptable peer-reviewed metric until the early 2000s when organizations such as AMEC and the Institute for Public Relations raised awareness to relegate AVEs to the past. To a large degree, their anti-AVE campaigns succeeded, as evidenced by the declining popularity of AVEs, but for those who continue to use them, they are a quantitative metric (assuming that one measures only positive stories). Their use is discouraged but, as stated earlier, "I'd rather be approximately right than totally in the dark," and AVEs do provide a way to evaluate performance. If you choose to use them, I recommend that you take out the dollar sign and treat them as a relative measure of space, time and prestige of the media outlet as these factors are reflected in an advertising rate. The dollar sign, in particular, is what makes AVEs so objectionable.

- Cost per thousand or CPM is a better way to apply a simple financial element to evaluate a public relations effort. As opposed to advertising value equivalency, which is specious and seeks the highest possible number, a "cost per" metric is a sound defensible equation that seeks the lowest possible cost. The cost per thousand formula takes the out-of-pocket costs or "inputs" (press release production and distribution, for example) and divides the total expenditure by the number of thousands reached through that investment. A press release that costs $1000 that yields a reach of 1,000,000 generates a cost per thousand of $.01 ($1000/100,000 = $.01). If that release reaches an audience of 2,000,000, the cost per thousand drops in half to $.005. PR's typical cost per thousand compares very favorably to advertising or any other form of marketing communication. This relates to an objective to "do more with less and for less." Generally, public relations delivers extraordinary returns using CPM when compared with advertising. Consider what eMarketer reported in its 2019 end-of-year review in which the trade publication stated that the average CPM for a prime-time broadcast television ad in the United States was $36.19.[1] An average PR program usually delivers a CPM of under $1.00.

Qualitative measures provide context to the quantitative. Common qualitative output data points include the following:

- Tone/sentiment is usually designated using a 3-, 5-, or 7-point scale ranging from negative to positive (including variations for very negative to very positive) as well as assignments for neutral. Tone/sentiment reflects PR's "semi-controllability" in that the journalist controls the final presentation. Communications data scientists apply tone/sentiment at either the story level or the message or "entity" levels. The preferable approach captures individual messages to provide more detail as to which messages are working or not working. Story-level coding captures only the "overall sentiment" and usually results in a "neutral" rating, either because the story is, in fact, neutral or because the positives offset the negatives to appear as a "balanced" or "neutral" story overall. Message-level tone/sentiment represents the true nature of journalistic content to reflect all sides of a story, including positive, negative, and factual statements. What is more, message-level data provides the communicator with the levers to pull and push to elevate overall PR performance. The astute communicator draws prescriptive and actionable insights from the tone/sentiment data to reinforce the positive and fix/mitigate the negative messages. By identifying "friends and foes" among journalists, opinion leaders, and analysts, the relationships with the most receptive friends are reinforced, supported, and amplified. Foes are educated to alternative perspectives or, to the extent possible, isolated from future outreach for the next story. For example, the public relations team at a car manufacturer kept a top-tier list of automotive journalists who were given first access to the press fleet of new cars for test driving purposes. In one case, despite the importance of the publication, one journalist wrote only negative reviews, dredging up historical shortcomings that the car manufacturer had fixed years ago through a quality improvement effort. Despite the manufacturer speaking with the journalist to reinforce the new higher-quality production methods, the journalist continued to focus on past flaws and was subsequently demoted from "top tier" to "second tier" as the PR team concluded that offering any access to new cars only perpetuated negative references.
- Intended and unintended messages measurement is a concept developed by David Michaelson, PhD, Don Stacks, and Jennifer Clark in their paper "Message Delivery: A Revised Approach for Public Relations Measurement," published in the *Public Relations Journal*.[2] Their approach

introduced a unified message delivery-scoring model to account for the inclusion of intended messages, the omission of intended messages, and the presence of negative messages in media. In this way, an *intended* message is usually classified as positive. However, in a crisis, for example, a message generally perceived as negative may be intended and add value. For example, when a Fortune 100 CEO was forced from his position after an indiscretion, the company took the position that it acted responsibly by ousting him. The public saw the situation as negative but overall the messaging was intentional. In that case, it was unreasonable to expect a positive reaction, but at least the company's position was credible and its response set the stage for a quick recovery by indicating what had happened (the CEO was dismissed), why it happened (his indiscretion), and what the company was doing about it (instituting new policies and looking for a new CEO). The presence of an intended message benefits the organization while the omission of an intended message is an opportunity to add value in the future. The presence of a critical mention reduces value and is usually unintended. Identifying a message as either intended or unintended is a safeguard against "fake news" since accuracy is a factor in determining your organization's intentions.

Measuring intended and unintended messaging requires three output measurement steps: message development and prioritization (are the messages the right messages?), message inclusion (do the messages appear in your PR outputs?), and the delivery of the messages to the target audience through the media (did the media reports include these messages?).

- Spokespeople, opinion leaders, and influencers-tracking reflects another opportunity to refine your communications output. Your company spokespeople allow you to deliver highly controlled messaging. Opinion leaders and influencers are third-party sources who also shape public perception of your organization.

- Tracking your company spokespeople enables you to identify which are the most newsworthy and best at staying on message. In some cases, executives need media training to ensure that they deliver intended messaging thoroughly. What is more, we know from journalist surveys we've conducted over the years that reporters prefer speaking with senior executives outside formal channels. In other words, they prefer to bypass public relations representatives. To use this to your advantage, you must create an environment in which executives are informed, responsive and accessible to the media because the media will quote the executive verbatim. If the executive reflects your intended messaging completely, your organization will never experience completely negative coverage since at least the executive's quote will be positive and reputation building. Providing executives with media performance data enables you to help them refine their media presence. Finally, even media-averse executives respond to the call when they see that their competitive counterparts generate more reputation-building coverage than they do. Everyone wants to beat the competition—in this case, "score-keeping" inflames executives' competitive spirit.

- Tracking influencers and opinion leaders enables you to identify friends and foes who earn visibility and own third-party credibility. Sometimes the influencer is a sports hero, while in other circumstances they may be a politician or a recognized expert (a celebrated chef speaking on behalf of a branded ingredient, for example). Some spokespeople and influencers receive compensation for supporting a brand, in which case the measurement ensures the degree to which the person is compelling and credible when communicating the brand's intended messaging and whether the investment in that spokesperson delivers a positive return. Spokesperson tracking traces the frequency with which the media calls upon the spokesperson and the percentage of times he or she delivers the brand message. Some may be paid spokespeople for your competition, in which case tracking them may help your own messaging and paid spokesperson strategy. Other spokespeople and influencers are truly independent (think about a reporter for consumer reports), in which case measuring their commentary provides useful feedback to either engage or disengage with them to the degree you can elevate their perceptions of your attributes and benefits to improve your visibility by coupling with their third-party credibility.

- Media presence data reveals the likelihood of a reader, viewer, or listener engaging with your content. Research conducted in the early 2000s but still widely applied today examined which physical attributes of a news item led to awareness and recall. In the experiment, public relations pioneer Bruce Jeffries-Fox[3] from AT&T led a team of data scientists who exposed 1,000 people to a variety of news items and later tested them to determine whether they remembered the news, if the article mentioned a brand, and which brand they remembered. The experiment revealed that certain physical attributes of a particular story predicted the likelihood that anyone saw the story and remembered the brand mentioned. Of the dozens of possibilities tested, certain news item characteristics emerged as the best predictors of awareness and recall:

- o size of the article: bigger/longer news items draw attention over shorter/smaller news items;

- o presence of visuals: if there's a photo or graphic present, the article draws more attention than if there is none;

- o headline presence: if you're in the headline, people are more likely to identify your brand than if you are absent;

- o exclusivity: if the story is all about your brand, your brand is more likely to be remembered than if the mention appears in a round-up story, for example a gift-giving guide for Mother's Day in which a dozen gift ideas appear;

- o dominance: if your brand appears in a round-up story, what percentage of the story does the author devote to you?

- Then, of course, the frequency, reach, and tone of your media coverage determine the overall desirability of the story when combined with media presence: a story in which you're in the headline of a large story with a photo, that's all about you, is great if it's positive (and equally bad if it's negative).

- Share of voice measures your relative performance versus that of competitors and peers. Ideally, your brand beats the competition for positive share of voice, which is the preferred key performance indicator (KPI). While an organization may wish to track share of voice (SOV) versus every competitor, the relative cost for monitoring everyone makes the exercise cost prohibitive for manual coding and may not reveal as many insights as one might think. To identify which competitors to track, we recommend a group of three, comprised of 1) the biggest competitor, 2) the competitor who keeps the CEO up at night, and 3) the most innovative competitor, who provides the greatest opportunities to learn. Beyond tracking the traditional competitive set, organizations also track performance against most admired peers (or the aspirational set) and the opposition. "Share of" measures apply also for internal purposes where one compares one business unit with another to ensure that the most important division (highest revenue generation, profitability, or potential) garners an appropriate share. In every case, share of reporting provides opportunities for context and continuous improvement by benchmarking against competitors and with your colleagues in different geographies, business units, and brands. If you generate the highest positive share of voice, you should reinforce your strategy and tactics to widen your margin of victory. If you generate the highest negative share of voice, you need to fix the problem. If competitors produce a greater share of positive voice, study their methods, then adopt from and adapt to best practice.

- Media mix measures the degree to which your target media cover your stories versus those of competitors so you can focus resources on strengthening relationships with the media and journalists who cover you most favorably and frequently. Conversely, if a media outlet or journalist favors your competition, you need to dig deeper, determine whether you have a credible and compelling version of the story to share, and then work to mitigate your competitors' advantage.

Outcomes

Outcomes represent the results of your public relations programming and the generated effects in the minds and actions of your target audience. Outcomes measurement involves gauging the degree to which your communication affects awareness, understanding, preference, and behavior, elements that the marketing world refers to as "the sales funnel." While the concept of the sales funnel originated more than 100 years ago, marketers and communicators commonly apply the approach to represent a progression of conducive actions whether you're actually "selling" or not. Traditionally, communications data scientists apply survey research to uncover the effects of a campaign on the target audience. More recently, they look to social media conversations to provide unprompted or "unaided" indicators to gauge campaign impact. Like the other public relations data streams examined here, outcomes seek the answers to questions like "what" (do we seek to change), "by how much" (do we seek to change it), "by when" (the timeframe for change), and "among whom" (centered around your target audience).

OUTCOMES DATA POINTS

As mentioned, communicators commonly measure outcomes using either surveys or digital media tracking. After introducing common outcomes data points, we provide the details for their measurement and evaluation.

Recall and awareness reflect the degree to which people—preferably your target audience—recognize your brand and remember it from a direct or indirect experience. In the sales funnel, recall and awareness are important as means to an end, which, in this case, means the desired behavior. Even though recall and awareness come early on the path to behavior, the likelihood for business success is greater when people recognize your company and brand as it offers a foundation upon which to build trust and openness to receive your intended messaging. Recall and awareness statements include "I've heard of that brand." Consider the fact that Coca-Cola's Christmas advertising campaigns feature white polar bears on a red field... there's no mention of the brand at all! The colors alone are enough to spark the brand association.

Comprehension and understanding represent a level of engagement with the brand that leads the prospective customer to a better sense of what the brand offers and what it represents. For example, people understand that Walmart means "low prices every day" and Porsche translates into "high performance." This is the second stage in the sales funnel. Company comprehension and understanding statements include "I know what that company does."

Attitudes and preference mirror a consumer's position toward that company or brand. By this definition, attitudes and preference are completely subjective to the taste and experience of the individual. To earn preference, a company or brand must credibly align with the priorities of the target audience. Health-conscious people may prefer organic lettuce while people on the go may prefer lettuce in a bag. Depending on your objective and your offering, there may be a perfect audience match. Attitude and preference statements include something to the effect of "This company makes the best product of its type. When the time comes, I intend to buy one."

Behavior reveals the ultimate measure of success: did people do what you wanted them to do? Buy the product? Invest in the stock? Vote for your candidate? Apply for the job? Traditionally, the difficulties in tracking behavior were manifold: Some people buy a product if it's marketed or not. Some people prefer Pepsi over Coca-Cola regardless of the three-for-one coupon. They love the product and they're immune to marketing. Compounding the challenge, many marketing and communications agents work simultaneously and isolating the effects of one over the other can be difficult. The answers come in two forms: attribution analysis and marketing mix modeling. Attribution analysis uses new technology to track earned and paid media by following the clicks and subsequent actions, including visiting an e-commerce site and completing a transaction. Marketing mix modeling applies a statistical regimen across many forms of marketing and correlates marketing outputs with sales. By working backward, data scientists begin by looking at sales activity over time and by market before correlating the marketing activities in place at that time in that market. Through a series of advanced statistical analyses, the model reveals the relative contribution of each marketing component.

Outcomes data is derived using three approaches: one employs surveys, one relies on self-reported behavior, and the third applies digital analytics.

- Surveys, a form of primary research, ask people a series of questions to assess awareness, understanding, attitudes, preferences, and behavior on an aided and unaided basis. By asking the right questions, surveys uncover the impact of your public relations activity and its effect on the audience's thinking and behavior. The survey instrument confirms whether your audience received your intended message; if your message affected their thinking about your theme; whether the message affected them positively or negatively; why it affected them the way it did; and whether the audience was sufficiently motivated to act.

- Self-reported behavior is discoverable through social listening. In sharing their life stories, social media fans tell their connections about their awareness of, attitudes toward, and behavior toward products, services, and the like. Social listening delivers particular value in capturing extreme feelings: most people don't care enough to share routine experiences and opinions but they love to post complaints and rave reviews over what registers more deeply.

- Digital analytics include Google Analytics and Google Search to determine the effects of the campaign. Google Analytics helps communicators capture website traffic, or you can look for the concurrence of searches on your topic to help determine whether your PR campaigns are working. You can also monitor blog reactions and social shares to determine the extent to which people respond to your campaign. Social media analytics enable the communicator to evaluate the degree to which people engage with your company, brand, or issue by analyzing social conversations to gather feedback, responses, and insights to make better communications decisions over time. Since social media monitoring captures organic conversations, you can learn not just what people are saying but what motivates them, what they intend to do in response, and what they actually did. One of the most important and newest digital developments enables communicators to track conversions, which is when people click on a link that leads to your website, a review site, or even a competitor's website. Conversions capture where people go online and what they do after clicking on a digital media story.

The objective to measuring inputs, outputs, and outcomes is to help you determine business effects. The data should reveal new insights that enable you to drive a positive return on investment by identifying strengths and weaknesses so you can optimize future action as you dive deeper into the sales funnel.

Business Results

Business results are measured by communicators in terms related to return on investment. There are three principal ways by which public relations contributes a financial return: revenue generation or sales; efficiency by doing more with less and for less; and avoiding catastrophic costs. Too often, communicators confuse "generating a positive return" with "proving value." Whereas proving value is subjective based on the preferences and priorities of those executives who evaluate public relations performance, generating a return on investment is a financial measure that translates into money either gained or retained. Communicators must know the difference to earn credibility in the boardroom since the C-suite knows the difference between the two measures.

BUSINESS RESULTS DATA POINTS

- Revenue generation measurement relies on either attribution analysis, marketing mix modeling, or, in rare cases, occasions where public relations operates in isolation at a time and place where sales occur without any other explanation. Revenue generation is the sexiest business result and through attribution analysis, it is more accessible than ever (whereas market mix models are expensive and tend to be outside the control of almost every public relations practitioner).

- Efficiency measurement relies on inputs, outputs, outcomes, and business results to uncover ways by which public relations achieved more with less and for less. Efficiency is the most accessible measure of PR-ROI because it involves many decisions and behaviors already enacted by most public relations people. Like the automobile example earlier, lending the test-drive vehicle to the automotive journalist who is most likely to write a positive review yields more positive reviews per test drive than sharing the car with negative reviewers. Considering that the test drive car is a depreciating asset the moment anyone drives it, there's a material amount of money at stake (not to mention the instances when journalists crash the car or return it with scratches, etc). One car magazine test driver landed his vehicle in a tree (not just *hit* a tree, he vaulted the car *into* the tree). The challenge with the efficiency business metric is that it can only amount to a fraction of what is already a relatively small PR budget. Lowering the cost of your average press release distribution by switching vendors can only yield a relatively small saving in the bigger picture, but efficiency is a business metric and everyone owns the opportunity to make better efficiency decisions.

- Avoiding catastrophic cost represents the rarest but most impactful of all business results when one considers the cost of a reputation-damaging incident. The market capitalizations of companies in crisis cost them billions of dollars (and sometimes the company cannot survive and simply goes out of business). For example, in 2017 passenger videos showed three security officers forcibly removing a passenger from an overbooked United Airlines flight.[4] The videos generated extraordinary visibility—all of which was alarmingly negative. By the next day, shares in United Airlines closed down just over 1 percent after opening down 4 percent as the company scrambled to address the incident. A mea culpa from the CEO helped the stock recover from its worst losses, but its market value was still off by $250 million. Following the reaction, United CEO Oscar Munoz issued a statement calling the incident "upsetting" and apologized "for having to re-accommodate" customers, which failed to appease customers and investors alike. The company's response was widely criticized. In his third attempt at an apology, Munoz called the event "truly horrific" and promised to "fix what's broken so this never happens again." While the PR team at United didn't drag the passenger from the flight, it might have helped to mitigate the scale of global criticism by advocating a genuine mea culpa in the first apology to de-escalate the cascade of criticism and negativity (not to mention helping to avoid a serious hit to the company's market value).

The communications data and measurement process begins by determining and understanding the objectives of the program and ends with measuring results, all within a reliable framework, to determine the degree to which the communication met or exceeded the goal. At the same time, it should provide important insights to determine the best path forward.

Some public relations experts focus solely on the importance of outcomes and business performance while others focus on the more accessible measurement of inputs and outputs. A friend puts it this way: "Why try to resolve which came first, the chicken or the egg, when you need both?" To paraphrase liberally from the warrior philosopher Sun Tzu, measuring outcomes without measuring outputs is the slow path to victory. Measuring outputs without measuring outcomes is the noise before defeat. Measuring both enables you to navigate your performance to higher levels of achievement, including measuring business results, which is the way to win the war.

Understanding PR Data

The data points we referenced at the beginning of this chapter include quantitative, qualitative, comparative, and attributive measures. A fully formed public relations measurement program employs all four elements to answer the key questions required to drive the data-informed, continuous improvement process.

- Quantitative measures represent volume.
- Qualitative measures reflect subjectivity.
- Comparative measures denote relativity.
- Attributive measures assign credit.

Let's explore each more fully.

Quantitative metrics reflect amounts, including the number of hours invested in a campaign, awareness, story volumes, and the number of social media shares. Quantitative research applies to a variety of communications research but with slightly different meanings. For example, when examining the definitions for survey research and content analysis, two popular forms of communications data science, the difference becomes clear. In a survey, quantitative data means the data is projectable to a broader population. In media analysis, the term applies mainly to reach and frequency. The likelihood for success requires a combination of quantitative analysis with other variables, including quality.

Qualitative metrics most commonly focus on words, images, and videos, and seek to uncover the nuances of what's on people's minds as well as what they read, watch, and hear in the media. Like quantitative research, qualitative research holds a different meaning in attitudinal research than it holds in media analysis. In attitudinal or market research, qualitative research usually refers to a type of research that cannot be projected to a general population. The opinions of twelve people in a mall—also known as a focus group—helps set the stage for projectable quantitative survey research by reflecting the language and priorities of the target audience but it isn't suitable for business decision-making. For content analysis, qualitative research represents the qualities of the content analyzed, including the words and images conveyed through media coverage and the degree to which they are positive, negative or neutral, intended or unintended, organic or placed.

Comparative data relates one data set with another. For example, among the most common comparative metrics are performance versus competitors and year-over-year results. Comparisons like these add context and understanding to either quantitative or qualitative analysis while satisfying those who may not understand the intricacies of communications. As such, one of the most accessible ways to communicate PR performance is to apply a combination of quantitative, qualitative, and comparative analysis to report to executives in the simplest and most compelling of terms.

Attributive data connects public relations with a behavior by attributing an action or a behavior to an event or a touchpoint. The most common form in corporate communications is attribution analysis of digital earned media content. New technology indicates how many people clicked on a story, follows their subsequent actions, and quantifies conversion by attaching a website visit, an information download, or an e-commerce transaction to the earned media content that triggered the behavior.

The combination of quantitative, qualitative, comparative, and attributive data provides communicators with a holistic approach to data analysis for public relations.

Data's Role in Corporate Communication

For those communicators just entering their journey to research-based communications, data comes from either primary or secondary sources. Each has a role in uncovering essential information, but one may prove more attractive depending on the relative importance of speed, budget, and data quality as well as the desired outcome.

Primary Research

Primary research usually involves testing a hypothesis or answering questions through the responses of a target population. As such, primary research is customized to a particular need, such as gauging the potential of a new product or assessing corporate reputation. The data scientist collects information directly from predetermined sources through interviews, surveys, focus groups, polls, and observation. Each approach has its advantages and disadvantages. Let's explore a few of these:

- Research interviews by phone or in person are relatively expensive and time consuming yet they yield detailed results. Interviews may be structured or unstructured while providing the researcher an opportunity to directly engage and probe further.

- Some survey options offer low cost and accessibility. Digital survey software enables do-it-yourself survey design, execution, and tabulations. Usually administered via digital and social media as well as email, proper surveys are "projectable" to a larger population when using rigorous sampling methods. Surveys with a sample size of 500 respondents will yield a margin of error of only +/–4 percent—good enough for most situations.

- Observational research can be structured or unstructured, controlled or uncontrolled. For example, retailers apply observational research to optimize the effects of store design, traffic patterns, and product displays on sales behavior. While informative, it can be expensive to create appropriate test marketing environments.

- Focus groups are a semi-structured, moderated dialogue with a small group of people, and are widely misunderstood. Unfortunately, many communicators apply the findings of these conversations to a larger population rather than using them properly to gather "the voice of the stakeholder" insights for quantitative survey questionnaire design.

- Polls, by definition, involve only one question. As such, they are less expensive than surveys and faster, simpler, and easier to execute, tabulate, and analyze. However, with only one question, polls greatly limit the depth of analysis and understanding one achieves with a survey.

Secondary Research

Another source of data is secondary research, wherein the researcher acquires and applies data collected by other organizations, such as census data collected by the federal government. While such data stems from studies whose purpose may differ from yours, you can take advantage of the convenience, accessibility, and low cost of publicly available data. Secondary research has its advantages and disadvantages. Some advantages of secondary research include the following:

- **Inexpensive:** Given proper attribution, preexisting data comes with few strings attached. While another organization expended resources to gather and analyze the data, it's often available online for free.

- **Convenient:** With internet search, many thousands of research studies from businesses, government, and academia are a single click away.

- **Efficient:** Since the data has already been gathered, calculated, and analyzed, it's available and ready to use immediately online.

- **Ubiquity:** Governments, industry associations, and non-governmental organizations (NGOs) conduct research constantly and consistently over time. As such, secondary research may be found from years ago with regular trend analysis over time. What's more, the ability to attribute your data to well-known and respected institutions adds credibility to your own research.

- **A useful guide for primary research:** Since primary research is resource-intensive, secondary research can help to guide your questionnaire design, sampling, and analysis methods. It may also uncover unexpected problems before you encounter them. What's more, the right secondary research may preclude the need for primary research overall.

- **New interpretations from existing data:** While secondary data is gathered to meet the explicit needs of another organization, you may find a more applicable perspective by reanalyzing the existing data to arrive at new and more relevant conclusions.

Just as there are advantages to secondary research, it also comes with disadvantages. The researcher must be careful to avoid the traps hiding behind low cost, easy access, and fast turnaround. For example:

- **Data quality:** Secondary research depends on the data generated by the primary research of another party, so beware of any hidden biases.
- **Insufficient relevancy:** The data may look great on the surface, but we must remember that a different organization sponsored the research to meet its needs and objectives (not your needs and objectives).
- **Incomplete information:** Some forms of publicly available data may hide underlying details of the methodology and the findings that may affect your use of that information.
- **Obsolete information:** Check the currency of the data and the experiment. Publicly accessible data may not be up to the minute, so it's important to work with the most up-to-date information available.
- **The need to compromise:** Once one commits to secondary research, one must be prepared to make reasonable compromises while protecting the integrity of the primary data and your application. With customized primary research, the study design is tailored to your needs and with the additional cost come fewer compromises.

Conclusion

Data without context and absent of actionable insights amounts to trivia. Your data analysis program must be based on your objectives, your resources, and your ability to execute. Through advancements in technology, public relations data and analytics are more accessible than ever. As such, employing a data-informed communications program is now purely a matter of choice rather than inability. In the next chapter, we discuss how communicators convert data to the actionable insights which provide a foundation for business and communication decision-making as well as positive business outcomes.

QUESTIONS PR INVESTMENT DECISION-MAKERS MUST ASK

- Where did the data originate?
- What methods did we apply for the analysis?
- How accurate and reliable is the data?
- What does the data tell us? What is it *not* telling us?
- How can we apply the data to uncover new ways to improve?

Endnotes

1 Benes, R (2019) TV year in review: advertising remains strong, but road ahead is murky, eMarketer, https://www.emarketer.com/content/tv-year-in-review-advertising-remains-strong-but-road-ahead-is-murky (archived at https://perma.cc/2KN6-9TCY)

2 Michaelson, D, Stacks, D and Clark, J (2020) Message delivery: a revised approach for public relations measurement, *Public Relations Journal*, 11 (2), https://prjournal.instituteforpr.org/wp-content/uploads/MessageCompleteness Formatted.pdf (archived at https://perma.cc/YV68-HCDG)

3 Weiner, M (2006) *Unleashing the Power of Public Relations*, Jossey-Bass

4 CNN (2018) Backlash erupts after United passenger gets yanked off overbooked flight, https://edition.cnn.com/2017/04/11/travel/united-customer-dragged-off-overbooked-flight/index.html (archived at https://perma.cc/ZSD7-QVT8)

03

Insights

For decades, executives demanded that their public relations departments apply research and analysis to set objectives, develop strategy, and evaluate performance for continuous improvement. Unfortunately, most PR professionals didn't know enough about research and measurement to respond and management didn't know enough about PR to offer guidance. As a result, the movement toward data-informed corporate communications stalled.

Today's PR professional is surrounded by data and technology, and as a result, more communicators measure their impact than at any time in the past. Unfortunately, data and technology alone won't suffice. Tools by themselves are not "insights engines" despite vendor claims. Data without context amounts to trivia. Tools and data embolden many communicators to "check the box" for PR measurement, which is not a bad development, but it's only the beginning. Beyond the simplest functions and without human expertise, communicators are unable to achieve what executives expect now: a data-driven hierarchy leading to actionable PR insights and demonstrably positive business outcomes. The ability to connect PR performance to organizational performance persists as a professional rarity.

Even with data and technology tools, PR research, evaluation, and insights remain less common than top executives and clients expect. At its foundation, the progression begins with PR *measurement*, which is tantamount to counting clips and tabulating audience reach, a task which PR software performs well. One level higher in the sequence, PR *research* involves gathering, analyzing, and interpreting data about a market, a company, or a brand, and its past, present, and future potential. This step requires practiced human involvement to succeed. Higher still, PR *evaluation* requires expert judgment to draw data-informed conclusions about quality, merit, or worth. Together, these elements provide a map to actionable insights and a path toward business results. To evolve as a profession, our skills, experience, and expertise remain essential even if data and technology bring out the best of our human attributes.

The Current State of Technology-Driven Data-Informed Public Relations Insights

Armed with technology to execute and data to inform, advanced communicators aim to elevate their position by adding their unique experiences and expertise to arrive at actionable insights. Nowadays, almost every PR person subscribes to a platform and everyone has data. As a result, the current challenge to achieving actionable intelligence to guide better communications and business decisions becomes "who manages the technology?" and "how do we think about the data?". Insights reflect the progression communicators make from measurement and real time to research, analysis, evaluation, and ultimately, actionable insights in right time, all of which, when taken together, result in a deeper understanding and an ability to generate more meaningful organizational outcomes.

In his text "Statistics means never having to say you're certain," Philip B. Stark, Professor of Statistics at the University of California at Berkeley, declares insights arise at the intersection of three elements:[1]

- **Technology:** This enables us to produce data and to act on that data with consistency and speed. For communicators, this means that our technology platforms enable us to monitor media coverage and survey responses, analyze traditional and social media content, and survey respondent data quickly and reliably.

- **Subject matter expertise:** This ensures that our findings are relevant to our hypotheses. For public relations practitioners, this translates to a keen understanding of the industries in which we operate and the stakeholders we serve; familiarity with the theories and practices of public relations; and experience and a firm grasp of the media and the needs of journalists, influencers, and the interested parties we and our organizations serve.

- **Statistical acumen and critical thinking:** These ensure that our findings are accurate, fully vetted, and repeatable. For public relations professionals, this transforms our innate talent and creativity into objectives which are reasonable, meaningful, and measurable; messaging and targeting strategies designed to optimize outcomes; campaigns that deliver our positioning to the right people at the right time, and to accurately measure our performance and the degree to which we met or exceeded the objectives we set at the onset.

Insights based on these three assets allow us to discern which factors are most likely to generate success by reinforcing the aspects that create competitive advantage, minimizing those factors that underperform, and optimizing our resources for even greater success in the future (see Figure 3.1).

To illustrate Stark's concept and bring it to life, the following award-winning case study from software company Adobe shows the effects of the Stark model. The Adobe communications insights team, led by Jennifer Bruce, PhD, with support from Susanne Sturton from Adobe and Dave

FIGURE 3.1 The three elements that lead to insights

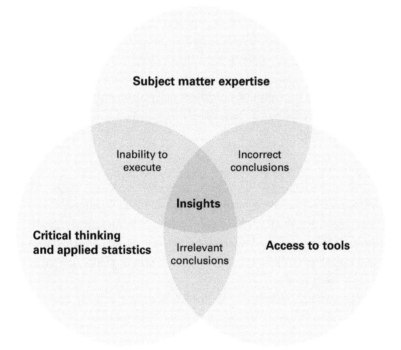

NOTE Philip B. Stark, PhD, simplified the insight recipe when he created a Venn diagram to visualize the ingredients for achieving a higher state. The diagram applies to public relations as well as every other endeavor.
SOURCE Stark, P (2017) Statistics means never having to say you're certain, https://www.stat.berkeley.edu/~stark/Java/Html/Venn.htm

Reynolds from Cision Insights, recognized an opportunity to realign the organization's perceptions of PR value while aligning Adobe's desire as an organization to simplify processes and gain efficiencies. Each member of the team contributed all three of Stark's requirements for insights generation: Jennifer Bruce's doctorate in social psychology and her involvement in social media research for more than a decade provided statistical rigor to the study; Susanne Sturton's knowledge from managing Adobe's media content analysis programs for more than a decade represented Adobe's institutional knowledge of past approaches; and Dave Reynolds brought more than a decade of experience driving research-informed communications consulting through tools and technology. All three team members shared enough knowledge to contribute on every requirement to achieve the desired insights. Together, the team combined the best of talent and technology to quantify PR's unique ability to drive meaningful business outcomes while sparking a new appreciation for PR among senior executives. The profession recognized this program as an example of "best use of research and insights" in awards competitions sponsored by AMEC and *PR News* in 2020.[2, 3]

The section below reflects the submission that requires each entrant to describe the program in ways similar to how we describe the public relations continuum in this book: objectives, strategy, tactics, and evaluation. These competitions give extra credit to entries that quantify the link between public relations input, outputs, outcomes, and business results. The Adobe award submission checks all the boxes.[4]

Here is their story.

Adobe's executive team believed that competition for its Experience Cloud business generated greater visibility in key media outlets reaching critical audiences. They also believed that a higher volume of coverage across *all* media drove better business results than a lower volume of high-quality coverage in *target* media.

To test the validity of these beliefs, the Adobe communications team conducted a data-informed, factual, objectively based communications analysis program. The goals of this analysis were to:

- assess Adobe's relative performance against the key competitor;

- impartially measure key topics and reputation attributes such as *innovation* and *leadership* to assess performance relative to the key competitor;

- provide share of voice on both the quantity and quality of coverage versus the competitor;
- identify key media outlets that covered the competitor's product offering while omitting Adobe;
- uncover new opportunities to either mitigate the competitive disadvantage or reinforce Adobe's advantage where either occurred.

As part of the research initiative, the insights team also focused on one of Adobe's new business lines: in 2019, the company entered an emerging product space—customer experience management (CXM)—at the same time as a number of competitors. The company set the objective to achieve dominant positioning in this new category. These leadership objectives included:

- to achieve the greatest CXM share of voice in target US media;
- to attain the highest quality of coverage among competitors;
- to ensure that media coverage across the CXM category aligned with Adobe's recognized strengths (rather than the competition's).

A third emphasis focused on the desire among Adobe's communications leadership to simplify its public relations performance program, to provide consistent holistic analysis and insights throughout the organization, and to quantify the company's PR return on investment.

To achieve these objectives, Adobe collaborated with the Cision team to implement a pioneering media insights framework using proprietary media analysis software. The structure applied proven traditional and social media analysis methods supplemented by innovative data science approaches, including:

- N-gram (predictive computational linguistic and probability analysis);
- audience and media segmentation research;
- a hybrid of automated and human media analyses.

This measurement framework assessed the validity of Adobe executives' assumptions while providing actionable intelligence to inform ongoing messaging and targeting strategies for continuous improvement, simplification, and category domination.

The research debunked the executive team's belief and showed that a core set of defined media outlets—rather than a higher volume of coverage across all media outlets—drove the desired results and delivered the greatest return on investment for the software leader. Following the Stark model, the team applied technology to test a variety of hypotheses and execute on the best iteration; the team's statistical acumen ensured that the data was accurate and repeatable to provide a solid foundation; and their combined experience with public relations, the media, and the technology sector ensured that their recommendations were relevant and valid. The research incorporated the desired combination of outputs, outtakes, and behavioral outcomes:

- size of target C-suite audience reached vs. the competition (outputs);
- presence of unique Adobe product attributes vs. the competition's and generic attributes (outputs);
- degree of C-suite audience social engagement and amplification vs. the competition (outtakes);
- number of C-suite visits from earned media to Adobe's website using advanced attribution analysis (behavioral outcomes).

In one of the most striking findings in achieving the goal to simplify, the research revealed that 65 percent of the original target list of 3,000 media generated only one story in the past year while the more focused list of 550 media generated 76 percent of all quality coverage.

Because of the communication analysis, key stakeholders agreed with PR leadership to focus Adobe's media outreach and measurement program on the media that delivered optimal results: target C-suite audience reach, unique Adobe message presence, C-suite social amplification, and lead generation as quantified by the attribution analysis. In this way, the communications team strategy shifted to deliver greater efficiency, better results, and a higher return on Adobe's investment in public relations. In the outtake of the final report, Figure 3.2 shows how just 18 percent of the original list of 3,000 media generated the best results.

The Adobe communications team developed and executed four main tactics to drive the desired results. Audience-targeting research and analysis identified four C-level purchase decision-maker audiences: chief information officers, chief marketing officers, chief design officers, and chief financial officers. Through the attribution analysis, the research team sought those media with the highest level of penetration but also those media that prompted the highest levels of engagement and social amplification among C-suite occupants. Adobe placed a higher percentage of unique attributes among C-suite media at a fraction of the cost of monitoring and analyzing all media coverage. When combined with qualitative analysis, findings identified the topics and key

FIGURE 3.2 Key indicators of comms success driven by key media outlets

A retroactive content analysis proved that more than 75% of
reach, social engagement, and C-suite visits to Adobe.com were driven
by just 18% of Adobe's target media outlets

NOTE Through a combination of technology, sector expertise, and statistics, the resulting
insights from the program mirrored the Pareto Principle, also known as the "80/20 rule," which
states that 80 percent of desired results come from just 20 percent of the possible causes. In so
doing, the research identified the most productive targets and made them the priority.
SOURCE Weiner, M (2020) Proving the most accessible and efficient path to PR-ROI, *PR News*,
August (8)

drivers of coverage for different audience types and prominence. This inquiry
further reduced the target media list from the original 3,000 to the first
reduction level of 500 and resulted in a proactive media relations target list of
just 150 media outlets.

After the targeting research, the team focused on messaging optimization to
identify the best themes for proactive outreach. The researchers tested
hundreds of potential subjects to reveal those that were most important to
C-suite buyers. The team made the determination using attribution technology
to compare the click-through performance of stories to isolate the themes that
appeared most commonly among the most popular news items. The second
factor involved a competitive content analysis to catalog the messages
communicated either by the key competitors or generically across all
competitors. The analysis revealed the messages that were important to the
target audience and uniquely strong for Adobe. Further, the findings
recommended avoiding messages that were stronger for key competitors or
most commonly attributed to all competitors. Finally, the team recognized that
the most engaging way to publicize Adobe's stories involved customers
communicating their own Adobe success stories from peer to peer rather than
sourcing from the company. Customer stories added credibility and higher
levels of engagement.

To meet the company's desire to *uncover efficiencies* and *simplify* wherever
possible, Adobe consolidated with a single source for international content
aggregation, analysis, reporting, and research-based consultation to deliver the

essentials for media content analysis. The four pillars are quantitative analysis including reach and frequency; qualitative analysis including tone, key message, delivery, etc; comparative analysis tracking performance versus the competition; and attributive analysis to tie earned media to business behavior, demographics, and firmographics.

The communications research and analysis team uncovered opportunities to drive better decision-making using a combination of methods, technologies, and know-how. To remove bias and enable "clean slate" message analysis, the team applied n-gram analysis, a linguistics model that assesses word sequences and probabilities to evaluate CXM coverage. The team also use attribution analysis to identify the media with the highest C-suite penetration based on demographics, firmographics, and media consumption patterns. For broad industry topics such as *innovation* and *leadership*, the analysis required a brand-agnostic approach. Keyword taxonomies represented each topic, aiming to avoid Adobe-centric definitions. This approach ensured a balanced, scalable methodology for benchmarking. Expert human analysts identified relevant product-topic coverage. As an emerging product-topic, CXM involved an evolving terminology and automated analysis would not suffice. Finally, the team measured proactive and organic coverage for Adobe and the competition, and designated the source of each story as driven by a press release, blog post, or an executive citation within coverage.

Senior executives, corporate communications leadership, and the research team judged the program as an overwhelming success. Beyond Adobe's evaluation, the profession deemed the research as extraordinary and awarded the effort with multiple forms of recognition, including awards and best practice case studies. The executives recognized the importance and ROI of quality of business engagement (and its related efficiencies) rather than volume of media coverage. Everyone agreed on the primacy of higher-level C-suite engagement over gross circulation. A clear definition of PR value enabled the PR team to prove PR value and improve PR performance by delivering more for less and with less. The research uncovered the opportunity to concentrate the number of media monitoring and content analysis services to a single provider after determining that the chosen partner captured 82 percent of all content while all other sources combined captured only 37 percent of coverage. The back-in-time landscape analysis which identified the opportunity to reduce the number of target media from 3,000 to 550 (and then to just 150) focused limited communications resources to the media that matter most, thereby saving time and money. By arriving at a single global methodology to enable greater PR performance data comparability, clarity, and insights, Adobe dramatically reduced the number of research reports from 900+ issued by a variety of providers. The new approach yielded time and cost savings estimated at 25 percent. The centralized approach to monitoring and analysis reduced billable agency hours by hundreds of hours, with related costs and reporting turnaround times reduced by 67 percent. The new approach to media monitoring and analysis formed the foundation for more fully integrated marketing and communications decisions. Impossible to calculate in the past, the new approach enables correlation analysis between news coverage and internal data such as Adobe.com visits, trial, and purchase behavior. Further, segmentation analysis revealed specific indicators for the optimal combinations. The communications team now knows, for example, the degree to which media are most likely to increase website traffic and conversions to product trials (and which do not). As a result, the team quantified the return on investment of corporate communications. Now that it's in place, the company's PR-ROI continues to improve.

Through a marriage of technology, statistical expertise, and industry knowledge, Adobe quantified the unique power of public relations to empower the enterprise as forcefully as any other marketing channel. As a result, Adobe executives control the levers to guide the company to even greater success.

The Public Relations Insights Discovery Process

The Adobe case study highlights the insights discovery process. Hypotheses led to testing which, when validated and refined, revealed insights that resulted in a substantial shift in public relations thinking and execution. What's more, Adobe's insights and data team made a direct connection between media-focused public relations and business results. Without the combination of technology, sector knowledge, and statistical acumen, the insights and the changes they sparked would never have happened.

An observation and an insight may seem the same but there's an important distinction. An observation is raw data such as social media likes and circulation tabulations without judgment or evaluation. Insights reflect a deeper interpretation and understanding of the data. Call it wisdom: an underlying truth that explains the fundamental motives that drive what stakeholders like, read, and listen to as well as what they say and do as a result. What's more, an insight helps to influence what people will say and do in the future. Observations are factual while insights apply experience, expertise, and knowledge to the facts. Finally, observations are thought provoking and enlightening while insights are illuminating and actionable.

Insights aren't easy to come by—beyond data, technology, and expertise, they require determination to go beyond the obvious to uncover the unexpected. Mastercard's experience introducing mobile payments technology reveals more about the insights discovery process. Here is their story.[5]

Mastercard is a global technology company working in the payments industry. It connects consumers, financial institutions, merchants, governments, and businesses worldwide, enabling them to use electronic forms of payment instead of cash and checks. Mastercard uses technology and data-driven insights to make electronic payments more convenient, secure, and efficient for people everywhere. Mastercard does not issue cards but develops advanced payment solutions and seamlessly processes billions of transactions around the world every year. The business has a global reach—extending to more than 210 countries and territories—and continues to experience growth in a world where retail transactions continue to be dominated by cash and checks.

One demonstration of Mastercard's ability to transform data into insights, actions, and business results relates to its efforts in mobile payments, an emerging form of commerce enabled through the use of mobile devices. When the mobile phone first became the consumer method of choice for making purchases and managing money, Mastercard was perfectly placed to help merchants provide their customers with a safe, simple, smart way to pay using their mobile devices. In a strategic drive, Mastercard led developments of standards and was among the first to launch mobile commerce technologies that let people "pay with a tap."

As part of this drive, the Mastercard executive team under the leadership of CEO Ajay Banga in 2010 embarked on a continuing journey to transform the B2B financial services giant into a more consumer-focused payments technology company. Among the most important discoveries at that time, data scientists uncovered a trend revealing consumers' great excitement and anticipation for the emerging mobile commerce technology. But those who tried it expressed two sources of anxiety: lack of acceptance and data security. Deep contextual analysis revealed concerns over data security centered on unfamiliarity with the technology and the possibility of personal data compromises. Frustration over lack of acceptance also arose over the inability of certain merchants to process mobile payments at point of sale.

Beyond the PR team, who listened, engaged, and refined their communication, social data insights profoundly affected planning and execution throughout the company. This "voice of the consumer" directly influenced marketing messaging, advertising campaigns, product development, and merchant training programs. Following the initial discovery, the company's market research tracking study confirmed the social media findings. In years two and three of the mobile payments initiative, Mastercard applied its research findings to lower barriers to mobile payments by interpreting the evolving social discussion of mobile commerce to inform marketing and communication targeting and messaging, providing a pulse of social opinion for the mobile payments industry, uncovering positive and negative drivers of use, adoption, and sentiment in global markets, and reporting on barriers to adoption of mobile technology for consumers and merchants to help Mastercard overcome them.

To generate earned media insights that could be trusted, upheld, and executed required a more sophisticated approach than a tool alone could offer. The social listening platform did the heavy lifting using complex, multi-language search string algorithms supplemented by human-validated analytics. The right streams of data were identified using search string methodologies to remove false positives, spam, and splogs (spam blogs), as well as ensuring the right geographical signals. Data scientists applied a layer of subject matter expertise, statistical acumen, and critical thinking to create the necessary insights.

The deliverables were real-time monitoring and analysis of online communications, including news, blogs, Weibo, Twitter, Facebook, YouTube, Google+, Instagram, boards, and forums. Mastercard employees could self-sufficiently access relevant content and human-validated data, as well as create real-time research and reporting. Mastercard generated regular timely reports, showing key metrics, SWOT analyses, key influencers, and industry themes. The aim was to help Mastercard set smarter objectives, develop better strategies, create more compelling tactics and execution, evaluate performance, and drive continuous performance versus objectives, competitors, and past performance.

Importantly, an annual study of social commentary around mobile payments was developed to assess people's willingness to adopt mobile payment services. The annual Mobile Payments Study aimed to assess people's awareness, understanding, attitudes, preferences, and behavior toward existing payment options throughout North and South America, Europe, Africa, Asia, and the

Pacific Rim. To assist in leading the industry agenda, visually compelling, sharable graphics were created to summarize the findings.

Using proprietary social media analytics expertise, methods, and technology, researchers identified millions of relevant social media posts each year on the subject of mobile payment innovation in the context of Mastercard and its industry peers. From the huge volume of posts, a broad sample of substantive comments was subjected to more granular expert human-coded content analysis. The resulting insights were converted into actionable business drivers. The findings were successfully applied throughout Mastercard and adopted across the wider industry.

In the year following Mastercard's strategic communication response, the company's "Mobile payments" study revealed that mobile payments transitioned from skepticism to adoption as 81 percent of conversations were driven by mobile payments users compared with only 33 percent the previous year. The social media analysis showed that conversations had gone from "problem solved" to "what's next?". In year three, consumers began to embrace mobile payments and asked banks and merchants to provide more mobile payment options.

Internationally, insights revealed that users based in Europe were the most vocal in expressing opinions about mobile payment technology, followed closely by Asia-Pacific and the United States. Some skepticism was evident in Europe as consumers discussed mobile payment security and general reservations about the feasibility of worldwide adoption. Across the Latin American and Caribbean regions, non-adopters expressed a need for clarification on the technologies offered as well as a clearer understanding of the cost implications on their current lifestyles. China, Thailand, Australia, Japan, and Singapore were the most active countries across Asia. Users discussed product experiences and shared opinions about news stories originating in traditional media. Discussions in the Middle East and Africa tended to retell or redistribute stories that originated in traditional media, with the highest shares of discussion stemming from South Africa, Saudi Arabia, UAE, and Nigeria. In the United States, users showed interest in the compatibility of mobile payments with other payment systems. Other drivers of discussion centered on value, longer-term benefits and security. These insights were fed back into Mastercard's global communications strategy and formed the basis of wider industry insight.

Mastercard used the in-depth global picture to inform messaging and targeting strategy. Mastercard's paid, earned, and owned communication reinforced high-potential themes on which it led the industry and elevated underperforming positioning which needed improvement. Mastercard applied the insights as an industry barometer for understanding consumer and merchant adoption. The study revealed significant year-over-year improvements on a number of key performance indicators:

- The 2015 "Mobile payments" study tracked 2 million global social media posts about mobile payments across social channels, up from just 85,000 posts three years earlier.

- Sentiment improved in 2015, with 95 percent of consumers feeling positive or neutral about mobile payments technology, an increase of 1 percentage point over 2014 and 18 percentage points over 2013.

- Safety and security of mobile payments continued to drive conversations, with sentiment improving further in 2015, now 94 percent positive or neutral, a 3 percentage-point increase over the 2014 study. This reflects an overall trend across all years of the study, where security sentiment was 77 percent positive or neutral in 2013 and 70 percent in 2012.

The 2015 study was revealed at the annual Mobile World Congress, one of the industry's most important events, where Mastercard appeared at the center of all mobile payment conversations. Striking data visualization assisted in the spread of the story and intensive media interest. Global media across traditional and social channels covered the story extensively.

As sentiment toward mobile payments improved significantly, the analysis demonstrated the user experience, technical quality, and acceptance network were improving for consumers. Most posts praised aspects including innovation, convenience, and speed, and findings were fed back into the business.

Despite improving consumer sentiment, *experience* remained an opportunity for improvement as it ranked as a high frustration point for users. The research highlighted *transaction experience*, *technical functionality*, and *consumer security protection* as areas for education and product improvement. Merchant acceptance was the most visible topic identified early on in the program. Over time, merchant availability went from a barrier to entry for non-adopters to the most discussed positive topic. The findings were consistent with discoveries about merchant engagement. Merchant conversations were driven by those who had implemented mobile solutions; non-adopting merchants increasingly turned to social media to seek mobile payments advice from other merchants. Many merchants discussed the benefits of mobile payments, in many cases as a differentiator for their business.

With confusion over security highlighted as a barrier, consumer education efforts in particular were identified as critical to the success and adoption of mobile payments. The research identified an opportunity for education: despite robust security, confusion existed on how mobile technology could reverse fraudulent and unauthorized charges. Consumers using Mastercard for mobile payments are protected through Mastercard's zero-liability policy, but the policy wasn't widely known or understood as it related to mobile payments.

In a world where many global organizations sit in limbo debating social media's impact on Big Data decision-making, Mastercard committed fully to research, uncovered insights, and applied the findings to become more strategic, efficient, and successful. The company's data and insights aid in the execution of communications campaigns in real time – whether identifying and responding to an issue or facilitating creative opportunities to position the brand with media, influencers, and consumers.

Over the course of four years, Mastercard's social insights have been used to successfully inform communications strategy, shape product messaging, and facilitate successful targeting. Mastercard effectively shifted consumer conversations from questioning available mobile options and the security of mobile, to the possibilities of enhanced experiences through tech innovations on digital devices.

As the Mastercard and Adobe examples demonstrate, the key to uncovering actionable insights is to recognize they come from hard work. Analytics platforms without human interpretive analysis promote the myth that insights are a function of a drop-down menu or a query. One doesn't need to be a genius. In fact, insights discovery is a skill that can be taught and learned, and when done properly, this talent transforms the tactician into a strategist (and a successful communicator).

While artificial intelligence and Big Data enable extraordinary computations to support the analysis, we, as professional communicators, must evolve to be smarter in harnessing the data to build efficient PR programs that achieve positive differentiation and success in the marketplace. Rather than an innate talent, insights generation takes practice. For example, as you read this book, you're not looking at letters as you did in the first grade; now, you instantaneously infer meaning from the written word in ways that are similar to the way a trained insights analyst interprets the data. Not so much numbers but substance, implications, and actions. And for them, the process happens just as quickly as you're reading the words on this page.

In my experience, insights emerge from a three-step process: defining the problem, mining the data, and developing hypotheses to test the result, which culminates in insights. The business need dictates whether these steps occur in order or independently.

Step One: Defining the Problem

If you can articulate the challenge you're trying to solve, you have the foundation for the insights discovery process. How one frames the business obstacle is the key to unleashing the power of insights because each assignment includes a number of assumptions, whether explicit or implicit. These assumptions may be based on the conventional wisdom or on any number of beliefs within the organization and across the business landscape. Often, they are predicated upon the beliefs of the culture in which they are formulated, which may make the problem definition step more difficult. The task of the research-based consultant is to convert problems into opportunity through data-informed insights.

To begin, list your problem statement and all the underlying possibilities. As a communicator, an example could be, "How do we generate more key message coverage in the media with the highest penetration among target audiences?" This assumes that a) you know the composition of your target audiences; b) you know which media offer the highest penetration among those audiences; c) you want to increase the volume of coverage. It also assumes that your messages are compelling and credible to target audiences as well as to the journalists and influencers at key media. Each assumption reframes the possible solution: for example, "confirm the composition of our target audiences" and "test our messages to confirm that they are compelling to the people we're trying to reach, and credible coming from our organization or brand." The same problem but framed in different ways that lead the communicator to explore alternative solutions through the research-informed insights generation process.

Step Two: Mining the Data

The second step is mining the data at your disposal. Very often, the challenge involves not just new information or "findings" but the ability to recognize an insight when you see it. An observation, even a new observation, is not necessarily an insight which sparks fresh thinking and new understanding. New information does not equate with new insights.

In this second stage, your communications team should mine for data and information available through secondary research sources like news, academic papers, and pre-existing research conducted by other parties with related challenges. Secondary research provides information about customers, the competition, the category, and your business landscape. Take note of trends, gaps, and novel perspectives. Social media offers a particularly rich resource for organic conversation and opinion on all this and more.

In advance of the formal research process, insights generation involves reading, listening, and gaining a sense of feel as you supplement the conventional wisdom with potential solutions and insights to test during the more rigorous formal research process. At this point, we've combined a creative process with a research process.

Step Three: Developing Hypotheses Based on Data

The third step involves collecting your problems, hypotheses, and assumptions to inform the execution of more rigid research methods. In our experience, the Strategic Cube Analysis, introduced to me by mentor Kevin Clancy, PhD, with whom I worked earlier in my career, provides a proven method to uncover insights, but more importantly, it uncovers *actionable* insights to help form strategic direction. Consider it a form of "communication engineering," which applies to message development and media planning. In the process described throughout the rest of the chapter, we relate an approach to creating unique and positive positioning for messaging. Using technology, statistics, and a keen understanding of your brand, your company, and your competitive landscape, you can approach message strategy more rigorously and scientifically. Most communicators rely solely on instinct and their experiences working on other campaigns or with other agency clients. The Strategic Cube provides a "clean slate" opportunity to develop fresh messaging to differentiate your company and brand from any other.

Bringing It All Together

One of PR's most enduring myths holds that messaging and positioning are entirely driven by creativity, ingenuity, and intuition, all primed to "break through the media clutter." While certainly important during the formative stages in advance of more rigorous approaches, research-based messaging constitutes the science beneath the art: fully optimized with limited risk, the positioning that arises from the message engineering process is pre-tested for success. To dispel a related myth, the research-informed messaging framework that results from messaging engineering actually sharpens the creative process by focusing an organization's limited resources on the winning messaging choices with the highest potential. And rather than performing only once at the beginning of a communications cycle or at the beginning of the year, the message engineering process using the Strategic Cube Analysis enables communicators to monitor and enhance performance over time and versus competitors to achieve or exceed predetermined objectives.

Using technology to manage data for insights requires a certain discipline that goes beyond what either technology or a human can do alone. The Strategic Cube Analysis enables communicators to test, review, and identify the most salient communications opportunities. The Cube parses through hundreds—sometimes thousands—of choices to isolate those few that offer positive differentiation. This form of analysis can be used to make a variety of communications and marketing decisions. In this chapter, we focus on message optimization, but the method also applies to media targeting, which we explore later in the book.

The Strategic Cube[6] is a decision-making tool that marries technology and data to empower insights that are more actionable. The method drives a systematic, target audience-based process of developing messages, confronting emerging issues, and tackling corporate positioning. In the case of marketing public relations, we define messaging or positioning as *giving the service or product significant meaning in the minds of prospective customers that positively differentiates your offering from others and motivates prospective buyers to purchase.* Of course, you can replace "buyers" and "purchase" with "target audience" and "desired behavior." Adding to this definition, the reference to "significant meaning" reflects what you and your organization communicate using PR outputs and market messaging, but also involves internal and external spokespeople, sponsorships and partnerships, visuals including the logo, and related causes which the organization supports. Your positioning must reflect your stakeholders' values and experiences—with the offering, the brand, the organization, the sector, and society in general—to elevate relatability even more. The "science of messaging" through research helps to uncover actionable insights for smarter positioning decisions.

Building on step one of the insights development process as it applies to the Strategic Cube and messaging, one begins with a list of problems and continues with assumptions. To move beyond assumptions, communicators require a rigorous and scientific process by which you augment and validate the creative process. The optimal insights-development process must enable the communicator to reach a variety of essential decisions. If you work in marketing public relations, your answers to the following questions provide a foundation for winning and sustainable messaging choices (and research enables many of the answers you'll need):

- Who is the optimal target audience for generating profitable sales? Since not all audiences are equal, to whom *should* you sell?

- What prompts this audience to do what you want them to do? How do you get them to act (and, perhaps, act differently)?

- To what degree does your proposition relate to the target audience's priorities and everyday reality in terms of relevance, credibility, and your profitability? To what degree can you sustain the proposition (everyone prefers three scoops for a nickel but your brand can't survive by continuously offering three-for-one promotions)?

- How well does your competition or opposition perform against the same criteria? What will you need to do to overtake them if you're not already in the lead (or at least mitigate any advantage they hold)?

- Does the message strategy align with the objectives of the organization? How will your brand message support the corporate entity and how will your corporate positioning reinforce the brand?

- Is your messaging consistent across all external channels? If not, what steps are required to align marketing, public relations, advertising, and social communication?

- Does the message resonate as strongly among internal audiences as well as it does in the marketplace?

- Do you understand your stakeholders, your positioning, your competitors, and your business environment sufficiently well to bring your message to life?

To inform the message decisions you need to make and the subsequent positioning choices, the message engineering process is proven, reliable, and sustainable when one follows these five stages, the first of which drives the others:

1 The process begins through collaborative ideation among your colleagues in corporate communication, but also your peers in marketing and sales along with the senior executives who lead your organization.

2 The second step in message engineering uses qualitative research to test your assumptions and to assemble additional propositional attributes and benefits—messaging opportunities—including future options as well as current approaches. Once the revised list is developed, your communications team, in collaboration with other vested parties within the organization, must decide on the preliminary options with the greatest likelihood for success. For the qualitative research, social media listening works as well as or better than focus groups because social listening is relatively fast, accessible, and inexpensive. What's more, it provides a broader spectrum of possibilities and insights than 12 random people in the mall on a Thursday. The next challenge is to select 25 or so potential winning messages to test through quantitative research.

3 The third step is the survey, in which you rigorously test the chosen 25 attributes and benefits by generating responses from no fewer than 300 but no more than 1,000 respondents. Online/digital surveys are fast and relatively inexpensive compared with other survey methods.

4 The fourth step is a scientific statistical analysis that aims to identify and probe the 3–5 winning possibilities derived from the survey (see Figure 3.3). The choices are made by examining the underlying motivation and intensity of the stakeholders' priorities and the insights gained from your competitive analysis. Winning messages are those which reflect the greatest need among the target audience, which are strongly, credibly, and positively associated with your brand, and those which competitors are unable to claim as positive, credible, or profitable.

5 The fifth step requires you to evaluate performance for continual improvement. Similar to steps 1–4 in miniature, evaluation should be constant and consistent to ensure that past decisions remain effective in the constantly evolving marketplace. Periodic pulse checks provide useful input for tactical execution to ensure that investments made in messaging continue to yield positive results over time versus competitors and in light of best practice. The cube in Figure 3.3 reflects the concept. Figure 3.4 reflects the actionable outcome from the Strategic Cube Analysis.

The sample table in Figure 3.4 reveals how the message engineering process transforms message development from the consideration and message testing phase to the activation phase. The top row shows those messages considered as high priority among your target audiences and the bottom row shows messages of lower importance. Each cell in the table indicates an action and a message against which one applies that action. From left to

FIGURE 3.3 Strategic Cube Analysis factors: relative importance to the target, your message performance, and the performance of your competitors

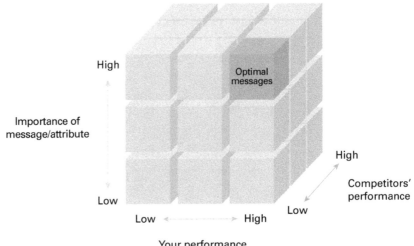

NOTE The optimal message is one which is important, on which you perform well (credible and positive), and on which the competition is weak. To visualize the process, the Strategic Cube illustration reveals the winning messages as those reflected in the shaded box in the corner of the cube.
SOURCE Weiner, M and Sarab, K (2016) Irreversible: the public relations Big Data revolution, The Institute for Public Relations

FIGURE 3.4 Strategic Cube Analysis: actionable outcome

			Uniquely superior	Parity: All Excel	Parity: None Excel	Key Weakness
Attribute/Message Importance	Value: High	Action	Immediate Opportunity	Price of Entry	Potential Opportunity	Fix
		Message	Winning Messages	Other Messages	Other Messages	Losing Messages
	Value: Low	Action	Potential Opportunity	Over Investment	No Action	No Action
		Message	Other Messages	Other Messages	Other Messages	Other Messages

Go   ● Caution   ● Stop

NOTE In this example, the optimal messaging opportunity appears in the upper left: High impact messages on which you perform uniquely well.

right across the high-value messages in the top row, we see the following actionable insights:

- The *Uniquely Superior* cell directs the communicator to reinforce the winning messages which are important to the stakeholder and uniquely credible and positive among your competitive set. Beneath the direction, the winning messages would be itemized. The majority of resources should be directed here.

- The *Parity: All Excel* box indicates that while these messages are important, all competitive claims are equally credible and positive. In this case, converting these messages from parity to a unique competitive position would require either that your competitors begin to slip and fall or that you invest enormous resources with little chance to rise to the top.

- The *Parity: None Excel* square indicates that even though these messages are important, no competitor—including you—can make positive or credible claims on these attributes. But if you can create an advantage by credibly and positively differentiating yourself from others, you jump from the "none excel" cell to the "uniquely superior" box with the potential to own the market. Look at Tesla, for example, which took electric cars and turned the industry on its ear by creating exciting, stylish, high-performance vehicles in compelling and credible fashion.

- The *Key Weakness* cell represents a four-alarm fire that needs a rescue: these are messages that your target stakeholders consider "important" but you alone among competitors perform the worst. In this case, you must fix the message. This may represent a problem beyond the powers of PR alone. If a company faces a crisis due to human error or malfeasance, it may be PR's mess to clean up, but as an example, finance needs to restore fiscal trust and manufacturing needs to fix the product flaw.

The second tier of messaging opportunities is less important but each cell prompts an action just like the cells in the top row. From left to right, these actionable insights include:

- The lower *Uniquely Superior* box indicates a message on which you are uniquely superior and credible but your target doesn't care. There's a potential opportunity because you have a choice, either of which may be constructive.

  o Choice one is to take that less important attribute and *make* it important. Until Apple elevated its importance, no one thought of a mobile phone that simultaneously accessed the internet, streaming media, and a camera along with impressive computing power. No one knew it could be done until Apple elevated the concept from the lower tier of attributes to the upper tier. Now, mobile devices are essential to most of the world.

o Choice two is to take that less important attribute and cut back, preserve your resources, and relaunch when the public's priorities change. Apple offers an example here, too. Take the Apple Newton, which was a very innovative gadget when it was introduced in 1993. Apple created a category known as "personal digital assistants" or PDAs. At that time, hand-held computers were the stuff of *Star Trek*. Among other firsts, the Newton featured handwriting recognition. As a product idea, the Newton was incredibly innovative, but consumers weren't ready for a keyboard-less computer. Consumers were drawn to the Palm Pilot, a competing PDA, and upon the return of Steve Jobs to Apple, the Newton was discontinued in 1998. However, the experience of the Newton is said to have inspired Steve Jobs to envision the iPad and iPhone, which recaptured Apple's reputation for breakthrough innovation—and retained it.

- The less important *Parity: All Excel* box is marked stop (dark grey) because everyone in the sector, including you, invests in the support of attributes that don't matter. If you're investing to sustain parity, you need to cut bait and let your competition waste their money supporting a concept that fails to excite or inspire your target audience.

- The secondary-level *Parity: None Excel* box represents messages which your public cares little about and which no competitor, including you, supports. The direction: do nothing.

- The lower-level *Key Weakness* box is one in which your competitors win on factors that aren't important. It requires no action on your part, but perhaps you'll gain advantage if your competitors blindly support a perceived advantage by supporting themes that are out-of-the-gate losers among your target audience.

While everyone talks about actionable insights, most of them are really offering advice based on intuition and past experience—what worked last time, what we did for that other client, and what qualifies as "edgy" and "disruptive." Perhaps they apply technology, but relatively few base their programs on data and even fewer apply a rigorous process to develop actionable messaging insights. Here's an interesting anecdote: a reporter once asked me, "You've judged a hundred PR awards programs, what is the worst PR program ever?" I thought and then responded, "The worst PR program is the one that hurt the brand, either through inexperience, neglect or by accident—after that, it's probably the one you never saw or heard of." Either way, the failed program certainly wasn't entered into an awards competition recognizing "the best of the best." Most people know enough to hope for the failed program to fade away. Yet, it continues to amaze me just how many of the award entries I've judged ignore the requirement to show research throughout the public relations process, from objectives-setting at the beginning to the evaluation at the end. Most entrants base their programs on the publicist's gut instinct and these programs almost invariably fail to register in the collective consciousness.

QUESTIONS PR INVESTMENT DECISION-MAKERS MUST ASK

- How well do we integrate technology and data to yield actionable insights and strategic guidance?

- What stage of the communications insights hierarchy are we: simply measuring? Analyzing? Evaluating? Are we reporting facts and findings or are we uncovering new approaches to positively differentiate ourselves in the marketplace?

- To what degree do we understand our business landscape? Are our objectives measurable and are they based on data-informed insights (or just vague goals based on gut instinct, conventional wisdom, and what we did last time)?

- What is our process for uncovering messages which reflect our unique advantages and that exploit our competitors' weaknesses?

- How do we organize and interpret data to uncover the often hidden tactical opportunities that human expertise reveals?

- Does our corporate and brand communications team employ a person whose experience reflects our desire for category expertise? An understanding of PR and the media? Is that person capable of leading a rigorous and scientific statistical analysis and applying critical thinking to go beyond simple observations to spark counterintuitive communication execution?

- When our campaigns end, are we capable of evaluating them in ways that reveal new approaches for continuous improvement and category domination?

Endnotes

1 Stark, P (2017) Statistics means never having to say you're certain, https://www.stat. berkeley.edu/~stark/Java/Html/Venn.htm (archived at https://perma.cc/92UH-RZ74)

2 AMEC (2020) AMEC Awards 2020 winners, https://amecorg.com/awards/ awards-2021-2/2020-announcement/ (archived at https://perma.cc/C4AJ-RSKR)

3 PR News (2020) Platinum PR awards, https://www.prnewsonline.com/go/2020- platinum-pr-awards/ (archived at https://perma.cc/VV27-PEQG)

4 Weiner, M (2020) Proving the most accessible and efficient path to PR-ROI, *PR News*, August (8), pp 12, 14

5 Weiner, M and Sarab, K (2016) Irreversible: the public relations Big Data revolution, The Institute for Public Relations, pp 18–24

6 Weiner, M and Sarab, K (2016) *Irreversible: The public relations Big Data revolution*, The Institute for Public Relations, pp 13–14

PART TWO

The Public Relations Continuum

In Part One of the book, we introduced technology, data, and insights as the building blocks of modern public relations practice. In Part Two, we apply these elements to the ongoing process through which every corporate communications program progresses: the public relations continuum. The process is cyclical rather than linear: every program begins with an assessment of the landscape in which it operates before progressing to setting measurable objectives, developing strategy, creating and executing tactical campaigns, and, finally, evaluation for continuous improvement. In each stage, technology, data, and insights play their part in making every stop along the cycle more productive and more efficient with each rotation over time. You may have practiced this routine hundreds of times, but the technology-enabled/data-informed version makes the process new again.

Most PR practitioners use purpose-built PR technology platforms that offer either a bundle of services or specialized services related to social media management or search engine optimization, for example. The software bundles usually include a database of journalists and influencers along with their areas of interest and relevant media data for the news and social media with which they are associated. The automation produces data used by communicators to inform decision-making and to evaluate performance. But routine use of these platforms and processes is no longer good enough. Members of the C-suite know that "best in class" data-informed public relations is available and they want it for the organizations they lead. Subscribing to the technology for an intern to run tabulation won't get you there. The new generation of CCOs and CMOs knows better since technology and data drive so many other aspects of business today.

Public relations insights reflect the brilliance and creativity of the profession, but we must ground our ingenuity in science. Rather than inhibiting the creative process, technology and data produce the insights that enable us to focus our human resources on the themes and media that matter most to our success. Each of us in public relations and corporate communication has a responsibility to deliver a positive return on our organization's (or client's) investment in public relations: we are duty-bound to create PR campaigns that efficiently avoid catastrophic cost, enable us to do more with less and for less, and foster positive behavior (sales, donations, votes, etc). In the current environment, it's almost impossible to say "no" when asked to quantify PR's ability to deliver.

In Part Two, we'll focus on each step of the public relations continuum to share ways to apply technology and data to achieve breakthrough business results. We begin with the Landscape Analysis.

04

The Landscape Analysis

Part of your role as a professional communicator is to know what external stakeholders want from your organization, what internal stakeholders value most from PR, and how well you meet these expectations. In addition, you need to have a plan for how you will exceed the preferences and priorities of these key audiences in the future. To begin the examination process, we suggest an approach and attitude we call "clean slate public relations." The mindset requires us to reject preconceived notions, discard conventional wisdom, and disallow tired approaches from the past. To succeed, you need an open mind to explore new avenues toward meeting and beating expectations while contributing a measurable return on PR investment. A clean slate outlook helps you prepare for creating, deploying, and managing a modern, data-informed, technology-enabled approach to the PR continuum. Clean slate public relations begins with the Landscape Analysis, an objective, dispassionate assessment of your communications and business environment and your position within it.

The Landscape Analysis is conducted every few years in order to answer such questions as: What is the current environment? What place do we hold within this environment? Why is this so? Is it likely to continue? What do we need to know now so that we can improve our position?

The "landscape" is your business environment. It is comprised of external actors like your customers, competitors, shareholders, regulators, journalists, social media influencers, politicians, and local community groups in cities where you conduct business. It also incorporates the changing business, cultural and societal norms that dictate what it takes to be an admired organization and preferred brand now. The landscape also includes internal stakeholders such as senior executives, employees, and peers to address in-house factors such as new developments and cultural shifts within your organization.

Executives within your organization balance some of what you may learn about external stakeholder preferences. Every customer wants a tasty hamburger for a quarter. And every vendor wants a 500 percent markup. Of course, your organization couldn't sustain itself if business answered only to customers and other stakeholders. Beyond balancing perspectives, you must fully understand your senior executives' preferences and values as they relate to public relations: what do they value most and least? And how do you perform against these priorities? To succeed, you must also uncover the specific metrics by which they choose to measure PR success (and yours). It will require courage to dig into this, but you must also reaffirm the professional attributes they consider most and least important, as well as how well you perform against those preferences. This part amounts to initiating your annual performance evaluation, but once you uncover their attitudes and partialities toward PR and your ability to deliver on their priorities, your path becomes very clear.

The philosophy of clean slate public relations helps you approach the Landscape Analysis with the right outlook. This research-driven process provides a fresh, objective foundation upon which to assess the status quo, to reexamine the organization's goals, and to analyze how these goals relate to public relations. It can also help you gain clarity as to what the PR function can do to make a quantifiable contribution to the enterprise's advancement.

The Benefits of a Landscape Analysis

The Landscape Analysis enables the communicator to:

- detect and evaluate the viability of new public relations opportunities;
- accurately forecast potential risks and opportunities;
- set objectives which are meaningful, reasonable, and measurable;
- adapt strategies and tactics to markets, trends, and stakeholder priorities;
- identify ways to differentiate the company's value proposition;
- reaffirm understanding and gain direction among internal stakeholders;
- evaluate competitors, opposition, and aspirational peers.

The Landscape Analysis Process

Bringing your clean slate attitude to your Landscape Analysis frees you from conventional wisdom and enables you to seek opportunities for innovation. To achieve meaningful and productive innovation, communicators must begin with a clear understanding of the internal and external factors that increase the likelihood of success (and failure). Before you can design and execute new ideas, you need a foundation for innovation. While every public relations challenge is unique, the Landscape Analysis provides the necessary understanding you need to assess, contextualize, and shape the actions you need to take.

The Landscape Analysis involves research and analysis to set the stage for what comes next: objectives-setting, which in turn leads to the subsequent steps in the continuum. Setting objectives in a vacuum is shooting in the dark. For example, let's say you lead an agency account team and you set an objective to generate a 10 percent increase in positive coverage in media read by high-income individuals in the first quarter of the fiscal year. Sounds like a solid objective reflecting the who, the what, the when, and by how much. But what if your Landscape Analysis reveals that your agency client's competitors are improving *their* performance by 30 percent every year? You can achieve the objective you set for that client and lose the account (and maybe put them out of business)! Without the intelligence derived from the Landscape Analysis, strategy development and the campaigns you execute may be similarly flawed. Then, only when it's too late, the evaluation of your performance reveals that your miscalculations led to irrecoverable failure.

To accelerate your Landscape Analysis and efforts to achieve a clean slate PR rebirth, here is an outline to jumpstart your efforts. Professional communicators should follow five basic steps to achieve this goal.

The first step in the Landscape Analysis requires you to clarify your objectives for the analysis. The most essential step in any discovery process is to know the purpose of the endeavor. What do you hope to learn? What questions must you ask and among which stakeholders to achieve your goal? In clean slate public relations, everything is on the table, but if you find yourself with a narrower objective, you need to know that, too. The tools we described earlier relating to surveys and media content analysis come into play at this stage.

The second step reflects the need for you to specify the scope of your analysis. Once you set your objectives, you need to determine the breadth of your research. In many cases, communicators tend to focus on a narrow set of factors within a broad category or a broad set of factors in a narrow category. As a clean slate initiative, we must cast a wide net at the outset to narrow down to the most meaningful factors to ensure success and efficiency in the end. One of the most meaningful factors to consider is the priorities of your organization, which may be different than the priorities of individual executives. Does the company or brand aspire to some greater purpose that goes beyond just sales? If you work for a company like Natura &Co, Patagonia, or Ben & Jerry's, for example, you would reflect the importance of sustainability in your analysis. You should also factor in the priorities of your internal and external stakeholders. For internal audiences, you need to focus on the priorities of those executives with influence over PR funding and the evaluation of the PR function, employees, and peers in adjacent departments. For instance, from employee stakeholders, you want to attract and retain the best talent and to advocate for their employer. From internal executive audiences, you probably want recognition for PR's unique contributions to the business as well as increased resources in the form of budgets and staffing. For you personally, a promotion and a raise would be nice, too.

When considering external audiences—whether they are investors, customers, partners, regulators, influencers, journalists, etc—you aim to get them to do what the organization wants them to do. So your goal would be to get regulators to vote favorably on the referendum, for customers to buy the product, for investors to accumulate the stock, and for journalists and influencers to report favorably on the company. To assess the current state and potential actions for the future you want to achieve, surveys, traditional news, and social media content analysis help you by reflecting current attitudes but also as vehicles to inform and shape attitudes and understanding in the future.

The Landscape Analysis should reveal the degree to which your messaging aligns with the objectives of your organization as well as the preferences and priorities of your stakeholders. What's more, you should aim to gain new insights into your competitors' activity and the extent to which they've succeeded or fallen short in reference to *your* objectives. Your aspirational peers help to benchmark "best in class" for whatever you seek to emulate.

The last consideration when determining the scope of your analysis is geography. Your geographic focus may be a continent, a country, a state, or a city. Communicators often make assumptions about which target audiences matter and the media with which those audiences engage. The underlying factors upon which these decisions were made must be revisited from time to time and the Landscape Analysis will reveal the who, what, and when within the "where."

The third step in the Landscape Analysis process requires you to identify the most important intelligence you need about each stakeholder. For each one, you will need to find out what's important and how you're performing on what's important. For example, when thinking about media coverage and social media activity, you'll want to know frequency, reach, tone, and the degree to which you delivered the intended message (as well as unintended and critical coverage). For customers, you'll want demographic and firmographic information as well as the media your customers and prospects favor. Earlier, we reviewed the technology you'll need to accomplish these tasks. Media analysis, social media listening, and surveys reveal the answers to these essential questions.

Step four involves digging deeper. Once you understand the objectives, the scope, and the data intelligence you need, it's time to probe the data with a variety of research tools and methods to gather data and conduct the analysis. An important factor for conducting the research is to answer the question, "what's good enough?" The research methods you employ can vary from a simple ideation session around the conference room table, to a Google search, to the use of secondary research, surveys, and media analysis. With the benefit of tools and research experience, you may choose to conduct the research yourself or, if you have the resources, you may choose to bring in an independent communications research provider who may be better able to instill objectivity into the process and interpretation of the data.

If you have the resources, and if you're about to launch a breakthrough product, I suggest hiring professional help from an outside firm which can manage the research and analysis for you and work with you to interpret results and contextualize them for your organization and your purpose.

Step five involves synthesizing and analyzing the data to uncover insights and explore the implications. In order to draw out the insights from your research, consider engaging marketing and human resources to develop preliminary conclusions since they target the same audiences you're evaluating. It's surprisingly common to learn that companies and brands offer conflicting information and calls to action for the same audience. By speaking with your peers, you'll learn more about the programs they're running or planning to run so all parties can leverage their respective efforts for even better results. Once vetted, and only then, you should present to senior leadership to discuss insights and recommendations along with implications for each recommendation. Your leadership's buy-in enables you and your communications team to proceed with minimal risk and with the most powerful tailwinds. Catalogue any conclusions drawn from the Landscape Analysis meetings with top executives and attain final authorization before executing the recommended steps. This helps to reduce the chances of resistance or memory lapses later.

The Public Relations Landscape Analysis Tool Kit

I recommend a series of PR-specific Landscape Analysis research methods. Each element is achievable through special tools, from outside communications research firms, or from within your organization if you know your colleagues in market research (who, in turn, may employ tools or outside services of their own, but you gain the benefit of their experience and statistical know-how). When deployed independently, each of the research instruments listed will yield data and insights while setting the stage for data integration and continuous improvement. When deployed together, they form a very powerful 360-degree view, with one element optimizing the other to achieve meaningful perspectives, insights, and actions. In the following section, I describe each research instrument or tool and share insights into their applications.

The Executive Audit

The Executive Audit is a 10–12-minute online survey with the executives who affect public relations funding, objectives-setting, and performance evaluation across the enterprise. It's related to step one of the Landscape Analysis process to help you clarify and prioritize your objectives. Typically, it involves members of the C-suite, business unit leaders, marketing executives, and even the board of directors. To ensure openness and honesty, the Executive Audit promises confidentiality and anonymity: no responses are connected by name or title to the respondent. Due to the high rank of each participant, the list of respondents caps at 30 or 40 even in large organizations.

The Executive Audit seeks to gain the feedback you need to set objectives, to achieve mutual understanding between the PR team and key executives, and then, once identified, to meet or exceed their expectations. Communicators apply the results to initiate and formalize the dialogue for setting objectives, determining the measures of success, and designing and deploying programs destined to deliver on executives' preferences.

The Audit allows the PR team to uncover the value that the public relations function holds in the minds of executives. It enables you and your team to assess current performance levels, to refine the team's interactions with executives, and to eliminate potential barriers to even better results. At the same time, and perhaps more importantly, the results enable you to negotiate with respondents to help align on objectives that are meaningful, reasonable, and measurable. With 30 respondents, communicators often find that their internal clients do not agree on what constitutes "reasonable, meaningful, and measurable," so the Audit sets the stage for the eventual one-on-one negotiation. When you combine a group of 30 executives who have PR oversight in their job descriptions with the general lack of deep understanding about public relations and the media among these executives, you will find discord. It's quite common for 30 executives to suggest 45 different measures of PR success, some of which directly conflict with one another: one executive loves the limelight and wants more exposure while another executive distrusts the media and refuses interviews. The Audit helps you reduce 45 disconnected individualized measures of success to a synthesis consisting of the three or four upon which you can get every executive to agree and approve. And that's where the one-on-one negotiation comes into play.

The first step involves identifying the participants. As mentioned, respondents should be those executives with either direct responsibility or influence over the allocation of public relations resources (staffing and budgets, primarily). These executives include the C-suite, the board of directors, and heads of business units. They should also include business-unit leaders, marketing executives, and brand managers who often control budgets on a more focused basis. Each of the executives receives an invitation, preferably from the CEO or the CCO to ensure compliance. The invitation should include key points such as the purpose of the exercise ("to inform our public relations people and programs to continuously elevate their contribution to our organizational success"), the importance of participation of the invitee, and the guarantee of anonymity and confidentiality. The invitation also features references to the schedules for receiving the questionnaire and the deadline for completion. Finally, the invitation should indicate the approach you're taking ("the results will be aggregated and shared in one-on-one meetings to capture your interpretation of the findings and to align on a path forward").

The second step involves populating the questionnaire. Our preferred approach looks something like this based on a sequence of "how important" questions backed by "how we perform" questions. We recommend ratings on a scale of 1–5 on both types of questions followed by an open-ended request for additional comments.

The answers will help you evaluate your standing within the organization. Note that some functions are inherently measurable (sales, for example) while others are not (HR, for instance). The executive responses enable you to network with the disciplines that fall into each camp to learn more about how HR quantifies performance if it doesn't come naturally and also to align with those disciplines that align with quantifiable results.

Here is a sample questionnaire outline:

- Rate the importance of the public relations function in relation to marketing, legal, HR, operations, sales, customer support (and so on). In the second part of this question, we ask executives to use a five-point scale, where a "5" means "excellent" and a "1" means "poor," to evaluate key indicators of success and the extent to which clients/competitors deliver on the same attribute.

- Identify three competitors/members of the opposition within our sector that matter most to our organization and why (could be "they're the market leaders," or "they're the most innovative," for example). Name one "aspirational peer" regardless of sector who reflects our organization's ideals.

- Rate the importance of each of the following corporate attributes as they apply to our organization now (plus performance vs. competitors) for the following: Leadership, Innovation, Financial performance, Quality of products and services, Workplace environment, and Corporate Social Responsibility/ESG.

- These general corporate attributes form the basis of many corporate reputation rankings, such as Fortune's annual ranking of "Most Admired Companies." While each attribute is important, its ranking may change from one year to the next. Within each category, there are supporting themes that you may want to explore along with other specific themes and product attributes that relate only to your sector and organization.

- Rate each of public relations' varied responsibilities on importance and performance on factors such as responsiveness to internal and external stakeholders, value and quality of counsel, creativity, quality and completion of tasks, accessibility to internal and external stakeholders, setting and meeting objectives, ability to contribute measurable results, and capacity to contribute to the organization's business objectives.

The answers to these questions enable the communicator to assess departmental performance on what matters most to this priority stakeholder group. To fulfill executive expectations, you may need to negotiate for more resources. If resources are not available, your executives may need to either reprioritize or at least agree on an appropriate alternative.

- Rate your preferences for PR measures of success as well as perceptions of PR performance vs. competitors on the same measures. Common measures embrace "output performance," including quantity of media coverage (reach and frequency) or quality of media coverage (presence of positive key messages to target media); "outtake performance" such as reputation awareness, understanding, attitudes, social sharing, and preference; and "business results" such as leads, sales, and other pro-business behaviors (passed the bill, avoided litigation, etc).

- Please rate the importance of each of these media channels for their ability to contribute to our organization's success (include consumer media, business media, trade press, TV, radio, digital, Facebook, Twitter, YouTube, etc). This may also include preferred journalists, social influencers, opinion leaders, and spokespeople.

Every PR program needs to identify its "tier one" media-based executive preferences as well as target audience penetration (see "Media Demographic Audit" below):

- Preferences for formal interaction frequency, participants, as well as frequency and composition of results presentations. Options range from an early morning news briefing via email to monthly top-line reports to quarterly in-depth reports, and may include in-person presentation of results or email.

- End with an open question: What single piece of advice would you give to any public relations professional within our organization who seeks to develop a closer and higher-value working relationship with our company leadership?

The third step in the Executive Audit process involves aggregating the data to assess the overall tendencies of organizational leadership. The purpose of this report is to present during your one-on-one follow-up meetings. In that way, conclusions are premature, as you need the input from each executive to achieve a consensus-based plan for authorization and implementation. A comprehensive report features interpretive analysis, implications, actionable insights, strategic guidance, charts, graphs, and all supporting data plus verbatim responses from open-ended questions.

Seek one-on-one meetings with all the executives on the original list (some may not have participated due to business travel or vacations) to share the results. Of course, the results are anonymous so you can't identify one respondent from another, but the purpose of this meeting is to present the results and get a reaction. Each executive will either agree or disagree with the consensus. This is your chance to educate the executive into alignment or to reinforce their position if they appear to be where you want them to be. For the executive who thinks that clip counts are the most important measure of PR, for example, you can include that measure but suggest others that are more meaningful. For the executive who expects PR to drive sales, that can be done, too, but it may cost more to accomplish that outcome than the executive thinks.

You can expect disagreement, and your job is to align the executives in your favor. Fair but favorable. After analyzing thousands of responses, the most common preferred measures for public relations are a) delivering key messages to target audiences through tier one media, and b) raising awareness. The second most popular answers are a) meeting or beating objectives, and b) quality completion of projects. Least popular? Volume of press coverage and driving sales. The three sets of answers provide insight. The most popular answers reflect an understanding of public relations and denote a preference for "quality measures." The second set reveals that executives need not understand the intricacies of public relations when they apply general measures that they apply to every other area of the enterprise. The first answer of the third set reveals that clip counting isn't meaningful and that tying PR to sales may not be reasonable. All helpful input when the time comes to transform Executive Audit responses into your communications objectives.

What is more, some measures are more complicated and therefore less common. As shown in Figure 4.1, the most common measures do not reveal much insight while the emerging practice uncovers the most meaningful. While mainstream thinking points to the simpler options, the measures to the right of the scale reveal business outcomes that will positively position public relations as a measurable contributor to business success.

FIGURE 4.1 The Executive Audit

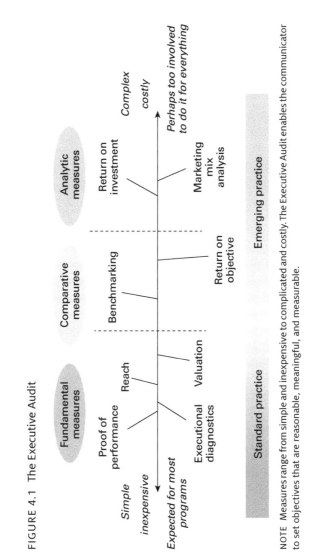

NOTE Measures range from simple and inexpensive to complicated and costly. The Executive Audit enables the communicator to set objectives that are reasonable, meaningful, and measurable.

The Journalist/Influencer Audit

Assuming that media relations plays an important role in the type of public relations you practice, the Journalist/Influencer Audit enables you to uncover the preferences and priorities of this important stakeholder group. As part of step three of the Landscape Analysis, you'll need to know what journalists think about working with communicators at your company and in your category. The method relies on a brief online survey or, if your budget and time allow for it, a telephone interview with journalists and influencers at "the media that matter." You must guarantee anonymity and confidentiality to all respondents; their responses will not be connected to their names and their opinions will only be revealed in aggregate. Certain media prohibit participation, including *The New York Times* and other leading media outlets. For those who are able to participate, you should be prepared to offer a donation in their name to their chosen charity (or, just as likely, to pay them directly).

Communicators conduct the Audit to gain the feedback they need to improve their media relations performance. With a better understanding of the needs and preferences of key journalists and social media influencers, you position yourself to meet or exceed their expectations. Your learnings contribute to competitive advantage and the opportunity to act as the first resource journalists and influencers contact, thereby preempting, perhaps, the need for a second call. As a result, you're doing everything you can to earn visibility in print and on air.

Here's an example of how an international consumer beauty brand applied its Journalist Audit findings to mitigate competitive advantage. In this media category, the wall between editorial and business is, shall we say, "porous." As such, brands that spend a lot on advertising reasonably expect to generate a proportionate amount of editorial coverage. What's more, even the brand's marketing team acknowledged that the editorial drove more sales than the ads, so a big reason to spend so much on paid media was to capitalize on the editorial/advertising quid pro quo. The PR team's hypothesis was that their brand spent more than any competitor but wasn't generating its fair share of earned coverage in key beauty magazines. A media content analysis of both editorial and advertising frequency confirmed the hypothesis. The research also confirmed that the volume of coverage the brand generated was lower and with fewer visuals ("tone" or "sentiment" is not a factor in this category— every article and review is positive). In conclusion, the media analysis findings suggested that either the brand had overinvested in advertising or the PR team underperformed, but the research couldn't determine *why* these magazine editors wrote what they wrote. Perhaps there was a gap between what journalists preferred and what the brand delivered. In this case, a Journalist

Audit revealed the answer: in response to this 10-minute telephone interview (which editors granted because they knew that the research was on behalf of "a major advertiser"), a typical response required much more time to allow the editors the freedom to criticize our client. One interview in Europe lasted 70 minutes! And it was all about how bad our client performed when compared to competitors.

We learned that the most important requirements for any PR department in the beauty-care category were *easy access to product samples, responsive PR people,* and *easy access to executives outside formal PR channels.* Our client, based in the USA, sent samples from the headquarters, while every competitor kept offices in the fashion capital of that country, which enabled them to cross the street with samples within 30 minutes while our client could do no better than "next day." What's more, PR requests faced a time zone barrier that competitors did not, and finally, competing brands made their local executives available, and when they connected, the executives spoke the same language as the reporter. Everything was faster and easier for journalists by working closely with the competition. The advertising spend was not enough to overcome the barriers the client put between themselves and the journalists they served. The client quickly made changes by establishing local field offices to match the competition and within one year achieved parity across all competitors. Had it not been for the Journalist Audit, the brand would have remained mired at the bottom, wasting its advertising investment and making cooperation difficult in every other way.

The structure of the Journalist/Influencer Audit mirrors that of the Executive Audit in that it asks respondents to rate the relative importance of key attributes and then to rate individual brand and company performance. Since we dove so deeply into the Executive Audit, what follows is a light telling of the details of the research.

The Audit process begins by establishing your hypothesis. In the last example, the client hypothesized: "Our competitors outperform us despite our greater investment in advertising." Yours will be different, but for the most part, the brand seeks to gain competitive advantage in some way that positively differentiates its media relations efforts. Decide what you want to learn. The objective of the research and everything else flow from there. While you can conduct this research yourself, the necessary anonymity and confidentiality may require a third party to protect *your* anonymity (not just theirs), otherwise respondents will be tempted to give the answers you want them to give.

The second step involves creating a list of journalists and influencers at the media that matter. Depending on whether you conduct the research by phone, digitally, or via email, you need their contact information as well.

Step three involves the creation of the questionnaire, which must be structured for the research instrument you intend to employ. The first wave of questions may involve the respondents' perceptions of corporate/brand reputation of the organizations in your sector using the same terms as the Executive Audit (and, as described later, the media analysis).

- Ask respondents to rate organization reputation-drivers. Attributes include Leadership, Innovation, Financial performance, Quality of products and services, Workplace environment, and Corporate social responsibility. The question should allow them to rank for your company plus three or four competitors, each presented equitably to protect your anonymity. Two additional questions follow:
  - What is it about the best company/brand that makes them the best in your opinion? and then,
  - How do these three companies compare to the best, "just as good," "almost as good," "slightly worse," or "much worse"? In this way, you learn what it takes to be the leader (assuming it isn't you) or what it takes to remain the leader by reinforcing all the things you're doing right and fixing any shortfalls.
- Ask journalists to rank PR departments performance vs. competitors using the same structure above of a four-part question rating importance and then performance on:
  - responsiveness;
  - accessibility;
  - understanding and anticipating your needs;
  - easy access to senior executives;
  - activities and tactics;
  - etc.
- Ask participating journalists to evaluate communications channels to gauge preferences for receiving alerts and news, including phone, text, email, press releases, website newsrooms:
  - Preferred points of contact when reporting on companies in this sector, including corporate communications, brand PR, agencies, company contacts outside of formal channels, financial and industry analysts that cover the sector, the opposition, the competition (of whomever they write about).

- End with an open question: What single piece of advice would you give to any public relations professional who seeks to develop a closer working relationship with you?

The resulting report should include actionable insights and prescriptive guidance on what to do next and what to do now. The findings will guide your actions and may give you more ways to consult with senior leadership who may not possess as fine an understanding of media relations and the media as you do.

Here's a second example from another consumer packaged goods company operating in what amounts to a "duopoly" market. This client ranks second and they sought to know more about their competitor, the market leader.

> The chief executive officer of one of the world's most recognizable brands strongly believed that this company fell victim to "media bias" among editors and journalists at leading business news outlets whom, it was claimed, favored the competitor. What's more, the CEO felt that only direct confrontation with journalists and editors would overcome their favoritism. The chief communications officer advocated for a more measured approach and sponsored research to test the CEO's hypothesis before confronting the editorial boards of some of the company's most essential media resources. The company had already invested in an ongoing media analysis tracking study, which confirmed that the competitor generated more coverage. The question was, "why?" To explore the attitudes and preferences journalists held toward the two companies, a Journalist Audit sought to a) uncover evidence of any purposeful and consistent bias, and b) learn what could be done to leapfrog the competition whether bias was present or not.
>
> The CCO hired us to field a survey among a core set of journalists to assess the category's public relations and to determine the extent to which any bias could be explained through root causes such as new-product introductions, general newsworthiness, and other content-oriented drivers, but also to examine the degree to which the composition, skills, and interactions of the two PR departments could be the cause of one-sided reporting.
>
> Within six weeks, the assessment revealed there was no systematic or intentional bias; in fact, the journalists preferred the "number two" company in many ways, including the quality of its public relations personnel who were found to be more responsive, more accessible, and generally better in serving

journalists' most important requirements. The journalists confessed that while they preferred working with the market runner-up, any story about the category required them to reference the market leader. What's more, most of the news originating from the #2 player required additional context about the category that naturally led them to report on the market leader. Until the #2 could take over market leadership, the research concluded, the #2's public relations team outperformed the market leader. The problem wasn't a PR problem, it was a sales and market share challenge.

As one would hope, the research findings went beyond simply answering the initial question, they generated insights and identified unique positioning opportunities which would clearly extend the client's advantages while addressing a core weakness. These key elements were as follows:

- Emphasize the CEO as a key asset. Within the organization, the CEO was self-conscious of overexposure. The survey showed that the CEO was a favorite among journalists. The media analysis assigned the CEO with the highest marks among all Fortune 100 CEOs (not just the competitor's), yet other CEOs were more visible. As a result, the CEO overcame concerns and fulfilled their responsibility to represent the company more frequently, with overwhelmingly positive results.

- Underscore the company's cross-category diversity. Unlike the competitor, the client had a more diverse product portfolio through which it could deliver more compelling corporate messages. Unfortunately, many brands operated autonomously and had not been required to support the corporate reputation through brand messaging. That changed when every brand was ordered to reflect corporate reputation as well as brand attributes.

- The client's business made them the subject of potential negativity related to environmental and health claims. The Strategic Cube Analysis revealed that all companies were weak in these areas, but the client had an opportunity to leverage compelling, credible story ideas to elevate their reputation and to distance themselves from the competition.

- Through the "deep dive" analysis, the CEO relented on the plan to tackle bias directly—a series of "confrontational" editorial board meetings was scrapped. Instead, the CCO embarked on a more collaborative approach to advance the CEO, promote the company's product and brand diversity, and emphasize the company's efforts in sustainability and nutrition.

- The research confirmed that the competitor generated a higher volume of coverage due to its inclusion in the Dow Jones Industrial Average, which meant it was included in more general economy stories. The media analysis confirmed over time that while the client generated more thorough, "high-quality" feature stories and exclusives, the competitor tended to appear more often in round-up stories, which are, by nature, less focused, shorter, and of lesser impact. The client reinforced their current media relations play book but added new emphasis on unique positioning opportunities.

- Through the ongoing media analysis study, the results showed that the three-pronged approach worked. One quarter following the implementation of its new strategy, which focused on CEO outreach, nutrition, and sustainability, the client's overall volume of coverage increased, as did its reputation in the media, so much so that they overtook the competition.

- The journalist survey provided the PR team with the necessary guidance to positively differentiate themselves from the competition while instilling confidence and recognition throughout the company that the PR team was "best in class."

Surveys

One way to understand your target audience and the effects your communications have had on that target audience is to ask them. Surveys provide public relations practitioners with a way to preliminarily assess, inform, and eventually gauge stakeholder opinions. Formative research happens at the beginning of the process during the Landscape Analysis stage. The findings and insights help set objectives, develop strategy, and create tactics. Summative research takes place after the conclusion of the campaign or program and tells you how well your public relations performed. Together they represent the scientific basis for all communication activity. A carefully crafted questionnaire looks at respondent levels of awareness, recall, understanding, attitudes, preferences, and behavior. Within the framework of PR's involvement in inputs, outputs, outcomes, and business results, survey results measure outcomes and, to a degree, business results. Over time and with repetition, surveys reveal shifts in your public relations, business, and societal landscapes. In addition to serving as an evaluation tool, the questionnaire can be used to test certain concepts such as receptivity to individual themes and issues, as well as to determine media preferences and to test possible spokespeople, potential events, and other aspects of the public relations and marketing communications process.

A communications survey provides analysis of and insights into the operating landscape through which the public relations professional investigates stakeholder characteristics, expectations, and needs. Surveys enable the communicator to mitigate risk by determining in advance the strategic and tactical elements for a campaign that audiences are most likely to receive positively. These elements include messaging, product, and service attributes that audiences find most compelling and most believable. Through surveys, communicators can gain the benefit of directly evaluating what's on people's minds and what's in their heads. In addition to stakeholder attitudes and preferences, the survey collects information about demographics, tendencies for pro- and anti-organization behaviors, competitors, media consumption, and other bits of useful information.

The purpose of the survey is to gain essential input from your stakeholders to empower your campaigns to win and retain favorable treatment toward the organization, in the form of sales and votes, etc. The survey results also reveal the most efficient way to achieve the results you seek. For a marketing communications survey, your customers and prospects will tell you what they find most attractive about your product or services, their preference for features and benefits, and their opinions about the competition. They'll tell you their preferences for learning about products and services like yours, whether that's through editorial coverage, social media, event sponsorships, or celebrity and expert spokespeople. They'll also tell you where you stand versus competitors in terms of what aspects are most important and how well you perform versus the opposition. All told, and in combination with the other elements of the Landscape Analysis, the survey prepares you to develop and execute the optimal public relations campaign.

Media Demographic Audit

The Media Demographic Audit consists of two parts. The first part involves identifying the audiences that constitute your target audience based on age, gender, family size, and income. It also specifies audiences by product usage, brand ownership, shopping preferences, car brand, bank by name, wireless and cable provider, airline and hotel preferences, favorite retailers, and much more (up to 800 consumer specifications). For B-to-B communicators, identifiers include industry sector, size of company by revenue, size of company by number of employees, and job title. The second part links these audience segments to the media they read, watch, and listen to. It's uncommon for a PR department to subscribe to this data, but your advertising department or media buying agency almost certainly owns it as a means to pinpoint their paid media investments. The same databases they use apply here, too. Using this approach to media targeting, we often find "counterintuitive" media targets that lead to uncommon results. Here are more details about the luxury sports car mentioned in Chapter One.

The high-end automobile manufacturer sought to identify which consumer media captured the highest penetration among people most likely to buy the car in the near term. The analysis covered all media types, including print, broadcast, social, and digital across national and local outlets. The brand, while well known, had a very small advertising budget compared with many of its larger competitors and focused its precious paid resources on one— and only one—media outlet in each of its top 15 markets. The Media Audit identified those media in the top 15 markets with the highest concentration of 1) high-income people and 2) people who intended to buy a new luxury sports car within the next 12 months. Another factor: the company focused its PR outreach on the media in which it did not advertise to manage a balance of paid and earned media in each market. It also relied solely on earned media activity in qualifying markets outside the top 15. The manufacturer sought to achieve two objectives: a) to augment paid media within the top 15 market in the media in which the company did not advertise, and b) to make efficient use of its earned media resources across all markets. If the company's advertising budget was small, the PR budget was microscopic, which made every PR decision that much more precious. By balancing paid and earned media, the company wanted to optimize both advertising and public relations to achieve the efficiencies and selling power of more fully integrated marketing.

The Media Audit findings revealed that each of the 15 top markets featured a much broader base than the PR team realized. While advertising could afford only one outlet in each market, PR had many more paths to the summit. In New York, for example, there were more than 30 additional outlets to pursue, most of which the PR team never considered.

Beyond targeting, the research findings revealed important clues about messaging and visuals. For example, while the PR team traditionally targeted media popular with luxury sports car enthusiasts, the probable buyers looked nothing like the car buffs the PR team had in mind—rather than gear heads and weekend racing enthusiasts, the most likely buyers were females of certain means who garage their sports car next to the family sedan. Imagine: the visuals changed from the car cornering on a racetrack to a middle-aged woman wearing a Chanel suit approaching her large house and pulling into a three- or four-car garage. Maybe she was carrying groceries to the front door.

No wonder many of the highest-scoring media targets came as a surprise to this PR team. In addition to the large daily papers and city lifestyle magazines, high-performing media included free weekly newspapers, and "society" and culture magazines. If the car brand chose to sponsor an event, it would more likely resonate with prospective buyers if it held it at the art museum than at the racetrack.

Retroactive Media Analysis

The retroactive analysis seeks to uncover trends in the media and to contextualize coverage patterns on media and messaging tendencies in target media. While not all media are available for this purpose, many are, through LexisNexis, Factiva, and Google. Broadcast coverage is limited to just 30 days in most cases. Among the major social media channels, Twitter stands out as making historical searches most accessible. Even if you miss some of your targets, this fact should not limit the integrity of the research or the quality of the findings.

The retroactive media analysis produces quantitative analysis like reach and frequency, as shown in Figure 4.2 (along with tone of coverage).

Reports also offer insight into which themes work well—and not so well—during the prescribed period. Once again, the communicator derives new ideas using the Strategic Cube Analysis to determine which messages from the past align with messages for the future based on the other elements in the Landscape Analysis. Figure 4.3 looks at the quality of coverage and the degree to which the company delivered its intended messaging over the past year.

FIGURE 4.2   Retroactive media analysis: traditional media targets

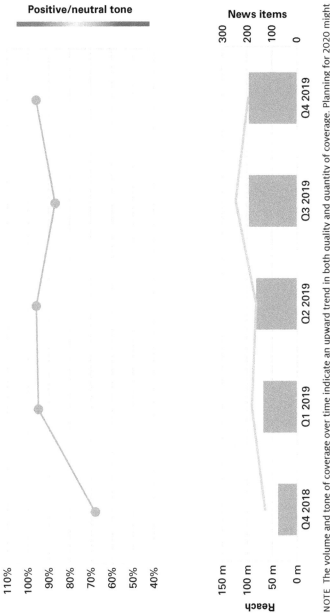

NOTE The volume and tone of coverage over time indicate an upward trend in both quality and quantity of coverage. Planning for 2020 might have begun with an examination of what caused the volume of news to decrease (even though the audience reach grew).

FIGURE 4.3   Key topics: reach and tone

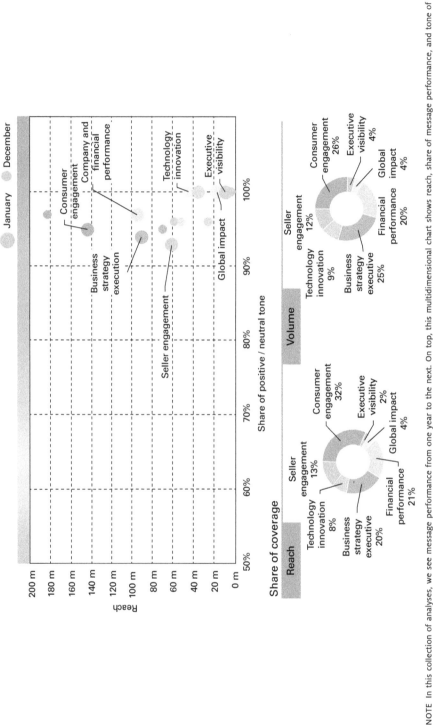

NOTE In this collection of analyses, we see message performance from one year to the next. On top, this multidimensional chart shows reach, share of message performance, and tone of coverage. Positive tone of coverage ranges from "less positive" on the left of the chart to "highly positive" to the right represented by the band across the top (the light tint represents "less positive" while the darker tint represents "highly positive"). The smaller bubbles represent the most recent trends. As indicated on the bottom "share of" pie charts, the tints represent certain themes across all charts. If, from other aspects of your Landscape Analysis, you learn, for example, that executive visibility is important to journalists and to your own executives, you see that your next plan must increase visibility and story frequency, especially since the top chart indicates that virtually all executive coverage is positive. Another message, "seller engagement," is improving in tone but slumping slightly in reach and frequency. As we learned earlier about the Strategic Cube, if seller engagement is an important message, it needs to be reinforced.

The Landscape Analysis Process: Insights

Each element of the Landscape Analysis gives insights into what's happening, why it's happening, and what should be done about it. And each element complements the other.

A domestic telecommunications and cable company, ranked third among its competitors, faced serious budget cuts and massive layoffs. The corporate communications team confronted similar challenges for staff and budget reductions that prompted them to embark on a clean slate public relations landscape analysis. The team began with the Executive Audit, from which they learned that top executives prioritized three measures of PR performance: 1) beat the competition, 2) generate key messages in target media, and 3) maintain excellent relationships with journalists. The media analysis revealed that the company beat its two, larger competitors by delivering a greater quantity of high-quality coverage. The Journalist Audit revealed why the company punched above its weight against the two much bigger competitors: while the larger companies reduced regional public relations staffing, the #3 provider did not. Keeping in mind that wireless and cable service is essential and touches almost every American, regional and local journalists knew there was only one company they could rely on for accessibility and responsiveness in the event of a service outage or storm preparedness. As a result of this Landscape Analysis, the company's leadership realized that the regional PR team that was on the chopping block was actually a vital advantage versus competitors. Not only were the local PR teams kept intact, the company increased funding to support them.

Conclusion

As you move forward in your quest to combine technology, data, and insights, the answers to your questions relate directly to the types of data you need to consider. Some of the information you need will certainly require human expertise and statistical acumen to supplement the "do-it-yourself" technology. Granted, this may require additional investment, but if the investment yields a positive return, which it should if you follow the guidance in this book, your executives won't ask, how much? but rather, how can we get more? If the necessary investment still isn't available, you must negotiate for common ground with the executives to either help them reprioritize their preferred measures of PR success or agree on a substitute measure.

This reflects the need to represent what's reasonable in the objectives-setting requirements reflecting goals that are meaningful, reasonable, and measurable.

QUESTIONS PR INVESTMENT DECISION-MAKERS MUST ASK

- Does our PR team rely too heavily on conventional wisdom and "the way we've always done it in the past"? What's fresh and new in our landscape to spark unconventional thinking?

- To what degree do our objectives align with the preferences and priorities of the business and the executives who lead it?

- To what extent do we understand the recent past and how can we optimize future performance as a result?

- When was the last time we aligned with journalists and influencers about what they need now that they're under intense pressure to stay vital (not to mention "employed") in their current newsroom environment?

- To what degree does our current situation reflect the inclinations and expectations of our stakeholder group?

- Do you know which media have the highest penetration among your target audiences?

05

Setting Objectives

In every organization, regardless of whether the enterprise is for-profit or not-for-profit, mature or a start-up, domestic or international, the business aims to achieve its objectives. While the type of organization and the organizational purpose dictate the objective, what is universally true is that everyone in the organization—including PR—needs to clearly understand the objective in order to achieve it. We in public relations share in the responsibility for helping the organization accomplish its targets. In order for you, your department, and your agency to elevate your primacy, you must set objectives that align with the business and support its purpose across all stakeholder groups. The Landscape Analysis created a platform for you to set objectives with confidence, clarity, and determination. Having committed to a clean slate approach, you are free from assumptions, preconceptions, and prearrangements. As long as your objectives relate directly to the organization's current and desired states, you are enabling your company to become the company it seeks to become. With the foundation provided by the Landscape Analysis, you now possess a keen and fresh understanding of the firm's priorities and your stakeholders' main concerns. You are in the unique position of knowing how those priorities and concerns relate to corporate communications and how PR's contribution advances the organization's standing.

Objectives-setting begins with an unemotional assessment of internal and external stakeholder opinions, attitudes, and behavior as well as historical performance, institutional knowledge, and competitive positioning. In other words, everything is up for discussion. The objectives you define now are a platform for new thinking in support of breakthrough opportunities and explosive growth.

The public relations process relies on technology, data, and insights to inform the objectives you set. Once you set objectives, these assets help to guide the progression of the objective as it becomes part of strategy development and tactical execution. At the evaluation stage, your PR data confirms the degree to which the program met or exceeded your objectives. The likelihood of achievement improves when you apply the consistency and accessibility of technology with the data it generates and the ingenuity of your insights to minimize risk and elevate performance.

As we continue to review the public relations continuum from the Landscape Analysis to objectives-setting, strategy development and tactical execution to evaluation, objectives-setting guides the entire process. Objectives are also the most direct means for executives to evaluate your performance because it's easy for them to compare objectives to results, even if they know nothing about public relations. Unfortunately, as important as objectives are, communicators frequently overlook the crucial role they play.

The Importance of Setting Objectives

Striving for success without objectives is like trying to reach a destination without a map or GPS. You may arrive or you may not—but chances improve and your journey will be more efficient, less costly, and more easily repeated with objectives as your guide. What's worse than no map? No destination. Too many public relations people can't specify their purpose to begin with, which means they will never know when or even if they've arrived.

Each year, hundreds of public relations professionals enter awards programs meant to celebrate "the best of the best." Professional communicators from corporations, nonprofits, PR agencies, and government agencies submit what they believe to be best-in-class PR programs for consideration to win the profession's most esteemed awards. Given the time and effort along with the entry fees, these submissions don't come cheap. Winners and also-rans recognize the allure of awards distinction. Agencies, for example, buy $10,000 tables for themselves and their clients and when they win, take full-page trade advertising to trumpet their victory. Reputations and businesses blossom under the spotlight of recognition that comes from winning the top prize. Everyone wants the prize—me, too—but complying with the rules is a prerequisite for winning (and that's how my colleagues and I have won dozens).

Based on my experience judging at hundreds of these awards competitions and evaluating thousands of entries, it pains me to say that low standards and slapdash methodologies infect our profession in the process for setting meaningful and measurable objectives. Despite the ubiquity of PR platforms and the cascades of data now available to communicators, more than four out of five entries neglect them entirely. In each of these awards programs, the rules for entry specify the need for specific, measurable objectives based on primary or secondary research. Still, many judges report that in categories ranging from Special Events to Corporate Communication to Brand Publicity, they eliminate 80 percent of the submissions straightaway because they contain no underlying research at all. What's more, half of those that remain after the first cut receive substandard marks for stating inadequate or incomplete objectives. When you consider the money, time, and effort devoted to preparing, winning, and marketing these awards, you'd think they would follow the competition guidelines and provide the measurable objectives the submission forms require. Surprisingly, most entrants do not, which leaves more opportunity for those of us who do.

Based on scores of awards judging experiences, I think the entries omit measurable objectives not so much as oversight but rather because the PR team was unable or unwilling to set them to begin with. Think about that: if judges disqualify the large majority of "worthy" entries due to improper objectives, what does it say about the thousands of communications programs that PR teams *don't* submit? It's hard to believe that companies and brands invest significant sums in PR without understanding exactly what they're striving to achieve and what defines success. Even if they choose to invest in vague objectives once, why do they make the same risky choices over and over again?

Most stated objectives are so vague that they represent a form of public relations malpractice. "Break through the media clutter," they say. Or they aim to "generate significant buzz." How do you know exactly when you've broken through from "insignificant" to "significant"? How do you define buzz, anyway? If you and your client can't agree on these points, you're in trouble from the start. Despite the best efforts and admonitions of the PR measurati, the "generate buzz" objective continues to hang on as a risky, indeterminate measure of success rather than the accepted, meaningful, and measurable objectives that PR investment decision-makers deserve.

Since so many PR departments and agencies sustain themselves without meaningful and measurable objectives, one can only speculate the reasons why. They may claim lack of budget, although we know that PR technology costs little or nothing. They may face a dearth of understanding of how to set professional objectives, although organizations like the Institute for Public

Relations in the USA offer hundreds of "how to" essays for free. They may prefer the creative rather than the scientific, or they may fear a scorecard. My hypothesis? Perhaps an educated client hasn't yet confronted them. Whatever the excuse, many PR people simply refuse to do it. Waiting for the client to say something reminds me of the two words that describe every business failure: "too late." If you force them to ask, you're already at risk.

The Technology-Enabled, Data-Informed Process for Setting Objectives

Each element in the research-based public relations approach is essential to the creation, execution, and assessment of your efforts. However, if such a thing is possible, the stage of objectives-setting is the *most* essential among the essentials because it concurrently serves as the foundation and the framework around which you build your strategy, execution, and evaluation. Unfortunately, communicators frequently and foolishly overlook its importance.

Objectives enable the communicator to:

- focus resources on where they contribute the most;
- enable alignment with executive preferences and organizational priorities;
- minimize risk of disagreements during the ongoing PR process;
- ensure clarity when executives evaluate the program performance;
- reinforce the importance of certain activities, audiences, and professional attributes to build consensus across PR teams operating across regions and business units;
- provide incremental milestones during the course of the public relations program.

Public relations objectives work best when authorized in advance. Based on the final negotiations following the Executive Audit and Landscape Analysis, your objectives must reflect three elements: they must be *measurable*. They must be *reasonable*. They must be *meaningful*. Many PR professionals set their objectives in earnest but may not know enough about how and why to set them. To satisfy the interests of the enterprise, to make it easier to gauge your performance without risk, and to make sure you can actually accomplish what you say you will, these three elements must be present. Let's look more closely at each of the three ingredients.

Objectives Should Be Measurable

Measurable objectives provide clear direction. When leaders specify the criteria for PR success, teams naturally work collectively to deliver the desired outcomes. Data-driven objectives enable everyone to "keep score" as you develop and execute the program. By providing direction and clear measures for success, measurable objectives make the decision-making process easier because once your aim is clear, your data drives decisions that lead to the desired outcome and quantify your performance. Technology enables frequent pulse checks to keep track of progress and the data measures progress.

In addition, when everyone is clear about the objectives and how they measure success, it minimizes the likelihood of disagreements within the PR team, with executives, and with everyone else within the organization. Assuming everyone aligns on the objectives in advance as we recommend, the chances for discord fade away. Just like the map and GPS analogies suggest, measurable objectives improve speed and efficacy by focusing budget and effort on the most direct paths to the desired outcome. As seen with Adobe in the last chapter, concentrated and purposeful effort reduces waste and inefficiency. As a result of measurable objectives, you're more likely to uncover opportunities for continuous improvement and successful outcomes. The objectives reveal elements that require refinement and reinforcement. With regular updates on performance vs. objectives, leaders and peers share in the public relations process, providing useful guidance and direction while keeping everyone aligned on the desired result. In this way, measurable objectives lead to greater communication and alignment at the beginning of, during, and at the end of each program. With regular updates throughout the program period, evaluation will be just another update (since you've been sharing performance vs. objectives all along). So while the big unveiling of superlative results may be muted, the opportunity for regular affirmation and engagement among interested parties increases, which reinforces the sense of partnership and collaboration even when results indicate some shortfall along the way.

To ensure absolute clarity among all parties, quantifiable objectives must include specifics on the *who*, the *what*, the *when*, and the *by how much*.

The essential questions for measurable objectives are as follows:

- **Who:** reflects your stakeholder groups. (Customers? Employees? Journalists? Choose one or many. The more you choose, the more resources you'll require.)

- **What:** reflects what you are trying to accomplish. (Savings? Media coverage? Awareness? Sales? Choosing several provides more ways to win.)
- **When:** defines a timeframe within which the objective must be reached. (This week? Peak selling season? Year end? You need one deadline for each objective.)
- **How much:** represents the desired degree of change on the what objective. (Increase positive share of voice by 10 percent in social media? Raise awareness by 15 percent? Improve PR's attributable contribution to sales by 20 percent?) This is where "reasonable" plays an important role.

Measurable objectives reflect and adhere to the elements of public relations measurement, research, analysis, and evaluation we described in Chapter Two: inputs, outputs, outcomes, and business results. Let's review them and put them into a measurable objectives context with examples for each.

Inputs

Inputs include the time and money invested in the execution of a program. When calculated against outputs, outcomes, and business results, your inputs objectives should communicate an improved cost per X against the other measures, with "X" representing measures like cost per thousand positive tweets, cost per digital conversion, or cost per percentage point of increased awareness. In other words, a cost per output, cost per outcome, and cost per business result.

Inputs objectives look like this:

- Reduce out-of-pocket expenditures by 20 percent during the slow summer months.
- Eliminate wasted effort by trimming our media list by at least 25 percent to include just the most essential targets before the end of the month.
- Work with regional PR offices to centralize local and regional media databases to a single source to reduce database costs by 75 percent by the new fiscal year.

Outputs

We defined PR outputs as press releases, events, executive interviews, and the media coverage they generate. Outputs reflect, for example, the number of people attending a press event, the number of placements from a press release, and the presence of intended messaging or the reaction to a social media post, each of which incorporate quality and effectiveness metrics. PR inputs drive PR outputs.

Outputs-based objectives look like this:

- Increase supportive media coverage of Graham Grainworks Sourdough Bread in top-tier gourmet magazines by 15 percent during the three months leading up to Christmas

- Improve our corporate ranking in *Fortune* magazine's "Most Admired Companies" by two places in the annual review by focusing our media messaging to elevate our weakest attributes.

- Raise social amplification of traditional media coverage from 10 percent of posts featuring a hyperlink to 20 percent during the Braden yoga pants product relaunch period.

Outcomes

We defined PR outcomes as awareness, understanding, attitudes, preference, and behavior. Outcomes objectives gauge, for instance, the degree to which your communication affects awareness, understanding, preference, and behavior, elements that demonstrate your contribution to the sales funnel. Outputs contribute to outcomes as, when effective, they spark change in the minds of the target audience.

Outcomes objectives look like this:

- Raise brand preference for Lesley Life Insurance among our competitors' customers in their top 20 markets by 10 points in six months.

- Increase the perception of Francis Electric Transformers as "the value brand" among procurement officers/decision-makers by 10 percent in the third quarter.

- Elevate attitudes about the workplace environment at Cameron Equities from 3.6 to 4.1 on Glassdoor by August to attract graduates from top-tier business programs.

Business Results

Business results as determined in financial terms relate to return on investment, principally by affecting revenue generation or sales, efficiency by doing more with less and for less, and avoiding catastrophic costs. Business results objectives reflect the degree to which PR makes a direct contribution toward the organization's financial goals and objectives. Business results occur as a culmination of positive outputs and outcomes.

Business results-based objectives look like this:

- Drive 1,000 attribution-based conversions from earned media to Clary Isles Luxury Resorts' online hotel reservations desk among high-income travelers during holiday planning season in October.
- Reduce costs for preparing the HB Electronics annual report by 20 percent.
- Before the ruling, educate regulators about our position on the river clean-up to reduce $20 billion in fines and avoid litigation.

Objectives Should Be Meaningful

Meaningful PR objectives ensure that your team and your agency reflect the priorities of the executives to whom you report. During the Landscape Analysis, your Executive Audit results provided a guide to executive preferences and focus. Do not assume that executive preferences are the same as business objectives. For example, a PR objective that focuses on executive interviews won't necessarily win over an executive who dislikes the media—you'll need either to plan an alternative approach or to convince the executive to embrace and respond to journalists and influencers. Meaningful PR objectives set the stage for more engaging evaluation by making the review easier for executives. After all, we set our meaningful objectives by seeking input from these executives and getting agreement up front. Objectives work best when program underwriters understand and authorize them in advance, and you've already done that. Once you set specific objectives and gain agreement at the start, there can be no doubt as to whether the program met or fell short of the desired outcome at the time of its conclusion (we've met some PR types who view this type of vagueness as a plus—they're planning for failure before they get started). I've had this experience in my career and maybe you have, too—you agree in conversation to certain goals but at the end of the review period, the executive doesn't remember that time you agreed over lunch. Perhaps the individual's priorities changed without you knowing. Once you agree on priority objectives and get authorization in writing, you greatly reduce the risk at the end-of-year review, especially if you've delivered regular updates on performance vs. objectives throughout the year at regular intervals.

When done right, meaningful objectives link the PR strategy and tactics to business objectives. If so, no one can argue whether or not they reflect the organization's priorities—the priorities came from the executives who evaluate your performance! As an example, consider that your company identified the success of one product as critical to overall success. Investing major time and budget in promoting any other product would be a form of death-wish public relations. Given appropriate support, you improve the likelihood of product success when you focus on that product as a priority. The success of that product was identified as "meaningful" and your objectives and subsequent actions supported that business priority. What's more, your ability to connect PR success to business success improves significantly when *meaningful* objectives are *measurable* (and measured). Meaningful PR objectives communicate simply and directly. Remember that not every executive to whom you report understands public relations as well as you do. Meaningful objectives translate your results to align with the value your executives place on PR. Keep it simple: some executives may need only to know that you set an objective of "12" (as a placeholder example). Last year, you achieved a "10." This year, your competitors achieved an "11" and you hit "13." You improved over last year, you exceeded your objective, and you beat the competition. How basic does it get?

Objectives Should Be Reasonable

To create a mutually beneficial arrangement between the enterprise and the public relations team, communications executives must align with others in the organization to ensure that your objectives are *achievable*. In the presence of executives who may not understand what's reasonable for public relations, we must negotiate the best approach to accomplish our objectives within the limitations of fixed resources and within a specific timeframe. Without reasonable objectives, there is an increased likelihood for disappointment and frustration—or worse (like unemployment).

As part of the Landscape Analysis, you established industry benchmarks to help in deciding what is and is not reasonable. As we learned in an earlier case study describing the duopoly company, it was unreasonable to jump from number two to number one for "share of voice" under the circumstances—until the Dow Industrials invite number two to replace number one, the runner-up will remain in its position. However, as demonstrated in that story, the number two company wins on many levels that are reasonable and that are conducive to success.

To ensure that objectives are reasonable, the Landscape Analysis aggregates the information you need for your conversations with leadership, which amounts to a stage for negotiation. After your one-on-one conversations/negotiations, you possess the information you need to create your proposed objectives-setting guide to share with the executives whose opinions you gathered. Through these one-on-one follow-up meetings, you'll share the aggregated results from participating executives at the same time as you'll share the results of your baseline research evaluating the attitudes and preferences of stakeholder groups, including customers, employees, journalists, and others, as well as the media content analysis results to support your desired position. This exchange is pivotal because you're educating and negotiating simultaneously. Rather than asking an open question, offer discrete options: quantity or quality? Domestic or international? For all brands or just one (and which one)? The executives with whom you speak may not know enough about PR to answer open questions like "what's the best way to measure PR performance?". During the process, and especially at the end, seek to reduce the number of priorities to an achievable number: if 30 executives provide you with the 50 ways they prefer to measure PR performance, you're in trouble. Steer them toward the center of what's reasonable, meaningful, and measurable. Simplify to the three or four "good" objectives on which you can forge agreement and then proceed to gain written authorization to proceed against those objectives. When you do that, the likelihood for success improves dramatically and proportionately by the degree to which you reduce risk.

Reasonable PR objectives are the product of your ability to negotiate. Prepare for your negotiation armed with the input you gained from the Landscape Analysis: know your budget history, the business's objectives, and your executives' preferences. Set the stage for your negotiations by allotting time for one-on-one meetings to share the Landscape Analysis findings, implications, and recommendations. When asking for the Landscape presentation, prepare yourself and the executive for the negotiation that lies ahead by letting them know in advance that the purpose of the meeting is to discuss next year's objectives. By making your objectives reasonable, you give you and your team a fair opportunity to achieve them. Executives who may not understand public relations or the media make assumptions about how easy it is to generate coverage or beat the competition. Reflect on the earlier duopoly case study where the CEO was ready to go to war with the editorial board over media bias. The Journalist Audit revealed the conditions that prevented the communications team from generating a larger share of coverage against the market leader. Beating the competition on the share-of-voice measure was unreasonable once the facts emerged. Instead, the CEO and CCO agreed to pursue different measures of success that were, yes, reasonable, meaningful, and measurable. To avoid disparity among individuals, reasonable PR objectives align key executives on the three or four objectives that matter most to the organization (not to the individual). Too often, a group of executives holds different priorities, some of which directly conflict with one another. Following these objectives guidelines helps you but also reduces friction among the executives and, in a way, the executives will negotiate what's reasonable with one another rather than you having to do all the heavy lifting. Reasonable PR objectives ensure you have the resources you need to succeed. If your executives agree on a particular measure of success that requires an outside consulting firm, you'll need to pay that firm. If the measure is important enough, executives must provide the funding or perhaps you can negotiate a more reasonable but still representative measure. Let's say executives agree that they want you to quantify PR's impact on the stock price. It's very hard to do, it will cost a lot of money, and require special expertise. If you can't afford to quantify PR's impact in that way, perhaps the executives will agree on a more reasonable alternative, such as "achieve the best financial analyst relations among competitors" as measured using a variation of the Journalist Audit (which would become the Analyst Audit). Finally, reasonable PR objectives reflect timing. You need sufficient time to accomplish certain objectives, so a perfectly reasonable objective becomes unreasonable if the timeframe prohibits your ability to succeed. Negotiate the timeframe with executives and then report on your progress regularly to avoid unpleasant surprises.

Setting public relations objectives that are measurable, meaningful, and reasonable brings many advantages. Conversely, the absence of objectives—or of any one of the three elements—carries significant risk to create conflicts between you and your superiors as well as tensions between you and your fellow communicators. These disconnects result in reduced productivity, diminished efficiency, and, worst of all, a loss of employment. Solid objectives are built using the tools we introduced in Part One. You'll rely on media analysis, surveys, attribution technology, and more.

When to Review Your Objectives

To ensure PR objectives synchronize with business objectives, we recommend one-on-one sessions with those executives as suggested in the Landscape

Analysis. However, in addition to "one big moment" once every year, you must continue to keep your objectives in mind throughout the year to reinforce alignment. The methods should remain consistent. Some measurement and evaluation elements of the objectives-setting process are constant to enable year-over-year or campaign-vs.-campaign benchmarking. Meanwhile, some objectives require the ability to fine-tune to developing situations. These questions, for example, provide opportunities to reconnect and align with business priorities. Sometimes, these amount to simple touching-base questions. However, changes in management, shifts in your operating environment, and other rapidly arising situations of significance require major shifts in objectives and resource deployment.

Questions to ask when you need to reassess your objectives:

- What are your/your management's business priorities now?
- From an enterprise standpoint, what will inhibit or facilitate our success?
- Which stakeholders matter the most now?
- What response does the business want to provoke from these stakeholders?
- What result do we anticipate if we succeed? If we fall short?
- What themes should we prioritize in our communication now?
- What can PR do now to achieve the objective?
- How do you envision PR success? In what ways will we calculate success? Are these success metrics meaningful, reasonable, and measurable? If not 100 percent, what's the best way to reconcile?
- What timeline do you require to achieve the objectives?

Management's responses to these questions help you prioritize current or short-term objectives with the overarching objectives you set in the beginning. If, for example, your long-term objectives for the Braden Istana Apparel Company include "improve sales of Braden brand bikinis during the warm-weather months," your objectives must adjust for the emergence of the pandemic and home isolation. Perhaps rather than bikini sales, your focus shifts to the Braden brand yoga pants to enable at-home workouts. Your overall goal—improving sales during the warm-weather months— stays the same although your focus shifts from one product to another. In so doing, we must build consensus and gain authorization from senior executives for the transition (in this case, they ought to be grateful for your agility in addressing such an unanticipated event).

The Do-It-Yourself Guide to Setting Objectives
that are Measurable, Meaningful, and Reasonable

Armed with this information, you have the basics you need to create your own objectives-setting. Here's a simple framework along with worksheets for your consideration. The guidelines we recommended so far lead to simple objective-setting statements. Just fill in the blanks: *Improve (what) by (how much) among (who) within (when/timeframe)*. Here are real examples (with fictional companies and brands) to illustrate the ease with which this stage of the process works.

We defined PR inputs as the resources you invest in your public relations programs. Inputs-based objectives look like this, with answers to the essential objective-setting questions underlined:

- Reduce out-of-pocket expenditures to paid spokespeople by 20 percent during the slow summer months.

- Eliminate wasted effort by trimming our media list by at least 25 percent to include just the most essential targets before the end of the month.

- Work with regional PR offices to centralize local and regional media databases to a single source to reduce database costs by 75 percent before the new fiscal year.

We defined PR outputs as press releases, events, executive interviews, and the media coverage they generate. Outputs-based objectives look like this:

- Increase the number of positive media reviews of Harlan Historical Tours among travel influencers by 20 percent by the end of May.

- Focus our media messaging to elevate our standing as a "good company to work for" in GlassDoor reviews from fourth to second among competitors prior to university graduation.

- Raise social amplification of traditional media coverage about Susan B. Moving and Storage from 10 percent of posts featuring a hyperlink to 20 percent among new home buyers during the spring home-buying season.

We defined PR outcomes as awareness, understanding, attitudes, preference, and behavior. Outcomes objectives look like this:

- Lift brand preference for Robert Pierce Handicrafts by 25 percent among woodworking hobbyists in our competitor's top five markets in the third quarter.

- Increase sales of Chelsea Baby Togs among new moms by 5 percent in the Midwest region by the end of the year.

- Elevate awareness of Cresta Bledsoe Fine Jewelry by 10 percent among fashion-focused women between the ages of 28 and 40 in the second quarter.

We defined PR business results as those effects that make a direct contribution toward the organization's financial goals and objectives. Business results objectives look like this:

- <u>Reduce manufacturing-area injuries among product assembly teams</u> to <u>zero by end of year</u>.

- <u>During the slowdown, elevate Investor Relations' responsiveness and accessibility</u> with our <u>top institutional shareholders</u> to <u>stabilize stock price and retain our market capitalization</u>.

Each example reflects the essential elements: they're measurable. Together with your executives, you will decide if they're meaningful. Through your leadership negotiations, you'll know if they're reasonable. Over time, as you track the interrelationships between inputs, outputs, outcomes, and business results, patterns will emerge to guide your decisions on the best recipe to achieve the desired results. How many news items or social media recommendations does it take to drive awareness? What degree of awareness is required to affect understanding, preference, and behavior? To what degree do these outcomes lead to a business outcome such as a purchase, a job application, or an investment? Over time and with your vigilance, the trends will become more evident to guide your communications decisions and the enterprise's business investments toward those that lead to the desired destination. In the following section we refer to a paper from the Institute for Public Relations white paper written by Forest Anderson, Linda Hadley, David Rockland, PhD, and Mark Weiner, entitled "Guidelines for setting measurable public relations objectives: An update."[1]

Figures 5.1–5.5 are taken from the paper and through the do-it-yourself worksheets, the process for transforming program elements to proper objectives becomes clearer.

FIGURE 5.1   Inputs relate to outputs and outputs drive outcomes and business results

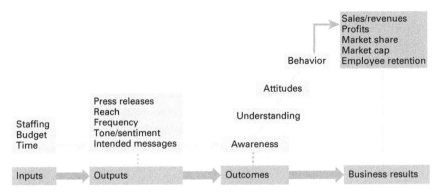

NOTE Try to include all of these when you set your objectives.
SOURCE Anderson, F, Hadley, L, Rockland, D and Weiner, M (2009) *Guidelines for setting measurable public relations objectives: An update,* Institute for Public Relations

FIGURE 5.2   To begin the process, review your inputs objectives

Inputs objectives
Articulate your input objectives (examples):   • **Accelerate**   Reduce turn-around times for release approval by one day by end of the year   • **Simplify/Save money**   Consolidate outsource providers to simplify processes and improve buying power within this fiscal period   • **Value**   Audit agency activity to ensure the account team focuses on the activities for which they are uniquely qualified to reduce waste and improve performance before the agency renewal
Your inputs objective(s)
• One: • Two: • Three:

NOTE We provide examples and a blank list for you to complete.
SOURCE Anderson, F, Hadley, L, Rockland, D and Weiner, M (2009) *Guidelines for setting measurable public relations objectives: An update,* Institute for Public Relations

FIGURE 5.3 Follow through in your objectives-setting process by specifying your objectives for outputs objectives

Outputs objectives

Articulate your output objectives (examples):
 	
• **Share of voice/market share**
  Generate at least 5 percent greater share of positive media coverage than our market share among top-tier media by the end of the year
• **Reach**
  By end May, secure 95 percent positive/neutral key message delivery related to the quality of our company's rotational management training program in media with the highest penetration among seniors graduating with a degree in finance

Your outputs objective(s)
• One: • Two: • Three:

SOURCE Anderson, F, Hadley, L, Rockland, D and Weiner, M (2009) *Guidelines for setting measurable public relations objectives: An update*, Institute for Public Relations

The Objectives Process and Workbook: A Guide to Setting Solid Objectives

Relying on the results of your Landscape Analysis, consider past objectives and the results they generated. For a reality check, compare your performance versus competitors, opposition, and aspirational peers to help you decide on the practicality of achieving the objectives you propose. Use these templates and share them with colleagues during your objectives-setting process. Review them together before sharing with senior executives for final authorization.

Objectives Formulation Workbook

Based on your review, formulate the objective(s) of your PR programs and activities. Keep in mind the essential elements: reasonable, measurable, and meaningful—articulating what you want to change, among which stakeholder groups, by how much, and within which timeframe.

FIGURE 5.4 Continue with your outcomes objectives by denoting the changes you seek to make within the minds of your target audiences

Outcomes objectives
Sample outcomes objectives, including *what, who,* by *how much,* and by *when*:   • **Awareness**   Raise awareness of antibacterial cleaning messaging among parents from 20 percent last year to 50 percent this year   • **Understanding**   Improve levels of understanding of sustainable growth by 10 percent among young urban professionals by the end of the campaign in November   • **Attitude**   By the end of the year, convince 10 percent of customers that the membership fees increase is acceptable   • **Behavior**   Between this year and next, increase from 15 percent to 25 percent the share of insured customers who recommend our brand to their friends or family
Your outcomes objective(s)
• One: • Two: • Three:

SOURCE Anderson, F, Hadley, L, Rockland, D and Weiner, M (2009) *Guidelines for setting measurable public relations objectives: An update,* Institute for Public Relations

Objectives-Setting Worksheets

When completed, the following worksheets give you a framework for setting strong objectives for inputs, outputs, outcomes, and business results. Tables 5.1–5.4 also originated in the same Institute for Public Relations white paper on setting objectives. The finished forms give the information and context you and your team need to propose objectives. They also provide perspectives for those executives who approve your objectives, evaluate your performance, and set your objectives to enable them to participate in an informed conversation/negotiation.

Inputs Worksheet

Table 5.1 represents a sample framework for you to create your inputs objectives. Using this template, add last year's staffing and budget numbers as well as those of your competitors (to the degree that you can get specifics or make educated guesses and get management to sign off on your assumptions).

FIGURE 5.5 Finalize your objectives by identifying business results and the impact you seek to make on organizational performance

Business results objectives
Sample business results goals: • **Sales** Generate $500,000 in attributable sales via earned media during the product launch period • **Save money** Uncover efficiencies to reduce out-of-pocket costs by 20 percent by year-end • **Pass regulation** Gain approval on pending regulatory action during the current session
Your business results objective(s)
• One: • Two: • Three:

SOURCE Anderson, F, Hadley, L, Rockland, D and Weiner, M (2009) *Guidelines for setting measurable public relations objectives: An update*, Institute for Public Relations

TABLE 5.1 Inputs objectives: sample framework

Specific input	Last year's objective	Last year's results	Last year's results: competition	Reasonable new objective
Staffing				
Staffing/turnover				
Budget: internal				
Budget: external/ agencies				
Budget: out of pocket				
Approvals/turnaround time				

NOTE The worksheet provides you with the context you need to guide decisions as you seek to meet and beat your objectives. At the same time, the completed worksheet enables you to negotiate the objectives-setting process with senior executives who expect greater perspective than just a list of objectives. Here, you show how your new objectives compare with last year's objectives, last year's performance, and your competitors' results (assuming you can obtain their information).
SOURCE Anderson, F, Hadley, L, Rockland, D and Weiner, M (2009) *Guidelines for setting measurable public relations objectives: An update*, Institute for Public Relations Outputs Worksheet

Table 5.2 reflects a do-it-yourself framework to set your outputs objectives. While this example illustrates annual objectives, campaigns, seasons, and events work just as well. Using this table, add last year's objectives (assuming you set them) as well as last year's results compared to your competitors' results. Based on what you know about the upcoming year, enter a reasonable incremental improvement for this year after negotiating with management.

As you review your responses, consider the technology and data upon which you measured last year's results to ensure consistency over time and versus competitors. Did you achieve last year's objectives? Did you beat the competition? What's the likelihood of improving performance year over year and against the best practices of your competition?

TABLE 5.2 Outputs objectives: do-it-yourself framework

Specific output	Last year's objective	Last year's results	Last year's results: competition	Reasonable new objective
Frequency of overall coverage (the big number)				
Overall circulation/audience (the big reach number)				
Target media frequency (the smart volume number)				
Target media circulation/audience (the smart reach number)				
Sentiment (share of positive coverage)				
Quality of coverage (exclusives, photos, size, etc)				
Prominence of brand (headline/lead paragraph, etc)				
Company spokespeople citations				
Key message delivery (prioritized by message)				
Advocacy and endorsements (influencer, expert, celebrity, etc)				

NOTE The outputs worksheet highlights the circumstances you faced in the past and how you plan to adjust in the future.
SOURCE Anderson, F, Hadley, L, Rockland, D and Weiner, M (2009) *Guidelines for setting measurable public relations objectives: An update,* Institute for Public Relations Outputs Worksheet

Outcomes Worksheet

In Table 5.3, identify the outcomes objectives set last year, the results achieved, the results achieved by the main competitor for comparison, and a reasonable incremental improvement for this year.

Did you achieve last year's objectives? Did you beat the competition? What's the likelihood of improving performance year over year and against the best practices of your competition in the future? As you review your responses, consider the technology and data upon which you measured last year's results to ensure consistency over time and versus competitors. In the case of outcomes, look to social media, surveys, and attribution technology/analysis to represent each stage. Social media indicates awareness ("Delta is an airline"), understanding ("Delta flies to and from my local airport"), attitudes ("Delta is the best airline"), and behavior ("I just flew Delta to London—great flight!"). Attribution analysis tells you which digital news item led a reader to your website to transact business. Consider the technologies and data-gathering methods you used last year to ensure consistency and compatibility with this year.

TABLE 5.3 Outcomes objectives

Specific outcome	Last year's objectives	Last year's results	Last year's results: competition	Reasonable new objective
Awareness				
Understanding				
Attitudes				
Behavior				

NOTE Your outcomes worksheet reflects the sales funnel or decision-making funnel.
SOURCE Anderson, F, Hadley, L, Rockland, D and Weiner, M (2009) *Guidelines for setting measurable public relations objectives: An update*, Institute for Public Relations Outputs Worksheet

Business Results Worksheet

In Table 5.4, complete the business objectives you set last year and the results, the results of the competition last year to compare, and a reasonable incremental improvement for the coming year.

Did you achieve last year's objectives? Did you beat the competition as far as you can tell? What's the likelihood of improving performance year over year and against the best practices of your competition in the future?

TABLE 5.4 Business objectives

Specific business results (attributable to PR)	Last year's objective	Last year's results	Last year's results: competition	Reasonable new objective
Revenues				
Market share				
Employee retention				
Profits				

NOTE The framework for developing your rationale for business objectives requires business information that you may need to acquire in earlier executions, but by working with other functions within the enterprise—finance, sales, and human resources, for example—you begin the process of elevating awareness among executives of PR's desire to complement the business data-gathering process. Some business information about competitors may be more widely available than you think. Just Google it as a way to start—work with your colleagues in the related functions for more information. A placeholder figure upon which everyone agrees may be necessary.
SOURCE Anderson, F, Hadley, L, Rockland, D and Weiner, M (2009) *Guidelines for setting measurable public relations objectives: An update*, Institute for Public Relations Outputs Worksheet

As you review your responses, consider the technology and data upon which you measured last year's results to ensure consistency over time and versus competitors. In the case of business results, look to social media, marketing mix analysis, and attribution technology/analysis to represent each stage. It's common to see references to purchase and investor behavior from social media and review sites, but it's unlikely that you'll be able to calculate the revenues related to the transaction or the number of shares purchased (or sold). For employee retention, HR has the data and you can track the content on employee evaluation sites like Glassdoor to correlate. Attribution analysis tells you which digital news item led a reader to your website to transact business and the details of that transaction. Marketing mix modeling (and other models) help to derive PR's contribution to revenue, market share, regulatory action, and profits by allocating a "share of contribution" to the business result.

If Management Wants PR Objectives and PR Wants to Prove Value, Why Doesn't Everyone Set Objectives?

Not everyone wants to be measured against a standard—in fact, I think it may be more a matter of human nature for people to feel that way given a choice. With all the upside of setting good objectives, why wouldn't everyone in public relations initiate the process? In my experience, it comes down to fear and ignorance (sorry): the communicators who refuse to set objectives do so to avoid accountability. At the same time, PR investment decision-makers don't require objectives in the first place. Finally, the public relations people and their clients may not know enough about objectives-setting to do it right.

Thoughts and Implications

As you begin your objectives-setting process, take advantage of the technology and data to inform insights and direction. When traps appear along the path to enlightenment, you'll possess the information and know-how to avoid them if you keep the following considerations in mind.

Define Useful Objectives

Rather than an account of activities, make certain that your objectives guide specific actions. Pitching influencers or inviting analysts to the earnings call do not qualify as objectives. Instead, they are activities that might help you meet an objective. In some cases, the Executive Audit included as part of your Landscape Analysis might indicate a desire among leadership for you to measure "quality and completion of tasks" and, in that context, you should measure those activities, but they will not lead you to the Promised Land. Quantifying a 10 percent uptick in the number of press releases you distributed versus last year indicates very little about your contribution to public relations success. A sponsorship alone means nothing if you can't specify what it accomplished. And placing that interview won't amount to much if your target audiences don't consume news from that media outlet. These examples belong on a to-do list. Checking off the boxes, however, doesn't amount to an objective met, nor does it relate to the overarching goals and objectives of the enterprise.

To make this easier, remember that objectives focus on ends rather than means. Study your objectives: if they begin with verbs like "distribute" or "pitch" or "create," you need to recalibrate them from activities to objectives. Activities help us accomplish our objectives but they are not objectives themselves.

Recalibration, in this case, means reviewing the stated activity and thinking about the outcome or business result you're trying to achieve. If the desired outcome is "raise awareness by 12 percent in the second half of the year" and the business objective is "generate $1 million in PR-attributable sales," holding executive interviews may or may not contribute to that result. However, if your target audiences consider these media outlets as credible and compelling, you're more likely to make the outputs and business connection you seek.

When Linking PR to Sales, Remember the Product You Sell

In shaping your objectives, account for the product, its life cycle, buyer, and the volume of sales in a given period. Ubiquitous products like bottled water sell billions of units each year. A specialty product like the Zenith Collector's Edition of the Rolls-Royce Ghost was limited to just 50 examples in 2019. Objectives must take into account the number of potential buyers. Volume of sales alone doesn't dictate the importance of the program or the objective. In this context, audiences and the media they read, watch, and listen to must be extremely narrow when compared with the audience for bottled water, which may be tens of thousands of media worldwide. Consider also the maturity of the marketplace. A new entry into a well-established market requires more resources to ensure positive differentiation.

Remember Your Existing Relationship with the Target Audience

What do you know about your relationship with the target audience and what can you reasonably expect to change? Do you seek to reinforce loyalty among current clients or do you want to poach clients from the competition? Here's an example: cola drinkers in Memphis overwhelmingly prefer Coca-Cola. If you plan to introduce an upstart cola brand to Memphis, you need to execute an extraordinary campaign that might cost more than it's worth. Perhaps it makes better sense to find a market that's more accepting of cola alternatives. It is also worth exploring what sort of relationship the company or brand wants to have with its target audience. Existing market research may provide targeting insights as well opportunities to collaborate for extra effect.

Make No Assumptions

Base your objectives on solid research to evaluate your landscape and to guide your objectives. Be sure that your objectives stand up to the current business environment. Use the Landscape Analysis results to test hypotheses before committing your objectives in stone. Align and get sign-off on the objectives before you commit to them.

Begin With the Desired Result in Mind

After you determine the business result you and your leadership seek, double check your objectives by working backward to confirm that your intended outcomes, outputs, and inputs ladder up to the business results to which you aspire.

Objectives Provide Direction, They Are Not Your Destiny

Objectives help you to focus public relations resources to help create the company you want to be in the future. Once you set objectives, you need to develop the strategies and tactics that enable success, but without objectives your journey will be much more difficult.

It's Worth Repeating: Get Agreement in Advance from Top Executives

Check before committing and provide updates throughout the program. The worst case is to set objectives and then announce the results after it's too late to affect them. Better to provide incremental updates to avoid big disappointments.

Too often, we in public relations depend on vague objectives to avoid scorekeepers and criticism. Our leaders expect more, and by avoiding measurable and meaningful objectives, we disqualify ourselves from enjoying validated success. By setting, meeting, and beating PR objectives in pursuit of business objectives, you and your colleagues will achieve the respect and professional standing you deserve within the business mix.

Conclusion

The problem with setting objectives is not entirely the fault of the public relations practitioner. The professional communicator aspires to improve and deliver good results for their employer and their client. A number of obstacles surround public relations, but it's our responsibility as professionals to overcome them. Professional organizations like the Institute for Public Relations, the Arthur W. Page Society, the PRSA, IABC, AMEC, and the rest do their best, but we, as professionals, must remain open to learning and teaching.

Professional Standards

Among the barriers we face as professional communicators is the absence of a common set of professional standards like those in other professions. Executives may consider ethical and moral behavior in public relations a matter of personal integrity, or maybe worse, that "exaggeration" comes as part of the bargain. How, you may ask, does ethical and moral behavior relate to objectives? Quite a bit, actually. Professional malfeasance is not so much an individual matter as it is a reflection of the implicit support of others. Objectives that are measurable and meaningful help to ensure that communicators put systems in place and accept accountability to those involved in public relations programs.

The medical, accounting, and legal professions uphold specific measurable standards; the professional associations governing these professions reinforce those standards with the threat of malpractice, suspension, and disbarment. Public relations identifies as a profession but rarely "disbars" a member (it's happened a few times in the past 30 years). Ethical and moral shortcomings revealed in the name of public relations happen when PR practitioners ignore accepted business standards. Yet, there are no required licenses to either practice or forfeit. As such, few are held accountable. As examples, consider promises made during agency pitches ("Our account teams know how to break through the media clutter"). What about seemingly simple claims ranging from "New and improved!" to "Made in America!" and "All natural!" Then there are more egregious revelations. British PR agency Bell Pottinger was ousted from the Public Relations and Communications Association for its work in South Africa, and Fuel PR was barred by the PRCA for providing a case study to the media under false pretenses.[2]

A Common Language

In addition to professional standards, we need a professional lexicon. Our challenge as a profession reflects itself not so much in the absence of a dictionary (there is one but only one: the *Dictionary of Public Relations Measurement and Research*, by Don Stacks and Shannon Bowen) as in the absence of generally accepted terminology and shared definitions, which makes understanding and objectives more difficult to establish. Even though they exist in the awards programs, for instance, most entries ignore them.

Here's one example to illustrate the point: the difference between *goals* and *objectives*. While used interchangeably, they connote different meanings and implications.

GOALS

While important for every organization to determine the broader direction of the enterprise, *goals* are relatively vague, reflecting aspirations rather than a chosen destination and the most efficient pathway. They often appear in the form of organizational vision and mission statements without specific steps and timelines. Vision and mission statements help to focus public relations attention and resources to make sure PR initiatives integrate well with other disciplines within the organization and with the organization overall. Unfortunately, goals tend to be indeterminate and difficult to measure. The nature of mission statements thus makes it challenging or even impossible to determine success. For example, how would you determine whether you succeeded if your mission statement proposed, "We seek to continue providing world-class access to a diverse portfolio of services to remain relevant now and in the future." *Wha?*

OBJECTIVES

Objectives are specific and unequivocal, leaving no doubt when you meet or beat them. As discussed earlier in this chapter, the objectives of the enterprise relate to precise measures of business performance, including revenues, profits, and cash on hand. Elements of your business's objectives translate to public relations and they help to make overarching goals achievable by segmenting them into steps and delegating responsibility. Unlike goals, objectives specify the audience, timeframe, outputs, outcomes, and business results. We apply these elements to ensure that objectives are specific and success is quantifiable when the campaign ends. While goals and objectives differ, they must align.

QUESTIONS PR INVESTMENT DECISION-MAKERS MUST ASK

If you invest in public relations programming, you are entitled to ask tough questions. And you have the right to explicit responses about what your PR investment will yield, among which audiences, by when, and to what effect. Finally, you deserve to know the measures of success.

- Have we set our PR objectives based on a clean slate understanding of our business environment?
- To what degree do our PR objectives reflect the organization's business goals and objectives? How was this determined?

- To what degree are our objectives meaningful, measurable, and reasonable?

- Have we considered both long-term and short-term objectives?

- Do our objectives specify outputs, outcomes, and business results?

- Have we defined the best timeframe?

- Have we targeted the optimal audience?

- By what methods have we quantified and qualified our objectives?

- To what degree do we have authorization to proceed using the objectives we've negotiated?

Endnotes

1 Anderson, F, Hadley, L, Rockland, D and Weiner, M (2009) *Guidelines for setting measurable public relations objectives: An update*, Institute for Public Relations, pp 9–12

2 Burne James, S (2017) Bell Pottinger thrown out of PRCA after "bringing industry into disrepute," https://www.prweek.com/article/1443592/bell-pottinger-thrown-prca-bringing-industry-disrepute (archived at https://perma.cc/KJ5N-KW3V)

06

Strategy and Tactics

One of the most interesting dichotomies in corporate communications is that between strategy and tactics. Ask anyone in public relations about their role as a strategist or a tactician and almost everyone identifies as a strategist. But if everyone is a strategist, how does anything get done? This may remind you of an earlier contradiction: that of outputs and outcomes. Just as it is true that you can't achieve an outcome without an output (despite the profession's emphasis on the primacy of outcomes), you can't enact a strategy in the absence of tactics. It seems that to earn respect, professional communicators feel compelled to position our function as "strategic." The inferences are clear: strategy requires greater mental and managerial oversight while tactics belong to the strategist's deputies. To put it simply, it's a false premise, and in failing to recognize the interconnectedness and interdependency of the two, you put your reputation at risk (not to mention that of your company or your agency).

If the Landscape Analysis reflects the terrain and objectives tell us our destination, then strategy and tactics show us the way. In preparing your strategy, you must consider your landscape and your objectives, but you must remember that the only path to success relies on the ability of tactics to bring your strategy to life. If tactics focus on outputs alone, you may generate tons of visibility through disruptive social media, but it may not relate to your organization's objectives. Strategy and tactics belong together: inseparable and inter-reliable. In *The Art of War*, the Chinese warrior philosopher Sun Tzu stated it succinctly in 500 B.C.: "Strategy without tactics is the slowest route to victory. Tactics without strategy is the noise before defeat."[1] Smart communicators recognize how strategy and tactics go together and leverage each for the benefit of the other. Inviting strategists and tacticians to participate increases the likelihood for success by providing exposure, context, and insights for strategic planning and tactical execution.

Strategy requires expertise, vision, critical thinking, and respect for tactics. Tactics require brilliance, ingenuity, perseverance, and deference to the strategy. Technology, data, and insights enable speed, productivity, and differentiation for your organization by addressing your key stakeholders' priorities and preferences.

Strategy enables us to elevate how most executives define public relations and tactics deliver the results to sustain the higher position. As most professional communicators agree, public relations consists of more than just media and "buzz." Unfortunately, media relations continues to occupy most of the attention of practitioners and the executives for whom they work.

Separating Strategy from Tactics

The language of public relations is loaded with contradictions and confusion. The need for clarity extends to strategy and tactics. Here's an easy approach to separating a strategy from a tactic: if your key messages and target market are not known to you, if you're trying to isolate that message and the market, searching for new messages and markets, or even trying to refine your current understanding of your existing messages and markets, then you're developing a strategy. Alternatively, if you know your message, audience, and market precisely, and you're concentrating on developing a variety of activities to communicate your message to that market, then you are developing a tactical plan. So, you ask, "What more can you tell me to differentiate strategy from tactics... and why does it matter?"

Definitions of strategy relate mostly to chess and the military, but we apply these terms in many aspects of business and life. Stated simply, strategy equates with generalship. A PR campaign shares similar traits to a military campaign: the general must weigh a number of factors, including (as we know) the objective, the landscape, and the competitive position as well as strengths and weaknesses. The general must consider risks, alternatives, and timing to achieve the objective of winning the war. The general relies on technology, data, and insights. Similarly, a PR strategy also seeks to win the war by achieving long-term organizational goals and objectives by thoughtfully deploying one's assets through public relations tactics. So, for example, the objective of a PR strategy might be to launch a new product successfully using tactics that deliver salient messages to the target audience within a given timeframe.

Strategies tend to be more stable and longer lasting while tactics are the short bursts of activity that deliver the strategy, which in turn achieves objectives. To use a non-violent example in war, a country's objective is to win; its strategy could be to convince the enemy's population to disregard their own country's mission in favor of its opponent's cause. To accomplish the objective by applying this strategy, the country would employ tactics such as the use of leaflets, broadcasts, or humanitarian aid. If your personal strategy is to become a lawyer, your tactics would include earning good grades as an undergraduate, taking the right courses, getting an internship, and joining your school's law review. In public relations, the strategy may be to generate revenue by selling more units of Jamie branded golf balls. The tactics might include using a professional golfer as spokesperson, a tournament sponsorship, or a brand logo patch placed on a top professional's shirt collar. These tactics positively differentiate you from many golf brands and campaigns. Without a strategy to generate more sales, you risk uncertainty and aimlessness rather than making gains in the direction you seek.

As you see, a strategy may appear as a broad and general approach to achieving objectives. Tactics, meanwhile, intend to be extraordinary and exciting. For example, a strategy supports a business objective to generate incremental revenues of 10 percent in the coming year. If the target is achieved, the outcome is important, but it's not exceptional or unique. Conversely, effective tactics generate excitement in clever and singular ways. The business goal is to generate top- and bottom-line growth. The public relations objective should contribute quantitatively to that business result. The strategy guides audience targeting, media planning, and messaging/positioning—these elements are commonly found in marketing public relations programs. Tactics support these strategic elements through campaigns that command attention in compelling—even explosive—ways. In this way, tactics act as vehicles to transform strategy into energy and action.

Strategies feature many aspects, but a tactic focuses on specific approaches to convey strategic messages to target audiences in compelling fashion. Video game manufacturers and software companies, for example, employ a range of tactics to achieve their overall objective to drive revenue. These organizations participate in the premier E3 trade show extravaganza and use promotions, sponsorships, and major launch events to accomplish their objective to generate sales. In this hyper-competitive environment, each company invests large sums in positively differentiating itself. These tactics require creativity and execution to stand out in such a busy marketplace.

But when effectively conceived and carried out, they deliver the strategic message to gamers and prospective gamers by segmenting audiences along the lines of gender, age, and special interests, across sports, fantasy, and combat, for example. These themes work best when delivered through the media, spokespeople, and events that the target audiences find most credible and most involving. Those who do it right leave the competition behind.

Finally, a strategy creates and maintains a sustainable advantage. Tactics, on the other hand, optimize positive differentiation among competitors through brilliant bursts. This distinction explains why so many marketers rely on short burst/unsustainable tactics like two-for-one promotions. As soon as the price returns to normal, customers resume their regular buying behavior. Since a strategy functions at such a high level, it focuses on the outcome rather than on a particular tactic. The tactic, however, must aid the strategy and carry it forward. And once your tactic achieves its mission in sparking attention among target audiences, you must nourish the advantage for the long term.

The Benefits of Strategy

Strategy enables the communicator to:

- create a bridge between *objectives* and *tactics*;
- set the stage for continuity and stability over time;
- sharpen resources for greater efficiency;
- activate upon a North Star in case of unexpected events;
- improve the likelihood of success;
- provide a cohesive vision for activation;
- focus attention on the proactive rather than the reactive;
- build support among executive decision-makers.

How to Develop a Strategy

Developing a strategy involves making decisions to "do this/not that." Sometimes these choices are challenging. To avoid difficult decisions, many communicators mistakenly approach strategy development as a vision or a plan. They seek to make the most from the conventional wisdom or adhering to best practice. All of these may play a part but they don't lead to breakthrough public relations.

To a large degree, strategy consists of choices related to developing the optimal audience targeting, media selection, and messaging framework. Strategy development depends on your ability to make distinct choices related to what you want to achieve and how you will achieve it. Based on your technology-enabled data-driven insights, strategy development continues along the public relations continuum based on the Landscape Analysis and the objectives derived as a result.

Strategy Development Begins with a Strong Data-Informed Foundation for Targeting

Target audience segmentation is the key to a successful strategy and the tactics that follow. This chapter devotes most of its focus to targeting and media selection. The Landscape Analysis revealed a lot about audiences. Demographics databases and attribution technology told us what our target audiences look like by age, gender, income, and family size. They also revealed the merchandise and brands that people own and intend to buy, and how they prefer to shop, invest, and spend their leisure time. These databases feature hundreds of specifications and combinations—"homeowners with $500,000 in assets who invest in mutual funds," for example. What's more, the technology generated data to uncover the media people read, watch, and listen to, the events they attend, and their preferences for other participatory activities. In sum, the technology and data combine to provide you with detailed information about the audiences you need to reach and how to reach them.

The results often surprise communicators: everyone in public relations seeks the "big numbers" media outlets rather than the smaller media outlets that often offer a higher reach among target audiences. For example, *The New York Times* appears on everyone's top-tier media list and for the most part it merits inclusion. However, if everyone seeks the same destination, that path grows awfully crowded. In addition to aiming for the *Times*, smart communicators hedge their bets by targeting less competitive media targets that reach similar audiences. An ecotourism company targeting high-income, nature-loving travelers to tout exotic getaways should target *The Wall Street Journal*, for example, but should also aim for media in the wealthy suburbs. The circulation of the *Journal* may be close to 3 million, but the number of environmentally conscious adventure-seekers may represent a very small percentage of readers. On the other hand, an upscale suburban weekly newspaper's circulation of 50,000 may be comprised of a high percentage of the target audience and offer an appealing alternative that many communicators overlook. If 1 percent of *The New York Times*' readers reflect the target, that amounts to 20,000. If 70 percent of the suburban paper's readership match the target audience criteria, the target audience circulation is actually higher at 35,000.

Media Segmentation: Target Audience Reach is Better Than Gross Reach

When considering target audiences and the media they consume, you must apply data—not just the big numbers but the smart numbers. For example, a luxury products manufacturer/retailer whose campaign aimed to tout expensive women's jewelry to high-income individuals generated many placements in high-circulation outlets but inefficiently targeted the best audience. In an attribution analysis of target audience reach, the demographics of those people who clicked on the story revealed that the results were not as good as the raw audience reach number preliminarily indicated—75 percent of consumers who clicked earned an insufficient annual household income to buy the product (see Figure 6.1).

Regardless of whether you specify target audiences by geographic markets or individual media outlets, you must build your media plan around foundational data science. Using a marketing PR consumer campaign for which the objective is sales as an example, ask yourself questions like these:

- What trends reflect the status of the target group: is the audience size increasing or decreasing?
- Are the consumers in the target group current customers (or do they buy what you sell from a competitor)?
- Is the target audience able to purchase what you sell (see the above example)?
- Can you reach this audience through conventional public relations channels? Which media do they consume?
- Who influences the audience?
- What events and sponsorships drive their interest?

FIGURE 6.1 Target audience: 25 percent of the readers have an average household income (hhi) of > $150k

Readership exhibits an unusually high share of consumers of coverage that are divorced

Hitting the right audience—one fourth of the total audience is likely to be able to afford the item based on their annual household income

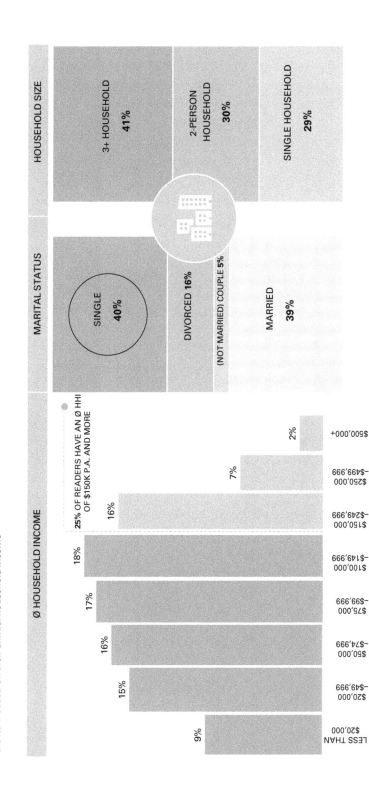

NOTE Not all media are created equal; even high-circulation vanity media underperform if they fail to reach prospective buyers.

After prequalifying the audience by answering these questions, we must prioritize your outreach to deliver positive results efficiently and effectively. Consider the case of Adobe, referenced earlier. By focusing on the media that matter—and *just* the media that matter—the software giant reduced its media management requirements from supporting 3,000 media to just the 150 whose readership matched Adobe's target audience. You might say that every one of the 2,850 other media represented inefficiency and waste.

Media Targeting

Too often, PR people rely on the conventional wisdom for media selection. Today's media databases make it easy to research and make the best choices. In some ways, they make the process *too* easy… so some publicists figure "it's only an email" and blast their pitch materials indiscriminately, regardless of whether a particular journalist or media outlet considers the content as relevant or not. Here's an example from an earlier time. In the 1980s when I was the editor of a newspaper syndicate overseeing 30 different topics and the columnists who wrote them, I received press releases through the US Post Office (sounds quaint, doesn't it?). Instead of "it's just an email," in those days it was "it's just a stamp"—and it showed. Managing 30 topics from auto tips and beauty care to sports and travel and everything in-between, half of the releases I received did not match our interests. In fact, many of those releases came from PR agencies which, for whatever reason, chose to put the agency's name on the envelope. After rejecting three releases from a particular agency, I never opened another of its envelopes, even though each envelope contained a press release from a different client (as if the agency brand superseded the client). What a waste! It wasn't just about me—how many deserving clients missed opportunities because the agency wasted my time with the preceding ten releases about which I couldn't care less.

Now flash forward and put my story into a contemporary context. Digital distribution is now simpler, faster, and costs less than the price of a stamp. Consider the fact that the number of media outlets is less than half what it was in the 1980s, and the population of working journalists is even lower. Today, a journalist's time is even more precious. If you were an overworked journalist, wouldn't it be a blessing to receive highly targeted releases aimed purposely to your audience? Targeted releases stand a better chance of seeing the light of day and they improve the probability that a more meaningful relationship between journalist and PR representative will emerge.

When I was a working journalist, I came to rely heavily on the professional communicators who knew my interests and anticipated my needs. They were invaluable. That word—*invaluable*—is the description every PR person seeks to earn in the eyes of the journalists who matter most.

There's no shortage of inept public relations, which is bad enough. But annoy or offend key journalists enough times and it leads to irrecoverably bad consequences. Even if the product is brilliant and you based your messaging strategy on thorough research, targeting the wrong audience with otherwise stellar campaign elements ends badly. At worst, a perfectly benign message for one audience may be offensive or insulting to another. Public relations people generate inspired ideas, but even the most ingenious message will fail if you miss the target audience entirely.

Journalist and influencer databases provide communicators with a fast and easy way to research journalists and influencers, to build media distribution lists, and, with a keystroke, send press releases in a variety of digital formats. But thinking in the larger context of strategy development, serious media targeting requires more than clicking from a drop-down menu. Uninspired media targeting—what do we have to lose? Why not *The New York Times*?—compounded by what I call "coffee table logic" leads to frustration among journalists who find you and your pitches easy to ignore. Even aids like demographics fall short in some situations when their scope leads to overly broad target audiences: "women aged 25–34" no longer serves as a useful target when so many other supporting factors emerge, such as living situation, shopping preferences, household income, and more. These aspects and more make audience targeting and media selection very challenging. You remember the luxury jewelry retailer and the imported sports car manufacturer who missed their target audiences? They generated coverage, true, but how much more could they have achieved if their messages properly targeted the highest potential buyers? How much more product could have been sold if the target audiences were effectively reached by their messages? Too many PR people forget to consider certain media choices because they run counter to common practice. Communicators bypass certain media because these media yield a low circulation or viewership. They overlook the concept of *target audience reach* in favor of *overall reach*. A broader scope that includes these "forgotten media" provides professional communicators with more opportunities to succeed on the merits of the story. Let competitors adhere to "big number" public relations thinking and annoy the same editors for whom you make life easier.

To some, the concept of a target audience strategy represents too much of a departure or suggests a process that's overly complicated. For many, concerns relate to the risky shift from big numbers PR to smart numbers PR. Indeed, there's the unknown reaction among senior executives who don't know the difference. The targeted audience reach approach will certainly lower overall media exposure, but can you imagine the CEO who prefers quantity over quality? Me neither, especially when quality leads to additional revenue accompanied by cost and time efficiencies. However, in certain regions—Asia and Latin America, in particular—big number media relations has a powerful hold on communications strategy. In one example, an international consumer goods company whose name you'd recognize initiated a global media research program, one part of which involved a focus on only those outlets with the highest target audience penetration. Of all the media in the USA, they chose 90 outlets, a tiny percentage of all media available to them. The team in Chile produced a list of more than 400 media... nearly all the consumer media in that country. Their list reflected an attitude that said "all publicity is good publicity" (which, of course, it isn't). Targeting your communications to your key audiences and the media with which they interact leads to heightened public relations thinking. As Adobe demonstrated, the media targeting and refinement process is continuous so performance gets better and better. In this case, "performance" translates to a balance of both quality and quantity.

The Strategic Cube described earlier for message development helps communicators prioritize media targets, too. While we apply the technique for media prioritization, as shown below, it also applies to events, sponsorships, and spokespeople. The Cube helps to optimize almost any communication decision. Besides making the most of your resources, the Strategic Cube provides an advantage over competitors who almost certainly do not apply the same logic. Journalists and influencers appreciate how you make their job easier by offering them the news and information their readers, viewers, and listeners value most. In fact, this approach, based on the audience profiles generated through attribution analysis and demographics databases, gives you an advantage over most journalists and influencers who probably know less about their audience than you do.

The Landscape Analysis—including the demographic analysis—revealed which audiences and media to target. Combined with your content analysis of traditional and social sources, the marriage of the two datasets reveals which media reach your target, which of them generates the highest volume of positive key messages, and which deliver extended reach through social sharing. When you combine the attribution analysis to determine who clicked on your content, you learn and refine over time. This scientific process combats conventional media choices. Let your competitors waste their resources chasing "vanity media" while you target customers and prospects who may actually do something with the information you deliver. What do I mean by vanity media? Here's an example. One of the world's most recognized food and beverage companies with a portfolio of a dozen billion-dollar brands instituted a rigorous communications and reputation tracking system. It identified key messages and target media. But when the company was profiled by *The New Yorker* magazine, they asked to include it in our analysis even though the publication was not on their list of target media. *The New Yorker*, an iconic literary and arts magazine, was so prestigious that the company wanted to take a detour just to include it. Never mind that the publication failed to match the target demographic or that they or their competitors would never appear in the magazine again, they were willing to skew years of consistent, reliable data to squeeze *The New Yorker* into the analysis. It was just too tempting given the magazine's status. Maybe the CEO subscribed… who knows. Instead of disrupting a highly controlled benchmarking study, we suggested instead that we devote a page in our findings to this exceptional story (which was positive, exclusive, and many pages long). That was vanity, not science.

To begin a scientific clean slate targeting exercise, employ the Strategic Cube to pursue a reliable and meaningful media strategy (see Figure 6.2). We recommend the following steps:

1 Conduct the Landscape Analysis using demographics databases to determine the best "unknown targets." The database identifies the media with the highest likelihood of success given what readers, viewers, and listeners say about themselves. You may have no history with these media outlets.

2 Pitch these media proactively and include them in your outreach (releases, story ideas, etc).

3 Monitor who runs your content (and the specific intended messages they use) by applying media content analysis to determine receptivity of intended messaging and quality of coverage. Assess which media drive amplification through residual pick-up (through either traditional or social channels). Consider adding the sources of residual coverage to your target list.

4   Use attribution technology to track click-through behavior and subsequent actions. Which media drive traffic to your website? Which media result in downloads and transactions (where transaction means applied for a job, made an appointment, or bought the product or service featured in the story).

5   Refine media targets to establish a more meaningful strategy. To draw on the logic of former US Secretary of Defense Donald Rumsfeld, use the findings to reflect the "unknown known" targets from the demographics database, "known unknowns" from your competitive analysis, and the "known known" targets from the attribution technology.[2] Continue to refine over time as patterns emerge and as your new targeting strategy takes root to uncover many new relationships and opportunities for even more coverage.

6   Apply findings to manage your communications team toward continuous improvement. Use the results as a sword and a shield to attack new media opportunities and to defend against vanity media and other emotions-based media targeting decision-making.

FIGURE 6.2 Media strategy: the Strategic Cube

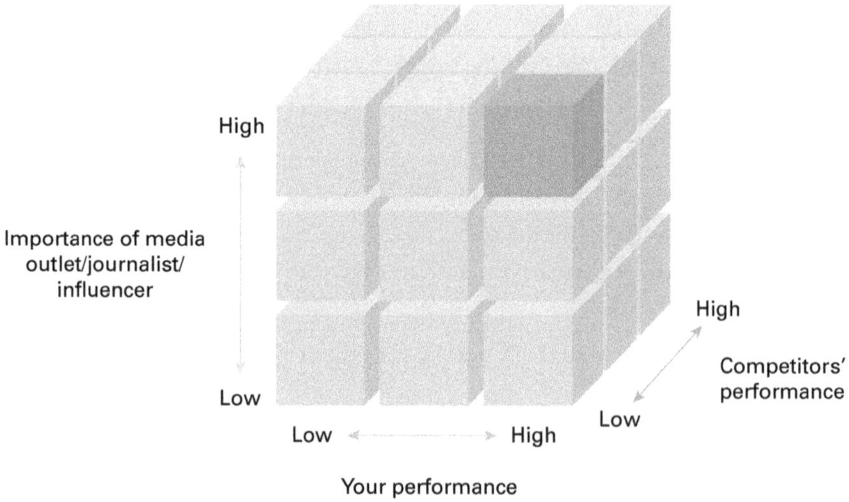

NOTE The optimal media targets are those that hit your target audience and spark behavioral responses by running positive stories about your company or brand and featuring them frequently. In the Strategic Cube, the desired outcome appears in the upper right: media that reach your target audience and generate the desired behavior; the media in which you perform best and the media in which your competitors either are absent or treated negatively.

FIGURE 6.3 The Strategic Cube applies to media optimization as well as message engineering

Tone/Volume

		Uniquely Superior	Parity: All Excel	Parity: None Excel	Key Weakness
High value	Action	Immediate opportunity: reinforce	Price of entry: sustain	Potential opportunity: elevate	Fix
	Media	Media titles	Media titles	Media titles	Media titles
Low value	Action	Potential opportunity	Over-investment	No action	No action
	Media	Media titles	Media titles	Media titles	Media titles

Media importance (left axis label)

○ Go   ◐ Caution   ● Stop

The media targeting process upends the coffee table logic of the past. In the top row of Figure 6.3 we see important media, with less important media at the bottom. Each box indicates an action and a media outlet, journalist, or influencer to whom you should apply that action. Across the top row from left to right, the Cube reveals the following actions:

- The *Uniquely Superior* cell identifies the media with the highest penetration among your target audience. When compared with competitors' performance in these outlets, the media, journalists, and influencers in this box generate a relatively high volume of positive coverage containing the messages that drive positive outcomes for your organization. Beneath the direction, list the optimal media, journalists, and influencers. You should direct resources at these media because they deliver what you value most in ways your competitors cannot replicate.

- The *Parity: All Excel* cell indicates a media outlet with a high penetration among your target audience. You perform well but so does your competition. Backing off these media equals surrendering to your competition. You must sustain the relationship and look for opportunities to positively differentiate with journalists and influencers. The media demographics analysis provides strategic insight into the best ways to micro-target to the interests of these readers, listeners, and viewers in ways your competitors don't know. You won't win in these media but you can't give up either.

- The *Parity: None Excel* square describes media outlets in which no one wins. Media analysis reveals the answers to "why" and "what should be done about it." Your audience recognizes the importance of these media but either your coverage skews negative or it generates low volumes. If you uncover the key to turning things around, you alone will occupy the upper left corner with a unique advantage over competitors.

- The *Key Weakness* cell spells danger. These tier-one media love everyone in your competitive set except for you. In this case, you need to examine your methods and refine your practices if you hope to rescue your reputation in these media that your targets consider important sources. If, for whatever reason, you can't educate or convert them, consider using paid media to deliver your message in a more highly controlled fashion than media relations enables.

On the bottom row of media, journalists and influencers matter less to your key audiences, but certain actions yield positive outcomes (even if it means simply cutting back). From left to right, your media strategy should include the following:

- On the lower left, these media love you but your audience cares little. The opportunity here is subtle: we can't change the demographics of the media, but perhaps we can elevate the importance of a traditional media outlet through social amplification or elevate the importance of a social influencer to increase relevance among tier one reporters and influencers. If you can't find a way to elevate the importance of this second-tier media outlet, consider either cutting back or transitioning to response mode rather than proactive mode in your outreach

- The *Parity: All Excel* cell may indicate a media outlet to which you devote significant resources but your target doesn't notice. If you excel on par with competitors in media that don't matter, reduce resources and devote your time and money to the media that make a difference. You won't win in these media, but unless your coverage is highly critical with the potential to spread negatively to other media, why bother?

- The *Parity: None Excel* square indicates a media outlet in which you generate low volumes or negative coverage but your target doesn't interact with the content. Low volumes don't matter. Highly critical coverage may matter if it spreads. So monitor for negative coverage and step in if required. Again, let your competitors invest precious resources to sustain their position in media whose content doesn't register with the target audience. Alternatively, consider switching from active mode to reactive mode and focus attention on top-tier media.

- The lower-level *Key Weakness* box is one in which your competitors win by generating content in low-value media. If you underperform in volume, let it slide and give these media over to your competitors. If you underperform due to highly negative coverage, continue to monitor the outlet to make sure the critical coverage remains isolated.

Message Development

Messaging and positioning come together with the audience targeting and media segmentation to complete the strategy progression. As described earlier, the message optimization process helps you to identify opportunities for positive differentiation. For strategy development, there are many ways to indicate a company is innovative, including new patents, technology breakthroughs, new product introductions, and more. Your media analysis will tell you which combinations of innovation messaging tend to win the most attention. As you plan your message strategy, your research will already have tested dozens of options for overarching corporate themes to find the three or four that work best. A typical corporate messaging hierarchy tracks attributes associated with companies in reputation-tracking attributes like those used by *Fortune* magazine's "Most Admired Companies" rankings. Attributes include Leadership, Financial Performance, Workplace Environment, Leadership, CSR, and Quality of Products and Services. Communicators reinforce each of these broad themes in a hundred ways, but your research should identify those messages that your target audience finds compelling, associate credibly with your organization, and differentiate you from your competitors. In Table 6.1, we share a typical framework for corporate reputation messaging.

Each of the primary and secondary messages shown may have dozens or hundreds of supporting themes. Within a given message category—take product reputation, for example—certain situations may prevail to elevate the importance of one message over another. Typically, a corporate seeks to reinforce all these broader themes throughout the organization wherever the organization conducts business.

TABLE 6.1 Framework for corporate reputation messaging

Corporate reputation themes (intended/unintended)	
Strategy/vision:	Product reputation:
• Quality	• Quality
• Safety	• Safety
• Effectiveness/usefulness	• Effectiveness/usefulness
• Innovation	• Innovation
• Market success	• Market success
• Social/environmental acceptance	• Social/environmental acceptance
Structure/positioning:	Management reputation:
• Quality	• Quality
• Safety	• Safety
• Effectiveness/usefulness	• Effectiveness/usefulness
• Innovation	• Innovation
• Market success	• Market success
• Social/environmental acceptance	• social/environmental acceptance
Business performance:	Corporate social responsibility:
• Quality	• Quality
• Safety	• Safety
• Effectiveness/usefulness	• Effectiveness/usefulness
• Innovation	• Innovation
• Market success	• Market success
• social/environmental acceptance	• Social/environmental acceptance
	• Emerging issues as they arise

NOTE A standard hierarchy of corporate positioning themes showing the first and second levels. Typically, an organization may have three, four, or even five levels if it chooses to disseminate, track, and evaluate specifics like brands, products, and product attributes.

For example, for an international company's message strategy relating to corporate social responsibility, the importance of *environmental responsibility* may overshadow *legal issues* in one country while the reverse may be true in another country. Similarly, every one of a company's business units needs to reinforce an overarching theme such as product reputation even though *innovation* may resonate better in one division while *safety* carries more weight for another division. Together, these country and business unit public relations departments elevate the reputation of the corporation, but the supporting messages may be more important at one point in time, in a particular geography, or in an individual business unit. In the case of a client, the company tried to elevate its commitment to the environment through its innovations in packaging. The environmental initiative first took root at the corporate level and expanded to business units, but the corporate reputation on this attribute plateaued and required further review. The analysis revealed that two divisions with high scores for their long-standing commitment to sustainability refused to identify themselves as business units of the parent company. On the one hand, the brand argued that the corporation's reputation was worse than the brand and that an association with the parent company would hurt the brand image. The corporate entity argued that to achieve its overall reputation goals, the brand needed to identify itself as a business unit of the corporation. The brand followed directions. Corporate reputation improved, in part, through the reputational lift provided by the brand. And the brand reputation did not suffer from the association with the parent organization.

Why Strategies Fail

In my experience, a large percentage of communications strategies either fail to deliver or cannot prove what they delivered at all. When strategies underperform, the communicator and the executives who funded the program should evaluate the presence of strategy torpedoes like these:

- There was an absence of suitable objectives upon which to develop a viable strategy.
- The communications team overlooked tactical execution during the strategic planning phase.
- Audience identification relied on conventional thinking rather than data-informed targeting techniques.
- The PR team missed cues for the best timing of the strategy.
- Positioning and media planning were fast-tracked without a clear messaging and media strategy at the beginning.
- Rather than applying data science to media and message development, the strategy relied on gut instinct, what worked last time, and "edgy disruptive thinking."

- The communicators never tested the messages for trustworthiness, persuasiveness, uniqueness, or the ability to accomplish the objective among the target audience.
- The PR person based their messaging and media choices on an insufficient number of options.
- Someone decided that research-based strategy development would tell them nothing that they didn't already know and simply ran with their hunch rather than pre-testing.
- Budget decision-makers allocated insufficient resources to succeed. Perhaps rather than basing budget and staffing on current needs, the planners allocated resources based on "last year's budget plus 5 percent," or some other false premise. Perhaps the idea was too big for the resources available to support it.

Tactics

Without PR tactics, we build a house of dreams and a life in limbo, relying on chance that the strategy will achieve the objectives and goals we seek.

Strategies are high level, broad, and directional, while tactics are temporal, distinct activities that ignite the overarching strategy. In this way, tactics represent a means to an end... a stop along the path from strategy to outputs, outcomes, and business results. In chess, individual movements and advances relate to the tactics the Grand Master deploys to win the game. While every contestant plays to win, sacrificing a bishop may make sense in the long term if it allows you to save your king in the short term. In the world of corporate communication, chess moves translate into campaigns, events, and sponsorships. Communicators deploy these tactics to reinforce certain messages to target audiences. When these tactics leverage your strategic intentions, the odds for success improve dramatically.

Tactical planning and execution rely on your creative decisions and your executional skill to drive the results you seek. Many of the technologies described earlier fall into this camp: communicators invest in video public relations, publicity surveys, sponsorships, and other visibility triggers guided by the targeting provided by media databases. When thinking about your tactical plan, these guidelines will keep you focused:

- Always keep track of your objectives and strategy; otherwise, you're opting for luck, chaos, and uncertainty.

- Integrate the strategy and objectives when specifying a supporting activity. Rather than PR for the sake of PR (ie breaking through the media clutter), weigh each tactic in terms of its potential to drive the desired objective, including outputs, outcomes, and business results.

- In all tactical initiatives, design your efforts around the same criteria as you did when you set your objectives: the *who, what, when* and *by how much*. Factoring tactics by timeframe, audiences, and what you want the stakeholders to do leads to desired outcomes.

- Make sure that you and your team execute on time and with quality.

- Track your tactical performance and measure using the real-time technologies referenced earlier to ensure that you meet or exceed expectations. If the analytics reveal a potential shortfall, adjust while time allows (without losing focus on the objectives and the strategy).

Tactical Public Relations

Communications strategy leverages your assets and resources toward the brightest possible opportunity. Public relations tactics apply technology, data, and insights to create openings to go beyond existing strengths to identify new ones. In this way, your public relations strategy and tactics add value even if they consume resources. Over time, tactics add to your strategic foundation to enable you to sustain your competitive advantage. The data-informed communicator recognizes the importance of research for both strategy and tactics.

As you consider the tactics to execute, keep in mind regional factors as well as the potential need to communicate in slightly different ways to each of your stakeholder groups (investors, employees, customers, vendors, etc). Also remember to align with tactics executed by your colleagues in paid, owned, and shared marketing, sales, and advertising to minimize potential friction points in the minds of your target audiences. In one notable example, a luxury car brand introduced a performance-tuned version of its venerable SUV. The PR campaign generated positive coverage among the right media. Journalists amplified their first-drive reviews through social channels. The click-through rate on earned media coverage was 300 percent greater than Facebook and Google ads. Unfortunately, the PR team never coordinated with the website team, so when interested consumers clicked on the article and proceeded to the car company's website, they couldn't find a reference to the new model. After a few minutes of frustration, the positive momentum evaporated when potential buyers went instead to the company's chief rival—the worst possible outcome... no media coverage would have been better than creating excitement and preference for your competitor.

The Benefits of Tactics

Tactics enable the communicator to:

- convert strategy into action;
- deconstruct the 30,000 ft strategic view into more digestible and actionable steps;
- connect our daily work to overarching communications and business strategies;
- involve the entire communications organization in your effort to achieve your objectives and communicate the value and ROI of public relations;
- experiment with different approaches to achieving the objective;
- test, reinforce, and refine your objectives, strategy, and future tactics.

In Chapter One, we listed a variety of technologies that power tactical public relations. The following rely on these technologies in tactical planning, execution, and evaluation.

Tactical Earned Media Relations

Media relations is an important tactical element in the arsenal of public relations. This is where audience targeting, media planning, and message development come together. While modern public relations involves a variety of associated functions, including investor and employee relations, social media, and events, a great deal of resources support media relations. The credibility of traditional media may be under attack, but it remains among the most credible institutions in the world, which explains why organizations seek the approval and support of journalists to convey intended messages to key audiences. Social media continues to rise in popularity, but it's not seen as credible or compelling unless the person posting is someone you know and trust.

As mentioned earlier, understanding the preferences and priorities of journalists remains critical to successful public relations. As you approach your media tactics, keep in mind what journalists want from PR people.

We've interviewed hundreds of journalists over the years to determine how to serve them better. Essentially, journalists want PR people to respond quickly and to provide easy access to senior executives. In other words, they prefer PR people to wait to respond when called upon. However, if the story is sufficiently newsworthy, every journalist wants to be the first and only contact on your call sheet. For the most part, PR people live in the "in-between"—they remain responsive and accessible but also proactively present journalists and influencers with content opportunities.

In my personal interactions with journalists, I find that true partnership leads to positive outcomes. Stacey Smith of Jackson, Jackson and Smith, my colleague on the Institute for Public Relations Measurement Commission, refers to this as "mutually beneficial self-interest." Unfortunately, too many public relations professionals practice "self-interest" that is not necessarily for the benefit of the journalist or the public. The strategy development process should prepare the professional communicator by identifying which media matter most to your target audience as well as the preferences and priorities of the journalists who work there. In an era of always-on, 24-hour news cycles, anticipating the needs of your key journalists positions you with a significant advantage over those who cannot and do not. Cross-promote and amplify your traditional media coverage across social channels.

Tactical Social Media and Influencer Relations

Basically, influencer relations involves aspects of paid marketing and earned media to generate advocacy and positive reviews among trend-setters and opinion leaders who possess a loyal following on social media and whom their devotees recognize as experts in their field. In addition to exclusive expertise, social media appeals because you tune in to those with the highest levels of believability: "people like me." Whether it comes from expertise or similar attitudes and interests, social media engenders high levels of trust, so an endorsement from an influencer generates interest, preference, and behavior. As a result, influencers work full-time on retaining their following and influence. As such, a class of professional influencers commands hefty fees for product features and endorsements (which explains the earlier reference to both paid and earned media). Influencer and social media targeting resembles the process for traditional media. As you consider your social media tactical plan, look for influencers and social media experts using the journalist and influencer databases commercially available, or do your own research by searching topics and tracking influencer preferences and favorite subjects, and then make contact. Follow through on your strategy to achieve your objectives and contribute to the business outcomes you seek. Cross-promote your social media success in traditional media outlets.

Tactical Print, Video, and Radio Press Releases

In addition to proactive person-to-person outreach in the form of emails and phone calls, communicators take advantage of press releases across all media channels. Once your tactics include release materials, you must factor the medium into your tactical plan by delivering information and materials to the journalists and influencers with whom you engage using the medium in which they operate. For example, it's better to distribute video content to TV journalists along with text. Many of the tools and technologies we have referenced enable you to identify the right media outlet to reach your target audience with the right message at the right time. Your ability to tailor your material to the individual outlet and journalist improves the likelihood that your tactics will achieve the desired outcome.

Tactical Photography and Visuals

Captivating photographic and visual assets command attention, and when the attention comes from your target audience, you fulfill much of what you aim to accomplish through public relations tactics. Media content analysis coupled with attribution analysis confirms the positive impact of visual imagery in generating higher levels of awareness, recall, and engagement. People wonder about the value of sending photographs to a radio journalist, but if you're promoting a resort location, it may help the journalist to visualize the destination and will capture their attention. In one case of visual tactics, a logistics client needed to positively differentiate itself in the media against its much larger competitor. The competitor was "monochromatic" and not particularly visual. The client's branding incorporated a wide palette of bright colors. Research quantified the degree to which the use of colorful visuals benefited the smaller competitor in generating bigger stories containing more intended messages. The visuals acted as a delivery mechanism for corporate messaging. Based on the data, the client featured visuals in every communication, even with "non-visual" events like quarterly earnings. In short order, the client overtook their competitor because they incorporate visuals in every tactic.

Spokespeople

The person who delivers your message using PR tactics adds credibility and appeal to whatever message they deliver. In certain situations, your CEO acts as your "spokesperson in chief," especially now that stakeholders expect CEOs to take positions on sensitive social issues. Paid spokespeople should embody the company, product, or service and should make it easy for customers and prospects to relate to the personality as well as what you sell. The spokesperson selection process begins during the Landscape Analysis where your brand personality emerges. Like almost anything in communications, spokesperson attributes can be tested in advance to identify the most appealing attributes: gender, age, field of expertise, and so on. It helps when the spokesperson is relatable and capable of articulating the brand message believably and authentically. Once you uncover the characteristics of an ideal spokesperson, identify the people who fit the criteria and test these potential candidates among target audiences to select the optimal choice. Ideally, the tactical application of celebrity spokespeople makes the tactic newsworthy, as with Michael Jordan and Nike, or Matthew McConaughey's enigmatic ads for Lincoln automobiles. Other times, the tactic turns the spokesperson into a celebrity, like Flo, "the Progressive Insurance lady" (played by the actress Stephanie Courtney). It helps when the spokesperson actually prefers or uses the product, as when pharmaceutical companies employ former patients whose lives improved through taking a particular medication.

Satellite Media Tours

A satellite media tour is a tactic that employs a spokesperson to deliver messages to television and radio programs using digital techniques originating from a single location. Rather than expensive and time-consuming in-studio appearances, the technology enables the spokesperson to sit in a highly controlled studio environment and conduct a series of virtual interviews. It's a common tactic. Like any form of media relations, targeting and a keen focus on the interests of the audience produce the best results. In one example, a large producer of carbon fiber materials sponsored a competition to design the most advanced bicycle using the company's product. Mass market tactics flopped until we identified local story angles including the locales with the highest concentration of bicycling enthusiasts and the cities in which the company operated manufacturing facilities. Granted, these locations weren't top markets, but the tactic succeeded when the local media ran the story and reached certain (but not all) target audiences. The client's PR team was happy (and relieved) with the results.

Why Tactics Fail

Regardless of how edgy the positioning and innovative the media plan, the most ingenious strategy will fail without excellent tactical implementation. Every campaign deserves a post-mortem review of what worked and what fell short. Consider these markers of failure before you begin. Tactics fail because:

- PR objectives were set without a practical way to achieve them;
- the strategy was flawed to begin with due to ineffectual messaging and ineffective targeting;
- the strategy and tactics were not fully integrated from the start;
- the tactics were designed with no regard for or understanding of the underlying objectives;
- the tactics were activated without a firm understanding or reflection of the strategy;
- the tactics were poorly timed;
- the tactics were undertaken without the target audience in mind;
- the tactics were underfunded and not allocated sufficient resources to succeed.

Conclusion

Strategy and tactics are interdependent: you need both if you plan to succeed. Data-informed strategy development and tactical execution reduce the risk of failure and enhance the likelihood for success. The resources that organizations invest in public relations are too precious to waste on strategies and campaigns that rely on pure instinct, gut reaction, or what worked for that other client. To make the most of your public relations research investment, applying technology and data to uncover actionable insights leads to better strategic and tactical decision-making and better return on investment.

QUESTIONS PR INVESTMENT DECISION-MAKERS MUST ASK

- Do we know how the program will be measured?
- How well do our positioning and targeting enable the achievement of our objectives?
- To what degree does our strategy interrelate with our tactics (and vice versa)?
- Have we employed audience-targeting technology and data to inform our priorities?
- How well do our target media represent the people we're trying to reach?
- To what extent does our positioning and messaging strategy reflect the priorities and preferences of our key stakeholders? Did we reinforce our unique messaging strengths? Did we fix our weaknesses? Did we convert opportunities from "no one wins" to "we win"?
- Did we check with our peers and leaders within the organization to confirm that our strategy and tactics support their objectives?
- How well have we considered the degree to which our strategy and tactics were created to yield a quantitative, meaningful, and positive return?

Endnotes

1 Sun Tzu (1994) *The Art of War*, Translator: Lionel Giles, Thrifty Books
2 https://www.youtube.com/watch?v=REWeBzGuzCc (archived at https://perma.cc/EX7P-CQC9)

07

Evaluation

To a large degree, the general state of public relations evaluation reveals widespread weakness in our profession, especially when one defines public relations success in the form of business success. Tens of thousands of corporate communications and public relations programs occur in a single year and fewer than 10 percent can quantify a subsequent return on investment. The overwhelming majority of communicators rely on the conventional measures like clip volume and impressions. While this may be a function of resources, high-level evaluation doesn't need to be overly sophisticated, complicated, or expensive. Certainly, resources help. Big companies across a broad range of industry sectors invest heavily in public relations and they take a scientific approach to evaluating their performance. They spend on public relations technology, data, and insights, but their investments yield positive returns. In addition, as a result, these organizations enjoy the benefits of a better reputation and all that comes with it. Even though some organizations invest more than you do to evaluate their performance, you shouldn't assume that your organization cannot evaluate (whether your organization is larger or smaller). In many cases, evaluation can be as simple as setting measurable, meaningful, and reasonable objectives and then beating them. But given the current state of objectives-setting, and in the absence of meaningful and measurable public relations objectives-setting and evaluation, I suspect that many public relations programs purporting great success are, in fact, wildly and widely overstated because they judge performance on either lower-value measures or no measurement at all. The irony is that effective public relations evaluation can be simple, accessible, and inexpensive even in small business situations.

In this chapter, I outline the right way to evaluate public relations performance and highlight case studies of organizations that lead our profession.

We evaluate each stage of the public relations process: the Landscape Analysis, objectives-setting, strategy development, and tactical execution. This allows us the opportunity to assess the degree to which we delivered value to internal clients and generated a positive ROI in the form of revenue generation, efficiency, and cost avoidance.

The Benefits of Evaluation

Evaluation enables the communicator to:

- measure performance versus objectives, competitors, and best practice;
- review objectives to make sure they remain meaningful and reasonable (assuming they are already measurable);
- assess the relative impact and efficacy of strategy and tactics to identify those which work best and to replicate them;
- gain insights into optimizing audience selection, messaging, media, and frequency;
- gain greater understanding of the trends affecting the enterprise to respond more efficiently and to either boost or mitigate anomalies while there's time to react;
- leverage opportunities proven to drive positive engagement and behavior;
- confirm PR's ability to drive a positive return on investment and uncover opportunities to drive even more;
- communicate public relations value and return on investment in the language executives prefer;
- inform the decisions of management and peers within the organization;
- power communications decision-making going forward.

The Right Way to Evaluate Your Public Relations Performance

The evaluation stage helps us deliver the directional guidance we need as we strive for continuous improvement over time, against objectives, versus competitors, and in light of best practice.

Technology, data, and insights emerge front and center at this stage. While these assets inform the entire public relations process, the evaluation stage requires you to revisit and challenge the formative research you conducted during the landscape analysis as well as every subsequent step that followed. Technology enables us to gather the data we need to evaluate our performance and the data fuels our insights to drive even better performance over time. Let's review inputs, outputs, outcomes, and business results and then revisit each step of the public relations continuum and explore the evaluation process in the context of the individual stages.

Evaluating Inputs, Outputs, Outcomes, and Business Results

Assessing Inputs

Inputs evaluation provides essential information in your ROI equation. Essentially, you must determine the wisdom of the human and financial resources you invested. For example, the Landscape Analysis is a type of input because it's an investment you make to set the stage for the planning and execution that follow. How much time did your team devote to the campaign? Did you assign the right people to the task? How well did your bought-in services perform? Did you hire the right service providers? Do you see opportunities for improvement based on this experience? How would you do things differently next time? Proper evaluation of inputs answers these questions.

Assessing Outputs

Outputs, you recall, are the activities and materials you deliver to generate a reaction from the media and, ultimately, your stakeholders. Media content analysis is a common type of evaluation and it comes in the form of quantitative, qualitative, comparative, and attributive. Let's review from earlier chapters common approaches to the evaluation of each form.

Quantitative media analytics enable you to judge earned media performance by measuring reach and frequency: how many news and social media items appeared and how many people were exposed to them as tabulated by circulation, audience, and clicks. You may also measure "mentions," where a single article may feature more than one. These forms of evaluation, while rudimentary, are within reach for almost every PR program. Better than total frequency and gross reach are target media frequency and target audience reach. Advertising value equivalencies (AVE) are discouraged as a way to quantify a monetary value for your media coverage. Instead, we recommend a more viable approach by dividing your frequency and reach by the out-of-pocket expenditure using your input evaluation. The equation produces a cost-per-thousand audience reached or a cost-per-mention. Still basic, but more defensible in the boardroom. In this case, the lower your cost per (whatever), the better. So, in effect, you seek to drive efficiencies as a way to show that you're delivering more with less and for less.

Qualitative media evaluation looks at the presence of intended and unintended messages, spokespeople, influencers, journalists, and opinion leaders. Importantly, good qualitative analysis also assigns a tone or sentiment to every reference. In your evaluation, probe for the subtleties and nuances: intended messages are almost always planned and positive. Unintended messages may be negative or positive: the negative speaks for itself as no one seeks to generate negative coverage about their organization. But sometimes, less important messages appear and even though they are positive, they are not the intended message, so there may be opportunities to either capitalize on them or to review the information you're disseminating to make sure you're not propagating secondary themes that may distract audiences from your key points. Some media analysis systems measure the quality of coverage at the story level rather than at the message level. Story-level analysis judges an entire story as a single unit. Since journalistic content seeks to present fair and balanced reportage, a single story usually contains a mix of positive, neutral, and negative messages. Typically, these evaluation systems rely solely on automation and the technology finds it difficult or impossible to code with greater precision. As such, these systems lack the capacity to inform future decision-making. It's entirely reasonable to expect that some messages in a story are positive and some are negative, but how do you optimize the positive and minimize the negative if you can't tell one from another? Further, you must track opinion leaders, industry analysts, and financial experts by name to determine who deserves the lunch at a good restaurant and who needs more information. Good evaluation tells you what elements worked and which did not.

Comparative analysis tells you more about your relative performance. A common measure indicates your share of voice, usually versus competitors. But comparative evaluation also shows how you performed against your measurable objectives and how much you accomplished over time. Without comparative evaluation, you never know how well you're really doing on one of the success measures that management values most: Did we beat the competition? Are we improving over time? Are we exceeding our objectives?

Attributive evaluation measures the ability of your earned media programs to affect behavior among your target audience. This measure applies to both B-to-B and B-to-C, and answers one of PR's most vexing questions: did PR drive market behavior? New technology makes this form of evaluation more accessible than ever and it solves so many of PR's mysteries about our ability to drive understanding, engagement, and behavior, including sales. The technology generates small PR data streams that flow smoothly into big data lakes to make for easier and more comprehensive integrated marketing and communications decisions. Given a solid foundation upon which to make the comparison, executives evaluating PR and marketing performance will see how efficiently PR drives the desired business outcome. What is more, the technology evaluates your performance in terms of demographic and firmographic audience profiling. This information tells you who clicked on your story and to what effect. Communicators use this information to pursue the strategies and tactics that deliver the best behavioral outcomes among the most profitable audiences.

Outcomes represent the results of your public relations programming and the generated effects in the minds and actions of your target audience resulting from a communication initiative. Outcomes measurement involves gauging the degree to which your communications affects awareness, understanding, preference, and behavior, elements that the marketing world refers to as the sales funnel. While the concept of the sales funnel originated more than 100 years ago, marketers and communicators commonly apply the approach. Traditionally, communications data scientists use survey research to uncover the effects of a campaign on the target audience. More recently, they look to social media conversations to provide unprompted or "unaided" indicators to gauge campaign impact. Like the other public relations data streams examined here, outputs seek the answers to questions like *what* (do we seek to change), *by how much* (do we seek to change it), *by when* (the timeframe for change), and *among whom* (centered around your target audience).

Assessing Outcomes

Outcomes appear in the form of awareness, understanding, attitudes/preferences, and behavior. Typically, assessing your impact in the minds and actions of your target audience requires a combination of surveys and attribution analysis, but social media provides some insights into the degree to which people share their thoughts in an unfiltered way to reveal their experiences with products and services (and life in general).

Evaluating recall and awareness enables the communicator to assess the extent to which audiences recognize your company and associate it with something (hopefully, something positive and accurate). You measure these outcomes by using surveys to determine the degree to which your company and brand reside in the minds of your stakeholders. Social media helps here, too, as people refer to you in their posts and social conversations. The same goes for comprehension, understanding, and preference, which appear further down the sales funnel. Google Analytics and Google Search trends tell a lot about people's search patterns, which reveal what's on their minds. Social media evaluation is a fast and relatively inexpensive approach, but surveys produce better results in terms of reliability and validity. Online surveys, and even the research companies that specialize in this form of analysis, are more accessible and affordable than ever. Assuming you have the resources, periodic surveys keep your hand on the pulse of your target audiences while informing future communications and business choices you need to make.

Evaluating behavior manifests the ultimate performance measure: did people do what you wanted them to do? Because many marketing and communications programs work simultaneously, isolating one driver versus another creates challenges. Surveys often seek to uncover the link from communications output to behavior, but there are too many ways to explain a sale, especially for "low involvement/low differentiation" decisions such as which bottled water someone bought and why they chose that water. Your communications evaluation program should seek better answers if you have the resources. In some rare cases, PR operates in isolation, so there's no other way to explain a behavioral change. In the case of a fast-food chain, a menu enhancement was communicated via earned media alone. The campaign wasn't big enough to warrant the budget for a survey, but we showed how the volume of Google searches on the menu item surged immediately following the announcement. No other answer made sense in that case. Too many people assume that behavioral evaluation costs a fortune or involves too much complicated research to understand. Not so fast. Even for campaigns where PR and other marketing channels occur in tandem, communicators isolate the impact of earned media using the attribution technology we described. While this form of analysis is new to public relations, it's quite common in other forms of marketing, especially digital advertising. The technology tracks clicks, whether the consumer clicks on an ad or a story. The data can be compared and the results segmented to determine the extent to which each form of marketing communication generated the engagement. To the extent that your resources enable you to do so, behavioral evaluation resonates loudly with internal stakeholders and it integrates neatly with other forms of marketing and communications evaluation.

Assessing Business Results

We've defined three forms of business results for public relations: PR that drives incremental revenue, PR that enables efficiency to do more with less and for less, and PR that avoids catastrophic cost. As described in the attribution evaluation above, the technology tracks behavior from click-through to transaction. If your company or brand enables transactions online, as it must, earned media can be traced from the digital news to a transaction page on your website to determine if people bought the product on your e-commerce site, whether they applied for a job on your company's career page, and more. Digital transactions are common and each one leaves a traceable digital trail. Efficiency can be evaluated by the degree to which your output and outcome performance improved while your input investments went down or stayed the same. Avoiding catastrophic cost requires a special approach because the focus of the evaluation is on something that perhaps didn't happen because of your acumen and dexterity. Your evaluation should get as close as possible to these forms of measurement—they don't cost that much and they quantify PR's ability to generate a positive yield.

Evaluating the Public Relations Continuum

Throughout the book, we've described an ongoing cycle referred to as the public relations continuum. Rather than a linear process, public relations evolves more as a cyclical progression as we plan, execute, and evaluate over time. In the course of a single year, the cycle may occur dozens of times as each campaign informs future action.

Evaluating the Landscape Analysis

The Landscape Analysis begins the data-informed public relations process. It provides a deep-dive analysis of your business and communications environment so that you may review and assess your position within your organization, among competitors, and in society. The analysis requires you to examine the priorities and preferences of internal and external stakeholders, including management and employees among internal audiences. You also assess what matters most—and least—to customers, investors, influencers, regulators, and community leaders, for example, to represent external audiences. At the same time, you assess the degree to which you meet or exceed their expectations.

Whether or not you think you know if and how your environment has changed, you should retest your hypotheses and key learnings once every year to make certain that your plans for the next rotation through the public relations continuum lead to even better results.

While many aspects of the original Landscape Analysis remain the same, certain events force us to revisit our understanding even if our assessment is only one year old. For example, a Landscape Analysis from January 2020 became obsolete just three months later when the pandemic led to an economic crisis, high unemployment, and entire industries in freefall. 2020 was an extraordinary year, but even lesser events indicate the need for an "audit" of your communications environment. Consider the public relations implications that a new CEO, recent regulatory action, or an election bring with them. Upon completion of the evaluation process, you must remain open-minded to changes in your communications, business, and cultural landscapes to revise and plan for the new approaches you'll need to demonstrate and generate a positive return on your organization's investment in public relations.

In revisiting your initial Landscape Analysis, you'll want to consider whether there have been changes in your performance among external audiences, internal clients, employee communications, traditional and social media, and consumer behavior. As you review each of these areas, I outline below what to look for.

Evaluate Performance Among External Audiences

Look at audience data from demographics databases to uncover changes in your audience's situation, preferences, and behavior. Do they look the same? If not, what changed? Revisit gender, age, household income, product usage, and purchase intention for consumers. For business-to-business, double-check firmographic data to revisit your customer base in terms of company size, earnings, and revenues. How have they changed? Are your target audiences now in a better position to do what you wanted them to do? Will they buy your products and services? Will they vote to uphold your position in a regulatory action? Will they pledge to support your cause? Have changes in global, domestic, and local economies affected your target audience? Use secondary research to learn more about population shifts, macro- and micro-economic changes, and societal trends. Apply social media listening and analytics to track how your target audiences talk about you, your issues, and your opposition and the degree to which they changed over the prior period. What topics do people focus on now? Have their areas of interest shifted from the last Landscape Analysis? Which topics trended upward and which declined? To what degree has your organization's position shifted? Do your target audiences feel the same way about you? Compare your results at the end of the cycle with your original research at the beginning to catalogue changes and to plan for the next cycle revolution.

Evaluate Performance Among Internal Audiences

To do this, use low-cost survey technology to update your Executive Audit results by assessing the preferences and priorities of senior management. Again, changes in our economic climate require executives to reexamine what's relevant to them and the organizations they lead in both the near and the longer term. In some cases, economic changes brought fundamental transformation to certain industry categories, especially in the aftermath of the pandemic. Certainly, executives in the commercial real estate, travel, and hospitality industries have new priorities related directly to the survival of the businesses they lead. Unrelated to the pandemic but to innovations in technology, shifts in purchasing behavior and alternatives for personal transportation have forever changed the energy, retail, and automotive sectors to the degree that even one year may bring significant changes to which you must adjust. How do these changes affect public relations? What can public relations do to contribute to the vitality of the enterprise? Review the data from your original Executive Audit to assess any changes to management priorities and to factor these trends into your go-forward communications planning.

Evaluate Performance on Employee Communications

Consider survey technology to assess the most important issues among your employees. Your communications team may already have this data from their own assessments during periodic employee surveys, so begin by asking them and collaborating if you can. If executives feel the effects of the economy and business changes, employees feel the impact even more, especially when employment trends severely affect those working in the industries under siege. While the businesses may survive, their levels of investment in human capital may change forever. During the pandemic, many companies recognized the importance of internal communications as the way to inform employees of the factors affecting their workplace and to retain their loyalty through a difficult time. If internal communication resides within your communications purview, recognize its essential contribution among internal and external channels. During the pandemic and the racial strife of 2020, companies and CEOs made sure to let their employees know where they stood on critical issues related to workplace safety as well as sensitive social issues related to racism and sexism. Data from internal surveys will reveal shifts in the priorities of the workforce and what they expect from their employer. At the same time, the data will uncover what it takes to keep them informed and loyal. Apply your findings to generate insights into refining your communications timing, messaging, media, and spokespeople.

Evaluate Traditional and Social Media Performance

Apply your social listening and media monitoring analytics software platform to track media performance over the course of time. While the surveys referenced above support a frequency of perhaps four times a year before the respondents feel "over-surveyed," media evaluation using content analysis continues 24/7/365 over time for in-depth analysis and real-time top-line examination. Of course, the technology and the data it delivers must undergo human analysis to validate content relevancy and to ensure accuracy. Top-line analysis and evaluation should occur as often as necessary, even throughout the day, especially for social media. Expert deep-dive evaluation research occurs at the end of the month or quarter as well as at the completion of a particular initiative or campaign. The data reveals the degree to which you achieved success as planned and indicates whether you need to refine messaging to generate better media outcomes. Common measures for quantitative, qualitative, competitive analysis provide many revelations and affirmations on the volume, reach, tone, and intended messages you delivered versus those of competitors and your own past performance. Monitor trends regularly to ensure a timely response to changes while there's time to affect—or mitigate—emerging trends.

Evaluate Performance on Consumer Behavior

Use social media, surveys, and attribution analysis. Social media often presents people speaking in their own voices to report indications of awareness, understanding, preference, and behavior. Social media relies on self-reported behavior, so while relatively inexpensive, it offers only limited insights into whether the person posting their recent experience belongs to your target audience (or even if they're telling the truth). Surveys show PR's impact on awareness, attitudes, understanding, and behavior, but they depend on your stakeholders' ability to remember what they did and why they did it, and they tend to take time to field the questionnaire, collect results, and perform the analysis.

Attribution technology quickly delivers absolute results from earned media interactions, including whether they clicked on a digital media source, what they did next, and to what effect. In this way, communicators regularly evaluate earned media performance throughout the year rather than waiting for the monthly, quarterly, or annual report. Thoughtful attribution data analysis uncovers patterns of media consumption as well as a catalogue of the assets that make a story "click-worthy." Continuous review enables you to optimize your content to include more of what people find compelling and to eliminate those elements that people ignore. Use the analysis to determine the effects of visuals, spokespeople, and certain messaging attributes. Gauge the contribution and effectiveness of every trackable digital channel: do daily newspapers perform better or worse than business media? Do suburban media perform better than their big city counterparts?

Focus on the media that deliver the highest concentration of target audience involvement to generate better business results. Take what you learn to improve actions supportive of pro-transaction behavior and to lower the cost per conversion to improve your return on PR investment and to allocate precious resources more productively. Work with marketing counterparts to feed your PR data into their advanced Big Data analyses to enable more efficient marketing campaigns. If the analysis reveals that certain audiences, media channels, and events drive marketing outcomes more efficiently than paid marketing, then marketing can focus its more expensive paid efforts on the media that require advertising support. In this way, marketing budgets focus resources on the audiences, channels, and events that require a higher level of controlled communication.

Evaluating Objectives

One of the most direct and simplest ways to communicate the value and ROI of your public relations program relies on your ability to connect the objectives you set and the results you generated. Even for executives who know nothing of public relations, the media, or marketing, performance vs. objectives makes this an exercise in at-a-glance evaluation. For example, using placeholder numbers, if your objective was to achieve a 12 and you hit 15, you're a winner. If your competitor generated an 11, you're an even bigger winner. And if your performance last year resulted in a score of 10, you're an All Star: you beat your objective, you improved over last year, and you beat the competition. That's a win-win-win situation.

If you established meaningful, measurable, and reasonable objectives and gained executive consensus on those objectives, you likely will need to make only minor refinements at the evaluation stage. Conducting evaluations on a monthly or quarterly basis provides timely milestones to either step on the gas or hit the brakes. If for some reason you fall short, it could be that your objectives weren't reasonable and measurable at the start and you may need to work with management to revise objectives—especially if there's an anomalous event during the course of business. Sudden economic or social changes, competitive activity, and other situations turn otherwise solid objectives into mush, so you must factor these uncontrollable shifts into your objectives and recalibrate. You may need to continue sharpening your strategy and tactics to improve performance by replicating the tactics that worked best and discarding underperforming aspects, even if they are pet projects. In one case, a large conglomerate sponsored a fishing tournament to promote its portfolio of specialty fishing gear. The tournament was a favorite among senior executives who entertained clients and enjoyed the week at a Caribbean resort. Unfortunately, despite generating great media coverage and beating the objective for the volume of press coverage, we helped the client realize that the tournament cost more than the specialty fishing equipment generated in profits. The executives loved the fun, but once the reality set in, they cancelled the tournament and found better ways to promote their products. That program exceeded some objectives, but it failed to meet the most important: to generate a positive return on investment.

We spoke about objectives that are quantitative, qualitative, comparative, and attributive. By setting objectives for each element, you create more ways to learn and more ways to win. The Executive Scorecard in Figure 7.1 offers a simple way to evaluate performance versus objectives. This scorecard tells only "what happened" but requires the public relations team to provide insights into why it happened and what's being done about it. In cases like this, the communications team reports feature much more diagnostic and interpretive analysis, though for executives this may be good enough.

FIGURE 7.1 Executive Scorecard

WIN CUSTOMERS

	Q1	Q2	Q3	Q4
Build brand awareness	Green	N/A	N/A	Green
Build preference in enterprise	Green	N/A	N/A	Green
Gain mindshare with target audience (share of earned media, social media)	Yellow	Yellow	Yellow	Green
Drive sales accepted leads in ENT / SP as a channel	Green	Green	Green	Green
Drive certifications	Red	Red	Red	Red
Enable sales and partners	Yellow	Green	Green	Green
Launch and enable solutions portfolio	N/A	N/A	Green	Green
Web lead generation and registrations	Yellow	Green	Yellow	Green
Enhance channel performance	Green	Green	Green	Green

PEOPLE

	Q1	Q2	Q3	Q4
World-class organizational capability	Yellow	Green	Green	Yellow

Legend: ● Green ● Yellow ● Red

NOTE A public relations scorecard provides executives with a simple pulse check over the course of the year. These reports promote a dialogue about successes and shortfalls, opportunities and vulnerabilities, as well as opportunities to fix weaknesses and reinforce strengths.

Evaluating Strategy and Tactics

Under ordinary circumstances, strategy should not require major review. However, as 2020 proved, "ordinary" may no longer mean what it once did. Messaging and targeting priorities changed within weeks of the sudden emergence of new realities caused by the pandemic and racial unrest. Companies like 3M, with broad product portfolios, found themselves thrust into the headlines due to their ability to contribute to the pandemic relief effort. As a manufacturer of surgical masks, 3M found itself challenged to meet the unprecedented demand for its product. After lauding the company initially, President Trump attacked the company for its policies over global distribution. While masks represented only one part of 3M's product portfolio, that product line became the focus. The company had to pivot almost instantly.[1]

3M is not alone. The tumultuous events of 2020 forced many companies to rapidly refine their strategy to stay relevant during the Covid-19 pandemic and the Black Lives Matter movement.

Evaluating Strategy and Tactics During a Period of Unrest

Regardless of one's opinion or position on the matter, the Black Lives Matter movement brought enormous social change. In a way, the genesis of its effects on communicators began in late 2019, when an organization comprised of 181 of America's most significant CEOs redefined the purpose of a corporation. Because of its reexamination, Business Roundtable restated the focus of a company from *shareholders* to *all stakeholders*, including employees, customers, communities, vendors as well as shareholders. Black Lives Matter challenged the determination of CEOs and the companies they led to address and take action in response to George Floyd's murder on May 26, 2020 and the subsequent protests.[2] Diversity and inclusion feature prominently in most corporate messaging frameworks, but the environment demanded that companies reprioritize these themes. The renewed focus sparked a need for a tactical response to address the issue as it became among the world's most important themes overnight.

At the time, Floyd's death and a series of events that followed severely tested the determination of CEOs everywhere as well as the companies they managed. Almost instantly, executives and communicators no longer felt certain about what was appropriate to say and when to say it. Some companies elected to "stay the course" by avoiding the subject altogether. But as Business Roundtable understood, the public now demands that corporate leaders take a more dynamic position in leading the world toward a better future. In this scenario, staying silent speaks volumes. In the recent past, a number of sensitive topics associated with gender and racial prejudice forced companies to declare their standing. In some cases, the response simply came from the heart while other organizations conducted quick research to pretest different ways to address the difficult conversations they planned to encounter.

In June of 2020, *Forbes* magazine writer David Hessekiel highlighted 55 companies and brands and their responses following Floyd's killing and the subsequent protests.[3] These organizations represented a broad spectrum of words and actions. To assess their responses, media analysis expert Kyle Heatherly undertook an analysis of news coverage of the companies featured in *Forbes* and compared their positioning and performance from before, during, and following the shocking incident. He chose to conduct a media content analysis because of the media's ability to both reflect and shape public sentiment.

Among the organizations in Heatherly's analysis, most issued public statements, donated money, and made changes in their programs and products. Even iconic brands were not immune—PepsiCo promised a makeover for Aunt Jemima, and Mars, Inc. announced changes for its Uncle Ben's brand.[4] These transformations were not anticipated until events forced the companies to focus attention on the meaning and implications of their famous brands. In response to the need to shift their messaging strategies quickly, a number of company statements generated significant and positive visibility in traditional media channels by clearly stating their support. Ben & Jerry's, the frozen confection brand well known for social activism, generated a positive spike in visibility by declaring "End White Supremacy" on its website. Grindr, which describes itself as "the world's largest social networking app for gay, bi, trans, and queer people," announced the removal of ethnicity filters in support of Black Lives Matter. As a result, the company's media coverage rose by 285 percent.[5]

For Ben & Jerry's, social activism is part of its DNA. As a strategy, diversity and inclusion themes remain ever-present. Tactically, the brand mobilizes to make statements and take actions, including the 2018 introduction of a new ice cream flavor: Pecan Resist. The limited-batch confection supports the brand's campaign to "lick injustice and champion those fighting to create a more just and equitable nation for us all."[6] What's more, Ben & Jerry's made donations to four non-profits representing people of color, Native Americans, and women.

The analysis proved that companies and brands engender positive media visibility when they take strong positions on social issues. The organizations that performed best were those already associated with social causes reflected in legacy strategies. But the events of the day demanded a quick pivot to reprioritize individual messages and to deliver these themes tactically.

In many cases, CEOs felt compelled to address the issue directly and more personally through their social media accounts. The statements were not always premeditated tactics so much as simply written declarations of "what's right" and authentic representations of company positions. Leaders from Deloitte, PayPal, Novartis, Cigna, Salesforce, Nike, and more made real-time tactical decisions to prioritize their positions and make them public. They succeeded because they recognized the gravity of the moment to announce their stance authentically, credibly, and directly. What's more, they supported their statements with action. These situations required courage and wisdom to bring their corporate vision and messaging strategies to life.

Like messaging, targeting strategy usually remains constant over time. The year 2020, however, was anything but typical. During this tumultuous period, hundreds of thousands of people died, life as we knew it was gone, and the global economy suffered as people coped with Covid-19 and its effects. As such, agile communicators faced difficult decisions as target audiences confronted issues related to mortality, health, unemployment, underemployment, business hardships, and other issues that changed the way we lived our lives. Many organizations in the tourism, travel, and restaurant industries suffered, as did their employees. With their businesses shut down, their traditional consumer targets were unable to buy, so communicators shifted focus inward to provide information and context about the company's commitment to its workforce, workplace safety, and managing work from home. While employee communication plays an important role in every strategic and tactical plan, companies did everything they could to retain top talent during a difficult period.

Not every business suffered: more and more people invested in home delivery and at-home entertainment, including streaming video services and gaming, so companies in this category needed to target additional talent. These changes required a reprioritization of targeting strategies and tactics, too.

For media targeting, the pandemic created enormous disruption, which made traditional media relations almost impossible for any company or brand without a Covid-19 story to tell. If a communicator was unable to tie their products and services to front-line workers, healthcare technology, or health safety products and manufacturing, the media shut them out.

In an April 2020 study, top communications research consultants Karinne Smolenyak and Bernd Hitzemann conducted a media content analysis tracking pandemic trends in traditional and social media.[7] The study analyzed coverage in the USA, the UK, France, Spain, Italy, Germany, and China to chart the direction of Covid-19 in order to evaluate media coverage vs. infection and mortality rates. The US report revealed an enormous challenge for communicators: 92 percent of all coverage during the week of April 18 was devoted to Covid-19 and President Trump. The concentric circles in Figure 7.2 depict the extent of news devoted to a variety of topics, most of which would command attention under regular circumstances. The outer circle illustrates year-to-date media activity. The inner circle reflects the week beginning April 11, 2020. During that one-week period, 70 percent of all news related to Covid-19 topics and 22 percent focused on President Trump (these topics were highly interrelated at that time). For public relations professionals, the two themes amounted to 92 percent of the available news hole (defined as the space devoted to journalistic content across print and broadcast media). The probability of any story earning its place in the public eye was extraordinarily low, especially when you consider the US stock market was crumbling, the Syrian conflict had flared up, and the US Democratic primaries

FIGURE 7.2 Media landscape

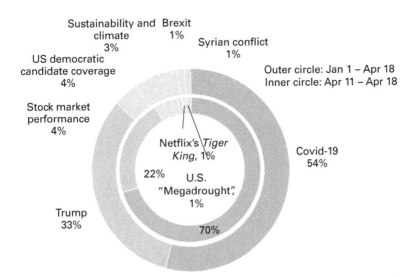

Media landscape shows little change even
as some countries pass peak infection

Sustainability and climate 3%

Brexit 1%

Syrian conflict 1%

US democratic candidate coverage 4%

Outer circle: Jan 1 – Apr 18
Inner circle: Apr 11 – Apr 18

Stock market performance 4%

Netflix's *Tiger King*, 1%

22%

U.S. "Megadrought", 1%

Covid-19 54%

Trump 33%

70%

NOTE The media devoted an extraordinary amount of its available news hole to cover Covid-19 and President Trump. As such, almost any unrelated topic stood only a remote chance of seeing the light of day.
SOURCE Cision (2020) Covid-19, a guide to professional communicators report, April

were underway. Each of these events might command front-page attention at another time, but during the first four months of 2020, they commanded less than 10 percent. In April, they were practically invisible.

Communicators faced enormous challenges: their employers and clients planned to introduce new products and announce other company news. Journalists and influencers considered what would ordinarily be a clever news hook as inappropriate. If your company wasn't producing or developing life-saving cures or equipment, you waited on the sidelines to fight another day. In this context, communicators told stories about how their companies and clients supported front-line workers by making donations in the form of either financial or material support. For example, Lowe's, an American retailer specializing in home improvement, shipped essential equipment to those in need. The company donated $25 million to support its employees, customers, and the communities in which it conducts business. Further, it donated $10 million in protective gear to healthcare workers. The company took these actions to express its deep appreciation for the actions and commitment of healthcare workers, but that was what was required to generate attention at that time. Promoting do-it-yourself home projects and gardening tips would fall flat and be considered inappropriate.

To evaluate news coverage and to add insights and guidance to communicators, the consultants created a synthesized monitor indicating trends governing news and social content to help public relations people recognize appropriate topics and timing during the most serious period of the outbreak (see Figure 7.3). The research team created a guide to the pandemic trends

FIGURE 7.3 Grading the probability of media acceptance

Key							
Infection rate		New infections		Mortality		Media focus	
Rate of cumulative confirmed cases over last 3 weeks as percentage of inhabitants		Weekly new confirmed Covid-19 cases		Weekly new confirmed Covid 19-related deaths		All Covid 19-related media coverage	
High	Above 0.15%	↗	Rising	↗	Rising	↗	Rising
Moderate	<=0.15% >=0.1%	→	Stable	→	Stable	→	Stable
Low	<0.1%	↘	Declining	↘	Declining	↘	Declining

NOTE This inventive system for grading the probability of media acceptance indicates the factors driving news coverage in April as the world came to terms with the pandemic.
SOURCE Cision (2020) Covid-19, a guide to professional communicators report, April

FIGURE 7.4 Public relations playbook

Phases	Media and audience	Corporate communications	Management communications	Product communications
Phase I **Detection**			No changes	
Phase II **Preparation and prevention**	• Media and readers in crisis mode • Majority of topics covid-related	• Corporate citizenship topics appreciated by readers and media • Reduce classical corporate topics to minimum • Important: Use time to create new, digital communications formats for Phase III	Management platforms: • Leadership • Transparency, reassurance and affirmation • Corporate citizenship	Important: • Unless directly relevant to mitigation, "promotional" and product coverage should be moved to Phase III • Channel-load Phase III • Create new, digital comms formats for Phase III
Phase III **Containment, mitigation and damage control**	• Increasing allowance for non-corona coverage • People still in quarantine with time for news consumption	• Begin to introduce a broader set of corporate stakeholder topics 　• Employees 　• Customers 　• Investors 　• Regulators/legislators	Management platforms: • Leadership • Transparency, reassurance and affirmation • Corporate citizenship	• Run new, digital formats • Provide your customers with alternative, new formats • Promote digital sales: Contactless business will be trending
Phase IV **Recovery and repair**	• Less time for news consumption • Back to work	• "Restart / reboot" topics: Start of production, sales, etc • Focus on the positive outcomes of the crisis	Management platforms: • Stronger out of the crisis	Important: There is no back to normal for product communications! • Brand events and sponsorships limited for next few months due to social distancing • Smaller interactions with journalists emerge: Product reviews, test drives, etc

NOTE The table provides a combination of diagnostic, preventative, and therapeutic action reflecting each stage of the Covid-19 crisis. Depending on the stage of the pandemic in a particular region, the communicator could better determine the appropriate form of public relations outreach within their news environment.

SOURCE Cision (2020) Covid-19, a guide to professional communicators report, April

affecting each country. Using data from the Center for Systems Science and Engineering at Johns Hopkins University along with the media analysis, the team's approach advised communicators on subject matter, timing, and tactics.

As a second step, the research team created a public relations playbook for what to say and when to say it (see Figure 7.4). The countries in the study faced different challenges depending on the stage of the pandemic at a given time. Each week we updated the research to evaluate trends and to provide guidance. We identified four communications phases: Phase I: Detection; Phase II: Preparation and Prevention; Phase III: Containment, Mitigation, and Damage Control; Phase IV: Recovery and Repair. With each phase of the pandemic, we offered guidance on the best audience targets, the best corporate topics, the best management themes, and appropriate product subjects. Phase I required companies to listen and remain agile. After that, the weekly evaluation (for some clients, we updated daily) indicated proactive tactical steps to gain "appropriate visibility" in the face of so much hardship.

The next piece of the analysis evaluated the environment in each country from which communicators assessed their situation and provoked thoughtful consideration for stories, activations, and timing. To return to "normal" public relations activity, the evaluation factored the four major considerations—infection rate, new infection, mortality, and media focus—to advise clients on preparedness and action. The snapshot in Figure 7.5 from May 12, 2020 showed that the communications backdrops in China, Italy, Germany, Spain, and France favored a broader range of stories, some of which were unsuitable only weeks before. Meanwhile, the UK and the USA showed a need to prepare and to communicate highly qualified content based on the phase they were in; it was not yet time to return to "normal PR" subject matter. Remember the circle chart from late April in Figure 7.2? The USA remained focused on rising infection rates even though the rate of new infections and mortality appeared more favorable than in the past.

The in-depth analysis of the USA evaluated the trends over time. While certain factors showed improvement, the country remained in a difficult period when routine PR pitches promoting non-Covid-related subjects would most likely result in disappointment. While Italy, France, Spain, Germany, and China proceeded to Phase IV: Recovery and Repair mode, the USA and the UK had not yet reached Phase III (see Figure 7.6). In every country, the initiation of lockdowns left people confronted with the grim reality, and media coverage on the pandemic spiked at that time.

Compare US trends with the UK where the lockdown-generated attention followed by the hospitalization of Prime Minister Boris Johnson added

FIGURE 7.5 Covid-19 scorecard

Covid-19 coverage continues to decline in most countries except the UK which increased and the USA which is stable

Only the USA and UK continue to struggle with efforts to gain control over the virus and the news. Spain improves to join other countries as an "all green" country but we recommend a cautious reentry around Covid-19 themes.

The public relations environments in China, Italy, Germany and France are favorable for more proactive PR activity.

Key

Infection rate	New infections	Mortality	Media focus
Rate of cumulative confirmed cases over last 3 weeks as percentage of inhabitants	Weekly new confirmed Covid-19 cases	Weekly new confirmed Covid-19-related deaths	All Covid-19-related media coverage
High — Above 0.15%	Rising	Rising	Rising
Moderate — <=0.15% >=0.1%	Stable	Stable	Stable
Low — <0.1%	Declining	Declining	Declining

Covid-19 scorecard

China
Infection rate	New infections
Low	
Mortality	Media focus

Phase: IV - Recovery
Action: Proactive outreach

Italy
Infection rate	New infections
Low	
Mortality	Media focus

Phase: III - Containment
Action: Proactive outreach

Germany
Infection rate	New infections
Low	
Mortality	Media focus

Phase: III - Containment
Action: Proactive outreach

Spain
Infection rate	New infections
Low	
Mortality	Media focus

Phase: III - Containment
Action: Start Phase III communications

France
Infection rate	New infections
Low	
Mortality	Media focus

Phase: III - Containment
Action: Proactive outreach

UK
Infection rate	New infections
Moderate	
Mortality	Media focus

Phase: II - Prevention
Action: Prepare now for Phase III to start

USA
Infection rate	New infections
High	
Mortality	Media focus

Phase: II - Prevention
Action: Prepare now for Phase III to start

NOTE Each country tracked in the study presented different indications to guide action. The USA and the UK lagged other nations in the media's readiness to run material unrelated to the pandemic.

SOURCE Cision (2020) Covid-19, a guide to professional communicators report, April

FIGURE 7.6 Covid-19: a US perspective

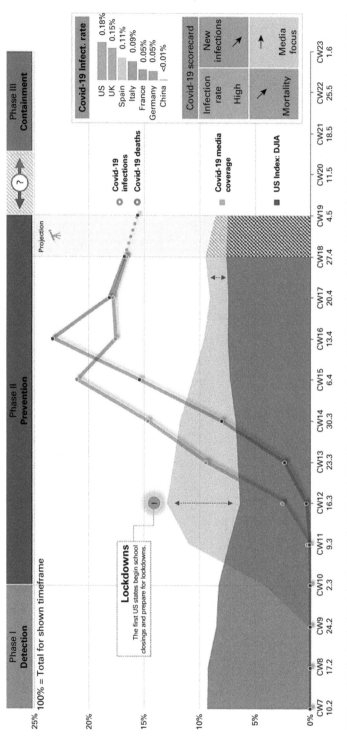

NOTE During the week shown here, new infections and mortality decreased in the USA compared with the prior week. The Dow Jones Industrial Average (DJIA), superimposed here, continued to recover from earlier levels although the pandemic's effects reflect themselves in the gradual decline starting in February.

SOURCE Cision (2020) Covid-19, a guide to professional communicators report, April

FIGURE 7.7 Covid-19: a UK perspective

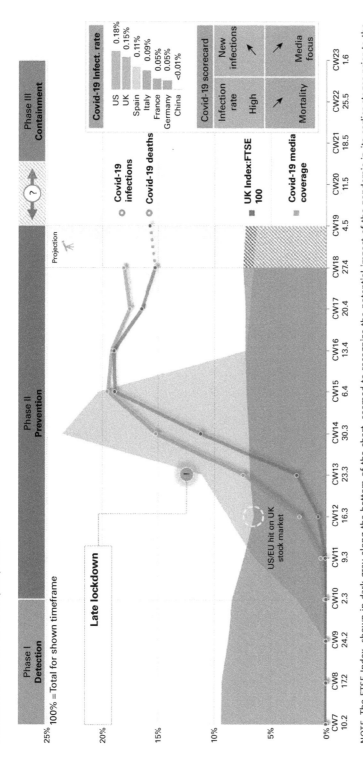

NOTE The FTSE Index, shown in dark gray along the bottom of the chart, seemed to recognize the potential impact of the pandemic in its earlier stages prior to the lockdown. The stock index remained relatively stable throughout the peak, even at the point of the pandemic's highest visibility in mid-March and early April of 2020.

SOURCE Cision (2020) Covid-19, a guide to professional communicators report, April

FIGURE 7.8 Covid-19: the Wuhan lockdown

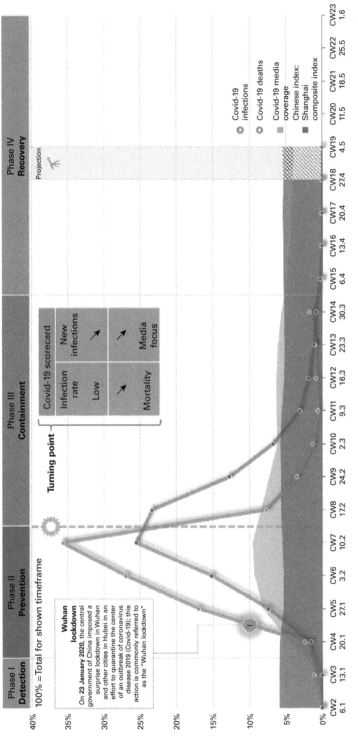

NOTE The Chinese government instituted the earliest lockdown to curb the rates of infection and mortality. By March, the environment for public relations returned to normal. The stock markets remained relatively constant throughout.

SOURCE Cision (2020) Covid-19, a guide to professional communicators report, April

enormous volumes of media visibility during the week of May 5. While infection and death rates trended upward, the media and the FTSE Index remained stable (see Figure 7.7).

Of all countries in the study, China's swift reaction created a faster return to normalcy (see Figure 7.8). Our advice to clients accounted for state control of the media in China and the possibility that certain sources questioned the accuracy of their pandemic data.

Evaluating Evaluation

As the Covid-19 example illustrates, good communications evaluation tells you more than just what happened. Design your evaluation to tell you why it happened and what should be done about it now to guide your performance to even greater results. Ideally, your public relations evaluation will combine assessments of inputs, outputs, outcomes, and business results. Now more than ever, executive sponsors seek to understand the degree to which your efforts generated a positive return on investment for your sponsors, whether the sponsor is an executive in your organization or a client of your agency. Your evaluation helps to identify and eliminate underperforming strategies and tactics to help improve performance over time. To make the most of your evaluation, schedule regular assessments throughout the year and after important campaigns. One way to assess your evaluation is to consider its frequency. In some ways, you make micro-evaluate decisions every day. The deep-dive appraisals should occur more frequently. One of the biggest mistakes you can make is to wait until the end of the year to evaluate your communications. By that time, you've lost any opportunity to eliminate wasteful initiatives, refine strategy and tactics, and improve your return on investment. It's been said before and it bears repeating—two words define every business failure: *TOO LATE*. Evaluate regularly to avoid it happening to you.

CASE STUDY
The Ford Mustang Mach-E: A Case of Excellent Evaluation From Start to Finish

Excellent evaluation comes from excellence throughout the entire communications cycle: you must set solid objectives; your strategy and tactics must combine to generate positive attention and a favorable business climate; and your evaluation must provide for the key measures for effective appraisal in terms of outputs, outcomes, and business results. One organization that did everything right was the

Ford Motor Company, which connected all the dots in its launch of the Ford Mustang Mach-E. The new car introduction combined outputs (media awareness), outcomes (awareness, preference, and behavior), and business results (sales). What's more, it reflected the three forms of PR's return on investment: sales, efficiency, and cost avoidance. Ford's evaluation represents a best practice example for communicators everywhere. Here's its story from the September 2020 issue of *PR News*:[8]

Ford unveiled its all-new Mustang Mach-E to international audiences in November 2019. Car enthusiasts and loyal Mustang aficionados looked forward with great anticipation as the car represented an inflection point for the company as well as the Mustang brand. For the first time in Mustang's legendary 55-year run, the Mach-E was the first version for which Ford extended the Mustang offering beyond sports coupes. Given the excitement and recent developments within the electric vehicle world, Mach-E enabled Ford to generate widespread visibility and awareness of the company's pledge to lead in the sustainable automobile marketplace.

Objectives

The new Mustang is Ford's first all-new electric vehicle but the Mach-E set another first by making reservations available online at Ford.com. As a result, Ford placed high importance on its ability to convert earned and social media coverage into website visits and online reservations. In addition to conversion, the company needed to preserve the reputation of the Mustang brand among loyalists. The car's performance warranted a place in the Mustang pantheon so the company considered it essential to promote its performance qualifications along with its sustainability credentials and innovative technology to foster highly visible positive media coverage.

In close coordination with Ford's communications insights team led by Global Manager Michael Young and his colleague Ben Kocsis, the public relations team set the objectives that were meaningful, measurable, and reasonable (even though they were very aggressive). The objectives touched all the bases:

- Business outcomes:
  - Generate unmatched demand in the form of reservations on Ford.com.
  - Apply attribution technology to achieve a conversion rate from earned media to the website of .7 percent or higher (a multiple of that produced by Google and Facebook ads).
- Outtakes:
  - Earn a high level of message retention and company recall, especially among younger audiences and key influencers as quantified by survey research.

- o Elevate Ford's reputation as an environmentally responsible company.

- o Rank among Google Trends' top 10 searches.

- o Set record levels of website traffic for a new vehicle landing page.

- Outputs:

  - o Produce at least 1 billion in media reach with positive tone in 30 percent or more of the articles among target media.

  - o Elevate the average auto industry engagement among females to 37 percent.

  - o Generate intended messaging in target media. Target: 70 percent penetration in support of three key messages: *Ford extends the Mustang family*; *Mustang cues evident in Mach-E*; and coverage of the *GT Performance model*.

Landscape Analysis

The manufacturer employs a full-time communications insights team of two as well as Cision Insights, a research-based communications consulting firm. As such, this effort combined the accessibility and speed of technology with the interpretive analysis, actionable insights, and strategic guidance that only human expertise provides. In addition, the company's insights team applied a variety of tools and platforms to optimize planning, execution, and evaluation:

- traditional media monitoring software to capture print, broadcast, and digital content;

- social media listening technology to track conversations and engage with fans and influencers;

- SEO technology to identify, test, and monitor key words;

- demographics software and the company's existing customer database to target the most likely audiences as well as the media they read, watch, and listen to;

- qualitative and quantitative analysis (focus groups and surveys) to capture and represent the preferences and priorities of the target audience. The team used the results to sharpen the messaging and targeting strategies;

- attribution technology that revealed the extent to which consumers clicked on an earned media story along with their subsequent behavior (visited the website, reviewed product specifications and photos, asked for additional information, and reserved a vehicle);

- attribution analysis to test and model the relationship to a variety of data streams to identify the optimal combination to reduce risk and maximize performance.

The communications, insights, and consulting team collaborated during the pre-launch, launch, and post-launch phases to consistently monitor, review, and refine throughout the launch period. As such, the combined team employed technology to enhance their ability to execute; relied on sector expertise to ensure relevant findings; and manifested their research expertise and critical thinking abilities to provide solid, accurate data as a foundation for making better strategic and tactical decisions.

Strategy

The Ford team defines "strategy" as the process of developing messaging to foster positive differentiation and encourage transactional behavior. Also, strategy represents the process by which communicators identify target audiences. Here, the team pre-tested hundreds of potential messages to arrive at the optimal positioning: compelling messages deemed credible for this brand by the target audience. The targeting prioritized audiences by the degree to which they matched the desired demographics, exhibited favorable past buying behavior, and identified their future purchase intentions. The data and insights team provided a strategic framework to meet or exceed their aggressive objectives. The insights team focused their attention on three primary areas:

- Target audience optimization:
  - Demographic, customer, and targeting databases provided a foundation for analysis to identify the audiences most likely to engage and buy the product.
  - Media databases helped the insights analysts to prioritize the media with the highest penetration, credibility, and engagement among the target audiences.
  - Media segmentation analysis to inform multiple event strategies: pre-briefing walkthroughs, company executive and expert interviews, and special event invitations.
  - Social media and influencer identification to ensure the traditional media coverage and social media conversations were further amplified through subsequent organic traditional and social media.
- Message optimization:
  - Preliminary message testing revealed positive affirmational themes to reinforce the positive attributes associated with the legacy car to speak with loyal fans.
  - In addition, the research uncovered new messages to positively differentiate the new car from the legacy model. These themes included "exhilarating

performance," "human-centered technology," and "effortless ownership experience."

- o The testing also answered the questions asked by any prospective car buyer, including "value," "maintenance," and "driving experience."

- Organic search engine optimization:

- o "Steal" search share away from electric vehicle manufacturers.

- o Apply SEO data to identify earned media targets with highest credibility around the electric vehicle discussion.

- o Make it easy for consumers to visit the company website and the new car pages.

Tactics and Execution

Using analytics tools and innovative research, the Ford communications insights team recommended the following tactics:

- Organic SEO:

- o Leveraged SEO tools to discover the most frequently searched keywords connected to "electric vehicles."

- o Analyzed opportunities for organic keywords versus paid.

- o Implemented high-impact keywords to increase search visibility of Ford web properties.

- o Identified earned media outlets with highest authority in organic search around electric vehicles.

- o Analyzed keywords "owned" by competitors to assess risk/reward of coopting theirs versus finding new opportunities.

- Optimized media target list:

- o Applied both qualitative and quantitative methods to find outlets with highest reach/frequency devoted to electric vehicle topics.

- o Deeply analyzed reach potential, particularly factoring difference between reach of homepage vs. automotive/technology-focused subpage. Outlets with the highest discrepancy were considered "high potential," which prompted special outreach.

- o Applied reader demographics with existing audience/customer profiles to identify optimal media targets and ensure that intended Mach-E messages resonated with target audience.

- Social media engagement:
  - o Identified the media outlets and headline keywords that drove the highest engagement across social media platforms around electric vehicles.
  - o Added data-informed insights and guidance into recommendations.

Results / ROI

The Insights team evaluated performance versus objectives, against competitors, and in light of past performance. By leveraging data-driven analysis and guidance, the communications team met or exceeded every objective, dominated automotive news and conversations during the launch period, and surpassed any launch in the company's history. Reviewing performance vs. objectives, the Insights team enabled their communications counterparts to deliver the following results:

- Business outcomes:
  - o Online reservations for the new car are officially "full"—the car sold out in advance of production.
  - o Earned media generated 78,000 conversions from the content to the company's website, a conversion rate of .99 percent (target: .7 percent).
- Outtakes:
  - o For those aware of the launch, surveys confirmed nearly 70 percent of respondents associated the vehicle with its manufacturer.
  - o Surveys revealed that nearly 70 percent of "opinion elites" were aware of the new car launch on an unaided basis.
  - o Surveys confirmed that about 60 percent of respondents reacted positively to the launch, primarily among target Gen Z buyers and "opinion elites."
  - o The car ranked among the top ten topics appearing in Google Search during launch.
  - o There were 2.5 million site visits in the first two months.
- Outputs:
  - o Generated 2 billion in potential media reach after the first week, with top media averaging eight stories each per week during the launch period (goal: 1 billion) with 30 percent positive tone (goal: 30 percent).
  - o 52 percent of Mach-E readers were women (goal: 37 percent).
  - o Intended message penetration achieved 72 percent (goal: 70 percent).
  - o The car was the third largest vehicle reveal by visibility over the last three years.

Beyond the launch, the Ford Motor Company's data and Insights team continues to inform communications strategy for Mach-E. Maybe most importantly to the profession, the Insights team confirmed what we in public relations believe in our hearts to be true: PR works. And the Ford insights team proved it.

Why Doesn't Every PR Person Evaluate Their Performance?

If you set objectives that are measurable, meaningful, and reasonable, PR evaluation may require little or no budget. And yet, measurement and evaluation continue to vex the public relations profession. If good evaluation is so accessible, why don't more PR professionals follow the process to set objectives, develop data-informed strategy, execute research-based tactics, and improve performance over time? Common excuses include the following:

- The costs will outweigh the benefits. Yes, research requires some level of investment if you plan to conduct a rigorous evaluation program. Smart communicators know better: they ask, "what is the cost of *not* proving and improving my value when our competitors are proving and improving theirs?"

- What could we ever learn that we don't know already? Isn't it worth validating what you know so you can defend your decisions and the achievements that follow? Even if you recognize your success, you can't be sure that your internal stakeholders will see it the same way. And who knows, you may actually learn something new and unexpected!

- It's too much work to follow all these rules to establish an evaluation program and to sell it to our internal stakeholders. True, setting up a new evaluation program takes time and a commitment to see it through to its highest potential. The process, however, provides a great opportunity to interact with senior management, to uncover their preferences and priorities, and to set the stage for better communication with them in the future. Plus, once you set up the program, it probably won't require nearly as much effort going forward.

- We only have limited control over the results. Why would I set myself up to be held responsible for things I can't control? Yes, certain elements of the public relations process are not entirely controllable, but most of it is "semi-controllable" and the only part that's not probably reflects the entire organization or activities initiated by the competition or the opposition. If you choose not to evaluate, you are electing to stand on the sidelines as every other department gets the resources that could be yours. And your peers who evaluate performance for continuous improvement see their careers move ahead while yours waits in limbo.

- The results will be used against us. The objective for PR evaluation is not "win or lose." It's "win or learn." It's true that some executives manage their teams using intimidation and fear, but proper evaluation gives you more ways to win. It's much worse to have no results at all.

- Research is too complicated. Some research is expensive and complicated. Not every company has the resources that Ford invested in the success of the Mustang Mach-E, but it doesn't have to be complicated. The basics for evaluation are really quite simple: set measurable objectives… and then beat them. In many ways, the research and evaluation clarify the public relations process and make it easier.

- Research and evaluation kill creativity. Nonsense. In fact, research and evaluation enable you to focus your creativity on where it can do the most good.

- Evaluation costs too much. Many steps lead to the summit, but all of them begin with a single step—much better to begin simply than to never begin.

QUESTIONS PR INVESTMENT DECISION-MAKERS MUST ASK

- Do we set objectives that are meaningful, measurable, and reasonable? Do we evaluate our performance against objectives? Versus competitors? In light of past performance?

- Does our evaluation focus on simpler quantitative measures or do we evaluate PR's impact on business performance?

- Do we seek to learn from every rotation around the PR continuum? How does our evaluation inform our progress?

- To what extent does our PR contribute to sales? Provide better results for less money? Avoid costs altogether?

Endnotes

1 Koenig, D and Miller, Z (2020) Trump, 3M clash over order to produce more face masks for US, https://apnews.com/article/cbed1f366882b07ecc5a45cdee9f4e1e (archived at https://perma.cc/CW48-34HM)

2 BBC (2020) George Floyd: Black Lives Matter protests go global, https://www.bbc.co.uk/news/av/world-52967551 (archived at https://perma.cc/B7JK-55XW)

3 Hessekiel, D (2020) Companies taking a public stand in the wake of George Floyd's death, *Forbes*, https://www.forbes.com/sites/davidhessekiel/2020/06/04/companies-taking-a-public-stand-in-the-wake-of-george-floyds-death/?sh=3e3110d72148 (archived at https://perma.cc/UMC8-C9QH)

4 Geller, M (2020) PepsiCo drops Aunt Jemima branding; Uncle Ben's, others under review, *Reuters*, https://www.reuters.com/article/us-pepsico-race-aunt-jemima/pepsico-drops-aunt-jemima-branding-uncle-bens-others-under-review-idUSKBN23O1V1 (archived at https://perma.cc/DT9K-2EP8)

5 Hessekiel, D (2020) Companies taking a public stand in the wake of George Floyd's death, *Forbes*, https://www.forbes.com/sites/davidhessekiel/2020/06/04/companies-taking-a-public-stand-in-the-wake-of-george-floyds-death/?sh=3e3110d72148 (archived at https://perma.cc/5D5D-H98G)

6 Kravitz Hoeffner, M (2018) Ben & Jerry's launches new resistance-themed ice cream pints, *Forbes Magazine*, https://www.forbes.com/sites/melissakravitz/2018/10/30/ben-jerrys-pecan-resist-trump/?sh=4e5b86ed649a (archived at https://perma.cc/CAF3-KSS8)

7 Smolenyak, K and Hitzemann, B (2020) Covid 19: a guide to professional communicators, *PR News*, May, https://www.prweek.com/article/1684292/digital-edition-may-june-2020 (archived at https://perma.cc/2D6K-NAR5)

8 Weiner, M (2020) The most captivating path to PR-ROI: making the PR-to-sales connection, *PR News*, 9 (September), p 13

EPILOGUE

We in public relations recognize the power of storytelling to engage audiences, influence change, and achieve our business objectives. As we end this book about contemporary public relations, I share an allegory reflecting our professional standing and our potential for a better future in the business world. In this story, we relate how the elements of technology, data, and insights combined in Shakespearean form to lift a small, under-resourced "band of brothers" to change the course of history.

The story is of Henry V, a young upstart English king who reigned from 1413–1422, and who earned great military success in the Hundred Years' War against France. In pursuit of claims made by his great-grandfather Edward III, Henry invaded France and because of his victories, England became the strongest military power in Europe at that time. Shakespeare's play immortalized Henry V as one of England's great warrior kings.

The play's climax is the battle of Agincourt, in which Henry's small army—sick, exhausted, and suffering from hunger—prepare to engage the larger, well-fed and heavily armored French opponents who will be fighting on their own turf.

France had every reason to be confident as they rejoiced the night before the battle: they outnumbered the English army six to one. The French army had access to food and shelter. Thousands of French knights wore heavy armor for protection.

Instead of celebrating their expected victory the following day, the French asked permission to bury their dead while the English rejoiced. For a while, France became part of England.

How did this unlikely victory happen? Here's a case where technology, data, and insights converged.

The English recognized the importance of technology. At that time, the long bow was new military hardware that enabled the English to shoot arrows from a great distance to cut down the French before they could more directly engage the smaller English army. The English anticipated the French generals' routine battle plans, an approach that made French soldiers easy targets for English archers.

Henry had the necessary "data" and foresight to assess the battlefield landscape. Weeks of heavy rain drenched the recently ploughed fields. The ground was muddy and soft. As such, the conditions slowed the heavily armed French cavalry and foot soldiers as they marched forward knee deep in mud.

Whereas the French relied on conventional wisdom rather than clean slate innovation, Henry had the insight he needed to anticipate the French routine and adjusted his plans to narrow the battlefield by placing soldiers at the place most disadvantageous to the advancing French.

English sources estimated the French dead at 11,000 and English deaths at around 100. Much of French political and military leadership died that day while Henry returned to London a conquering hero.

In many ways, Henry V and the English army reflected the challenges faced by public relations in earning our rightful place within the organizations we serve. Outnumbered. Under-resourced. Hungry. But we, like Henry, have the discipline, vision, and motivation to apply the technology, data, and insights at our disposal to take a more fitting place within the hierarchy of communications, marketing, and business.

INDEX

NB: page numbers in *italic* indicate figures or tables

3M 188
5G 6
"80/20 rule" 77

A/B testing 4
Addressograph plates 3
Adobe 156, 158
  communications analysis program – case
      study 73–79
      communications insights team
          members 73–74
      results 78–79
advertising value equivalencies
      (AVEs) 54–55
AirTran Airways 25
"always on" culture 9–10
Amazon 6, 34
Americans with Disabilities Act 41
analytics software 62
Anderson, F, Hadley, L, Rockland, D and
      Weiner, M 134
anti-globalization 9
Apple
  iPad 92
  iPhone 6, 91–92
  Newton 92
Art of War, The 149
Arthur W. Page Society 4, 16, 144
artificial intelligence (AI) 7–8, 26–31, 45, 84
  content creation 28–29, 30
  content ideation 30
  crisis identification 27–28
  in news 29
Associacao Brasileira de Comunicacao
      Empresarial (ABERJE) 16
Associated Press 29
AT&T 4, 5, 58
attribution analysis 4, 11, 32, 44, 61, 159,
      160, 184, 185
attributive data 65–66
  evaluating 179
augmented reality 37

Bacon's books 2
Banga, Ajay 80

Bell Pottinger 145
Ben & Jerry's 100, 189
Bernays, Edward 3
Big Data 24–26, 84
Black Lives Matter movement 15, 188,
      189
Bloomberg 29
Boeing 17
Bowins, Andrew 5
Bruce, Jennifer 73–74
Buffett, Warren 17
Burrelles 41
business results 63–64
  "catastrophic cost", avoiding
      63–64
  efficiency 63
  evaluating 181
  revenue generation 64
Business Roundtable 13, 188

Carnegie, Andrew 13
"catastrophic cost", avoiding 63–64
Center for Systems Science and
      Engineering 194
Chartered Institute of Public Relations
      (CIPR) 16
Cigna 190
Cision Insights 41, 74, 189, 201
  "Global state of the media" 31
Clancy, Kevin 86
"clean slate public relations" 97
  and the Landscape Analysis 97, 98, 99
  and objectives 121
  and Strategic Cube Analysis 86, 159
Coca-Cola 143
"coffee table logic" 157
communications, defining 5
comparative data 65
  evaluating 178
Consumer Reports 24
conversions 62
Coombs, W. Timothy 27
corporate social responsibility (CSR) 13–15
cost per thousand (CPM) 55
Courtney, Stephanie 171

Covid-19 pandemic
    communication during 15
    home video, use of 36
    internal communications 184
    and the Landscape Analysis 182, 183
    media acceptance during 190–99, 191
        Chinese trends 198, 199
        PR playbook 193, 194
        probability of, grading the 192,
            192, 194
        UK trends 194, 197, 199
        US trends 194, 196
    and strategy/tactics 188
    and trust 12
    video conferencing 37–38
    webinars 38

data 47–69
    attributive data 65–66
        evaluating 179
    and the boardroom 48
    business results 63–64
        "catastrophic cost", avoiding 63–64
        efficiency 63
        revenue generation 64
    comparative data 65
        evaluating 178
    defining 48
    inputs 50–52
        activities 51
    and objectives 49–50
    outcomes 60–62
        common data points 60–61
        measuring 62
    outputs 52–60
        advertising value equivalencies
            (AVEs) 54–55
        cost per thousand (CPM) 55
        factors in 53
        frequency 53, 59
        influencer commentary 58
        intended / unintended messages 56–57
        media mix 60
        media presence 58–59
        reach 53–54, 59
        share of voice (SOV) 59–60
        spokespeople, company 57–58
        target audience reach 54
        tone/sentiment 56, 59
        total mentions 54
    primary research 66–67
    qualitative data 65
        evaluating 178
    quantitative data 65
        evaluating 177–78

    secondary research 67–68
    and strategy/tactics 153–54
data mining 85–86
defining 48
"deli counter PR" 5
Deloitte 190
Department of Transportation 24, 25
Dictionary of Public Relations Measurement
    and Research 145

E3 151
Edelman Trust Barometer 12, 13
editorial calendars 34–35
eMarketer 55
environment, social, and governance
    (ESG) 14, 15
evaluation 175–206
    assessing your 199
    benefits of 176
    business results 181
    inputs 177
    and the Landscape Analysis 181–85
        consumer behavior 184–85
        employee communications
            183–84
        external audiences 182–83
        internal audiences 183
        media performance 184
    and objectives 185–86, 187, 205
    outcomes 179–81
    outputs 177–79
    and strategy/tactics 188–99
        Covid-19 pandemic 190–99
        social activism 188–90
Executive Audit 102–06, 107, 183
    participants, identifying 103
    questions 103–04
    results, presenting 105–06
Executive Scorecard 186, 187

Facebook 81, 104
    Facebook ads 167, 200
Factiva 41, 116
"fake news" 13, 42
Financial Times 41
Floyd, George 188–89
focus groups 4, 65, 67
Forbes 189
Ford 43
    Mustang Mach-E case study
        199–204
Fortune
    "Most Admired Companies" 104, 163
Fuel PR 145
Fullintel 27–28

Glassdoor 141
globalization 9
GlobalStats 9
Google 101, 116
    Google ads 167, 200
    Google Alerts 3
    Google Analytics 62, 180
    Google Search 62, 180, 204
    Google Trends 201
    Google+ 81
Grindr 189

HARO 33, 35
Heatherly, Kyle 189
Henry V 209–10
Hessekiel, David 189
Hussman School of Journalism and
        Media 11
hypotheses, developing 86

influencers 11, 34
inputs 50–52
    activities 51
    evaluating 177
insights 71–93
    data mining 85–86
    hypotheses, developing 86
    problem statement, your 85
    Strategic Cube Analysis 86, 87–92, 90
        actionable insights 90, 91–92
        collaborative ideation 88–89
        continual improvement 89
        qualitative research 89
        statistical analysis 89
        survey 89
    three elements of 72–73, 73
    vs observations 79–80
Instagram 81
Institute for Public Relations 16, 55, 144
    "Big Data revolution, The" 25
    "Guidelines for setting measurable
        public relations objectives: An
        update" 134
    Measurement Commission 26, 169
Institute of Directors (IoD)
    Manifesto on Corporate Governance
        14
    International Association for
        Measurement and Evaluation of
        Communication (AMEC) 14, 16,
        55, 74
International Association of Business
        Communicators (IABC) 144
International Public Relations Association
        (IPRA) 16

iPad 92
iPhone 6, 91–92

Jackson, Jackson and Smith 169
Jeffries-Fox, Bruce 4, 58
Jobs, Steve 92
Johnson, Boris 194, 199
Jordan, Michael 171
Journalist/Influencer Audit 108–13
    anonymity, importance of 108
    hypothesis, your 109
    participants, identifying 109
    questions 110–11

Kocsis, Ben 200

Landscape Analysis 97–120, 121, 129, 149
    audiences 153, 158, 159
    benefits of 98
    buy-in, gaining 101–02
    "clean slate public relations" 97, 98, 99
    evaluating 181–85
        consumer behavior 184–85
        employee communications 183–84
        external audiences 182–83
        internal audiences 183
        media performance 184
    Executive Audit 102–06, 107, 183
        participants, identifying 103
        questions 103–04
        results, presenting 105–06
    Journalist/Influencer Audit 108–13
        anonymity, importance of 108
        hypothesis, your 109
        participants, identifying 109
        questions 110–11
    Media Demographic Audit 114–16
    retroactive media analysis 116, 117, 118
    steps in
        insights, uncovering 101
        intelligence needed 101
        objectives, setting 99
        research tools and methods 101
        scope of, determining 99–100
    surveys 113–14
    when to conduct a 97
LexisNexis 41, 116
Lincoln 171
Los Angeles Times 29
Lowe's 192

machine learning 8
marketing mix modelling 4, 61
Mars, Inc. 189
Martha Stewart Living 33

Mastercard 80–84
    Mobile Payments Study 81–82, 83
McCarthy, John 26
McConaughey, Matthew 171
media advertising 11–12
Media Demographic Audit 114–16
media monitoring 40–42, 184
    broadcast 41
    executive briefings 42
    print 41
    real-time alerts 42
    social listening 41–42
Meltwater 41
messaging 163–65, *164*
    defining 87
Michaelson, D., Stacks, D. and Clark , J. 56–57
mobile technology 9–10, 11
Mobile World Congress 83
Munoz, Oscar 64

Natura &Co 100
New York Times, The 41, 108, 153, 154
New Yorker 159
Newman, Nick 12
Newton 92
n-gram 75, 78
Nike 171, 190
Novartis 190
NPR 41

objectives, setting 121–47, 149
    and audience relationship 143
    and audience size 143
    buy-in, gaining 144
    "clean slate public relations" 121
    evaluating 185–86, *187*, 205
    framework for 133–41, *135*, *136*, *137*,
        138, *139*, *140*, *141*
    importance of 122–24
    meaningful objectives 124, 128–29
    measurable objectives 124, 125–28
        business result objectives 127–28
        input objectives 126
        outcome objectives 127
        output objectives 126–27
    reasonable objectives 124, 129–31
        negotiation 130–31
        resources 131
        timing 131
    reviewing 131–32
    vagueness 123
    vs activities 142–43
    vs goals 146

observational research 66–67
Oliver, Gaugarin 27
outcomes 60–62
    common data points 60–61
    evaluating 179–81
    measuring 62
outputs 52–60
    advertising value equivalencies
        (AVEs) 54–55
    cost per thousand (CPM) 55
    evaluating 177–79
    factors in 53
    frequency 53, 59
    influencer commentary 58
    intended / unintended messages 56–57
    media mix 60
    media presence 58–59
    reach 53–54, 59
    share of voice (SOV) 59–60
    spokespeople, company 57–58
    target audience reach 54
    tone/sentiment 56, 59
    total mentions 54

Page, Arthur 4–5
Paine, Katie 27
Palm Pilot 92
Pareto Principle 77
Patagonia 100
PayPal 190
PepsiCo 14–15, 189
Pew Research Center 10
"Pinocchio counting" 13
podcasting 36–37
polls 67
positioning 163
    defining 87
PR News 74, 200
PR Newswire 35
PR training 16
primary research 66–67
problem statement, your 85
Procter & Gamble 15
professional associations 16
Progressive Insurance 171
Proof Analytics 27
Public Relations and Communications
    Association (PRCA) 16, 145
public relations gross rating point
    (PR-GRP) 53
Public Relations Journal 56
Public Relations Society of America
    (PRSA) 16, 144

Public Relations Student Society of America
        (PRSSA) 16
"purpose" 14–15

qualitative data 65
    evaluating 178
quantitative data 65
    evaluating 177–78

real-time tech 6–7
reputation management 17, 63–64
research interviews 66
Reuters Institute for the Study of
        Journalism 12
Reynolds, Dave 73–74
Rolls-Royce 143
Rolodex 2, 24
Rumsfeld, Donald 160

Salesforce 190
"sales funnel, the" 60
Samsung 17
search engine optimization (SEO) 18
secondary research 67–68
Securities and Exchange Commission 35
share of voice (SOV) 59–60
SIRI 7
smartphones 9–10
Smith, Stacey 169
social media 12
    social listening 4, 41–42, 62, 184
    as a source of news 10
    "unmediated media" 11
Sotheby's 47
Southwest Airlines 24–26
Stacks, Don and Bowen, Shannon 145
Stark, Philip B 72
Stouse, Mark 27
Strategic Cube Analysis 86, 87–92, 90, 158,
        159–63, 160, 161
    actionable insights 90, 91–92
    "clean slate public relations"
        86, 159
    collaborative ideation 88–89
    continual improvement 89
    qualitative research 89
    statistical analysis 89
    survey 89
strategy 149–66
    audience reach 154–56, 155, 157
    benefits of 152
    defining 149, 150–51
    developing a 152–54

evaluating 188–99
    Covid-19 pandemic 190–99
    social activism 188–90
media targeting 156–63
    Strategic Cube Analysis 158, 159–63,
        160, 161
messaging 163
pitfalls, common 165–66
Sturton, Suzanne 73
Sun Tzu 64, 149
surveys 4, 62, 66, 113–14, 183
    sample size 66

tactics 149, 151–52, 166–72
    benefits of 168
    defining 149, 151–52
    evaluating 188–99
        Covid-19 pandemic 190–99
        social activism 188–90
    guidelines 166–67
    influencers 169–70
    journalists 168–69
    other teams, coordinating with
        167–68
    pitfalls, common 172
    press releases 170
    regional factors 167
    satellite media tours 171–72
    spokespeople, company 171
    visual assets 170
technology ("CommTech") 2, 6,
        23–46
    artificial intelligence (AI) 26–31, 45
        content creation 28–29, 30
        content ideation 30
        crisis identification 27–28
        in news 29
    audience targeting 31–33
    Big Data 24–26
    engagement 37–40
        social tools 39–40
        video conferencing 37–38
        webinars 38
        website, your 38–39
    measurement, analysis, and
        evaluation 42–45
        surveys 43
    media monitoring 40–42
        broadcast 41
        executive briefings 42
        print 41
        real-time alerts 42
        social listening 41–42

technology ("CommTech") (*Continued*)
   media targeting 33–35
   persuasion, importance of 45
   production/distribution tools
      35–37
     audio and video 36
     podcasting 36–37
     virtual and augmented reality 37
   routine tasks, completion of 23, 45
teletype 35
Trump, Donald 15, 188, 191
trust, in the media 12–13
"truth-o-meters" 13
Turing, Alan 26
"tutor", data as 7
Twitter 81, 104, 116

United Airlines 17, 64
United States Postal Service 2

video conferencing 37–38
virtual reality 37
Visa 43

Wall Street Journal, The (WSJ) 17, 41, 54,
   153–54
Washington Post 29
webinars 38
Weibo 81
WiFi 6 6

Young, Michael 200
YouTube 81, 104